Odie Unleashed!

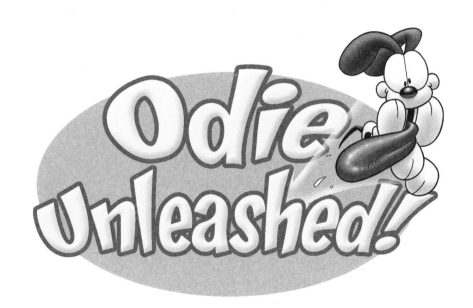

Odie Unleashed!

Garfield Lets the Dog Out

By

Jim "Top Dog" Davis

with his muttly crew

Mark "Atomic Dog" Acey

Scott "Veggie Dog" Nickel

Brett "Bulldog" Koth

Thomas "Hotdog" Howard

Ballantine Books • **New York**

A Ballantine Books Trade Paperback Original

Copyright © 2005 by PAWS, Inc.

Published in the United States by Ballantine Books, an imprint of The Random House Publishing Group, a division of Random House, Inc., New York.

BALLANTINE and colophon are registered trademarks of Random House, Inc.

"GARFIELD" and the GARFIELD characters are trademarks of PAWS, Inc.

Library of Congress Control Number: 2005904018

ISBN 0-345-46464-8

Printed in the United States of America

www.ballantinebooks.com

9 8 7 6 5 4 3

CREDITS

EDITORIAL
Mark Acey and Scott Nickel

ART DIRECTION
Betsy Knotts

DESIGN
Thomas Howard

ILLUSTRATION
Gary Barker, Mike Fentz, Brett Koth, and Lynette Nuding

PRODUCTION
Lori Barker, Linda Duell, Larry Fentz, Kenny Goetzinger, and Brad Hill

INTRODUCTION

I'm going to let you in on a little secret. I don't like dogs. You're shocked, right? But it's true. From schnauzers to shih tzus, dachshunds to Dobermans, I can't stand the walking flea hotels. They shed, they stink, they barf on the carpet, and to top it all off, they sniff each other's rumps!

So why do I waste my time with Odie? Good question. Is it because he's so unfailingly loyal? Maybe. Is it because he's always there to give me a boost to the cookie jar? Partly. Is it because he lets me glue him to the ceiling, braid his ears, and shoot him out of a giant slingshot? Yeah, those are factors. But there's more. For one thing, Odie makes me look good. As I've always said, "If you want to look smarter, hang around with someone stupider." And, boy, is Odie stupider!

But Odie's different, too. He's not like other dogs. Sure, he's a slobbering, toilet-lapping bonehead. But he's *my* slobbering, toilet-lapping bonehead. And I wouldn't trade him for all the chow mein in China.

Being the generous, bighearted (and modest) cat that I am, I've allowed Odie to have his moment in the sun. So enjoy *his* book, but don't forget who the *real* star of the show is!

-GARFIELD

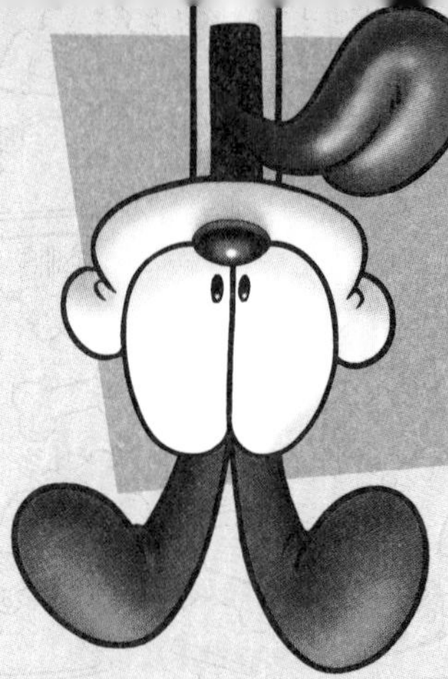

ODIE'S

Where did Odie come from?

He's such a brainless brick, maybe he evolved from rocks! Actually, the character of Odie was introduced into the Garfield comic strip on August 8, 1978, as the pet of Jon's friend, Lyman. Lyman eventually left the strip (don't ask me where he went!), but Odie remained—much to Garfield's chagrin.

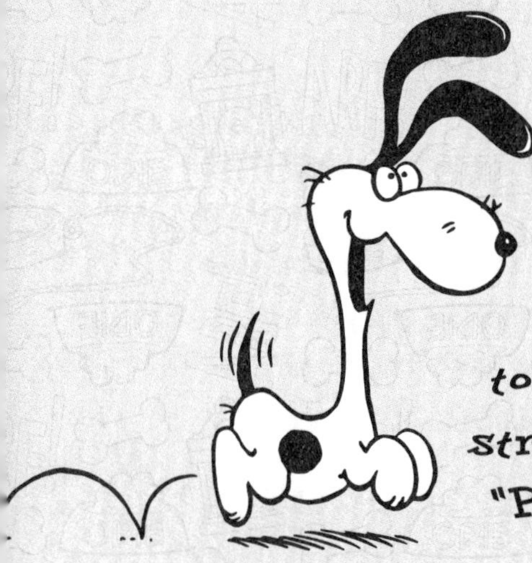

Like Garfield, Odie has changed over the years. Back then Odie was thinner (and goofier looking), and his ears were black. I changed the color of his ears to brown in October 1979 to avoid a conflict with a certain comic-strip beagle. (Hint: The pooch works for "Peanuts," but he doesn't work cheap.)

ORIGINS

I'm often asked how I came up with the names for the various characters. Garfield was named after my grandfather; Jon Arbuckle came from an old coffee commercial I remember hearing. The name "Odie" is really an inside joke. I chose the name because it connoted stupidity, at least to me. Back in my pre-Garfield days, I used to supplement my income by doing freelance advertising work. One job I did was writing a radio commercial for a local car dealership. The spot featured Odie, the village idiot. I liked the name, so I used it again. Hey, why reinvent the fool?

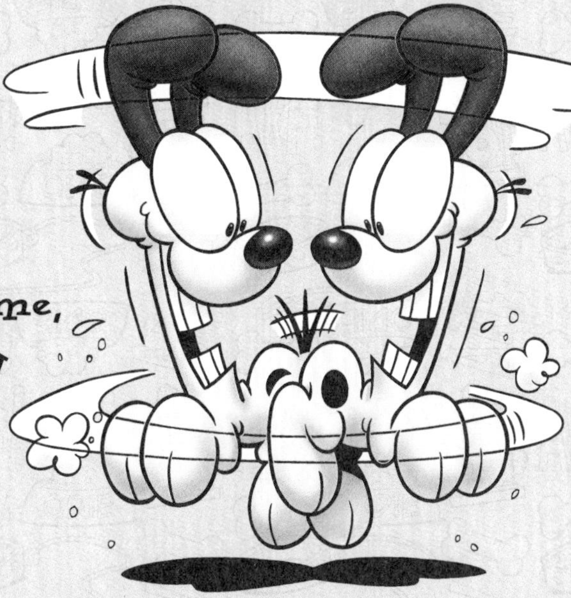

-JIM DAVIS

ODIE'S ORIGINS The first week of strips

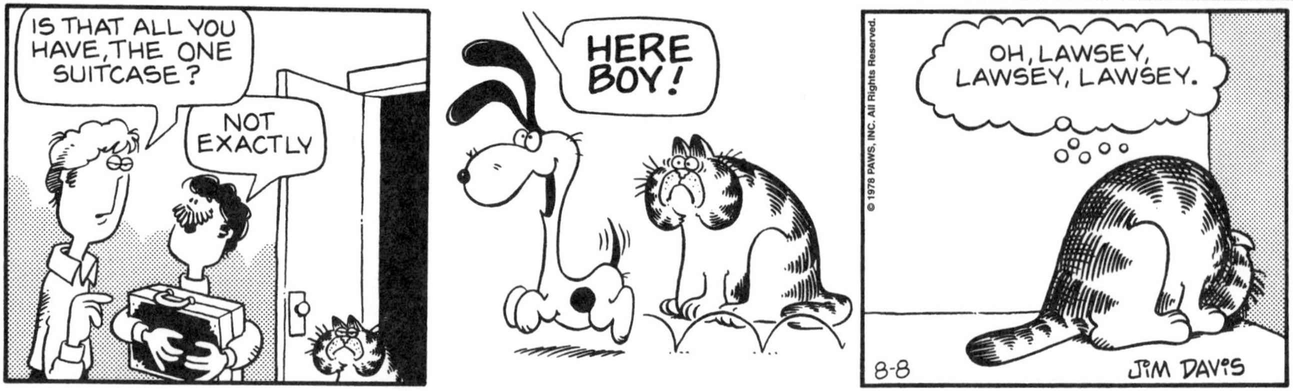

IS THAT ALL YOU HAVE, THE ONE SUITCASE?
NOT EXACTLY
HERE BOY!
OH, LAWSEY, LAWSEY, LAWSEY.
© 1978 PAWS, INC. All Rights Reserved.
8-8
JIM DAVIS

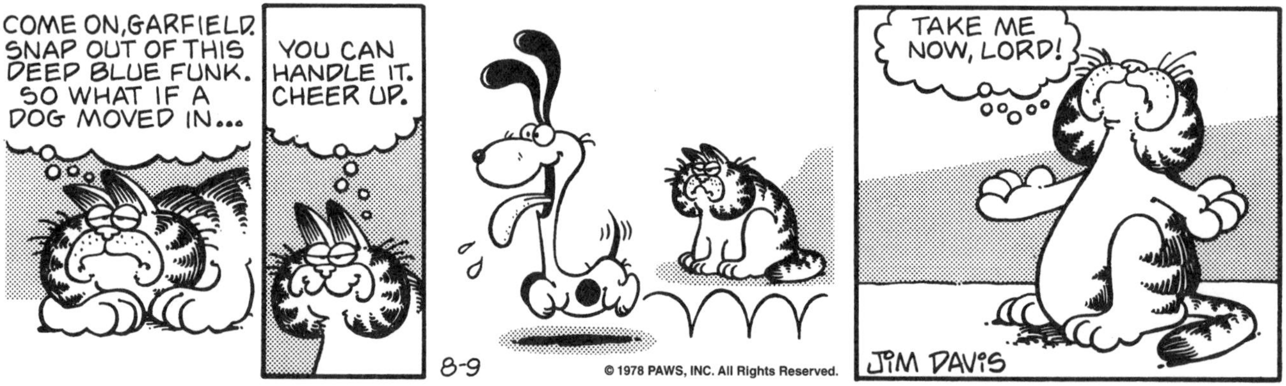

COME ON, GARFIELD. SNAP OUT OF THIS DEEP BLUE FUNK. SO WHAT IF A DOG MOVED IN...
YOU CAN HANDLE IT. CHEER UP.
8-9
© 1978 PAWS, INC. All Rights Reserved.
TAKE ME NOW, LORD!
JIM DAVIS

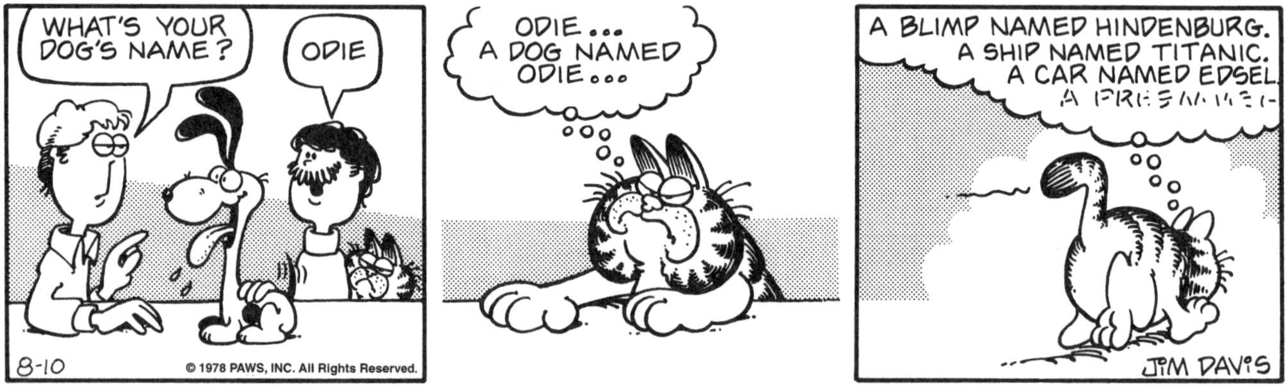

WHAT'S YOUR DOG'S NAME?
ODIE
8-10
© 1978 PAWS, INC. All Rights Reserved.
ODIE... A DOG NAMED ODIE...
A BLIMP NAMED HINDENBURG. A SHIP NAMED TITANIC. A CAR NAMED EDSEL.
JIM DAVIS

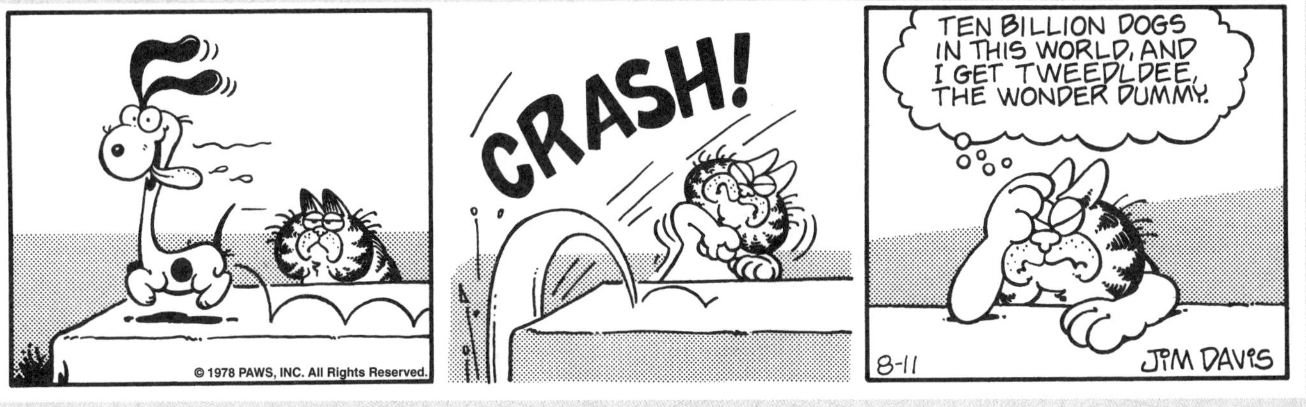
© 1978 PAWS, INC. All Rights Reserved.
CRASH!
TEN BILLION DOGS IN THIS WORLD, AND I GET TWEEDLDEE, THE WONDER DUMMY.
8-11
JIM DAVIS

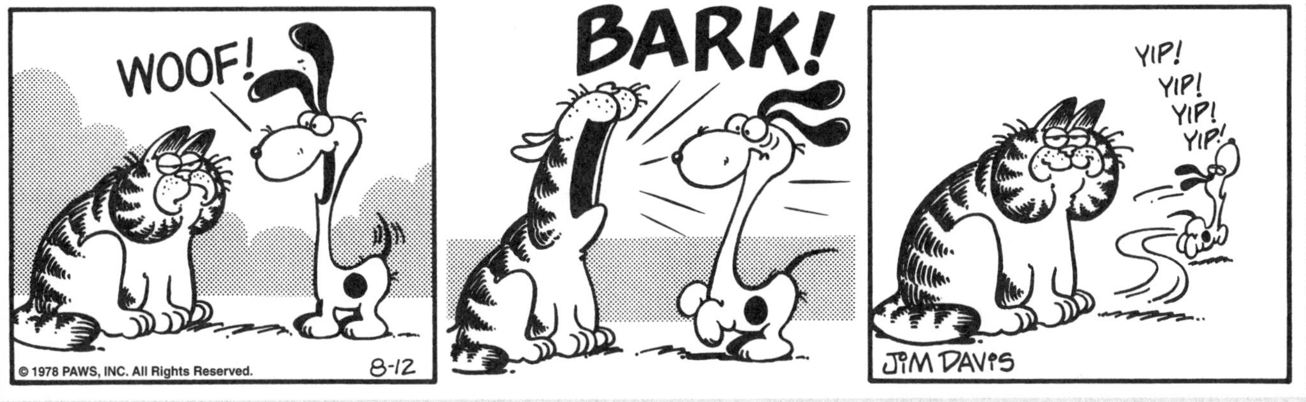
WOOF!
© 1978 PAWS, INC. All Rights Reserved.
8-12
BARK!
YIP!
YIP!
YIP!
YIP!
JIM DAVIS

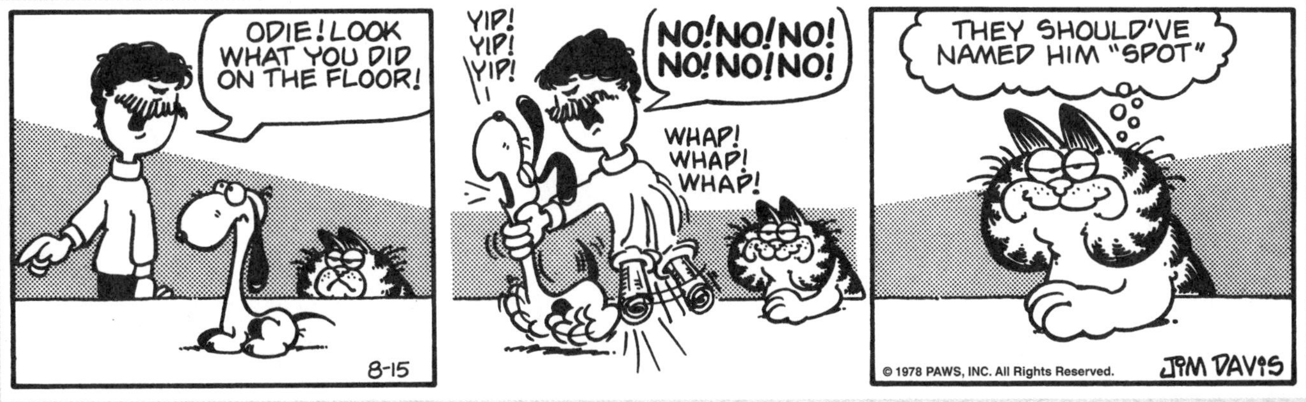
ODIE! LOOK WHAT YOU DID ON THE FLOOR!
8-15
YIP! YIP! YIP!
NO! NO! NO! NO! NO! NO!
WHAP! WHAP! WHAP!
THEY SHOULD'VE NAMED HIM "SPOT"
© 1978 PAWS, INC. All Rights Reserved.
JIM DAVIS

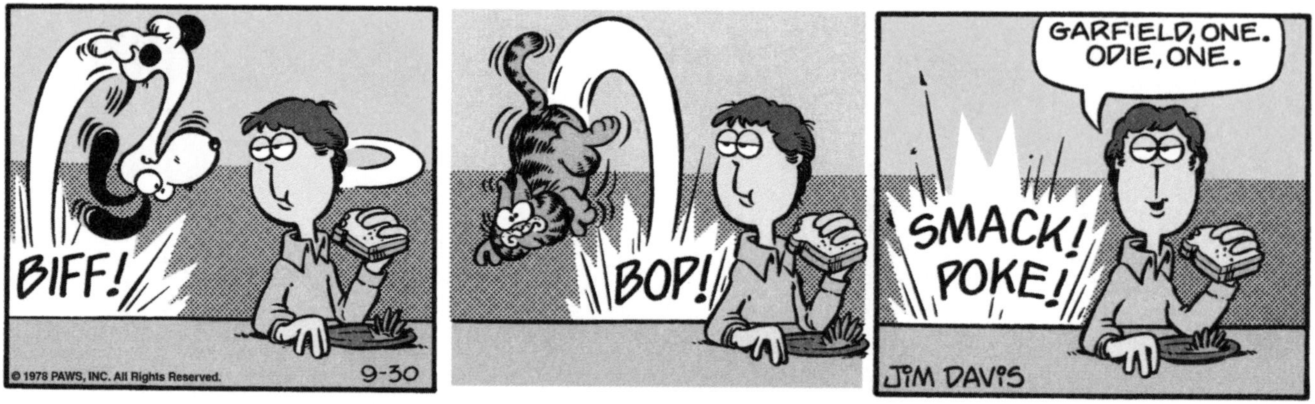
BIFF!
© 1978 PAWS, INC. All Rights Reserved.
9-30
BOP!
GARFIELD, ONE. ODIE, ONE.
SMACK! POKE!
JIM DAVIS

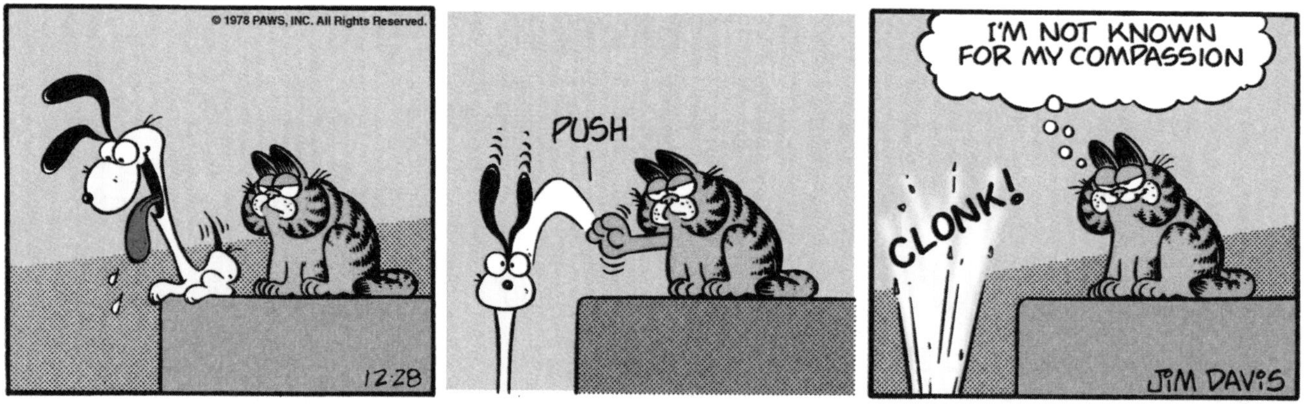
© 1978 PAWS, INC. All Rights Reserved.
12-28
PUSH
I'M NOT KNOWN FOR MY COMPASSION
CLONK!
JIM DAVIS

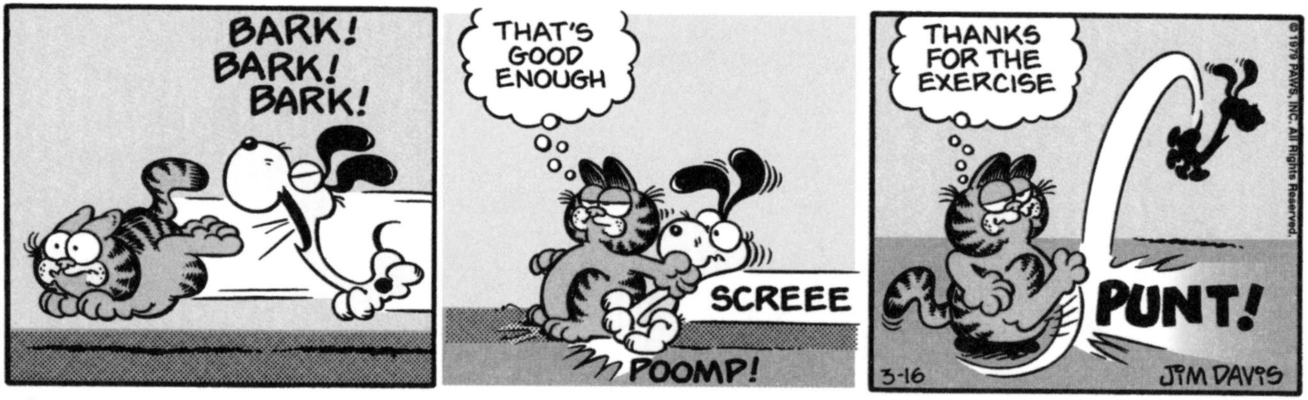
BARK! BARK! BARK!
THAT'S GOOD ENOUGH
SCREEE
POOMP!
THANKS FOR THE EXERCISE
© 1978 PAWS, INC. All Rights Reserved.
PUNT!
3-16
JIM DAVIS

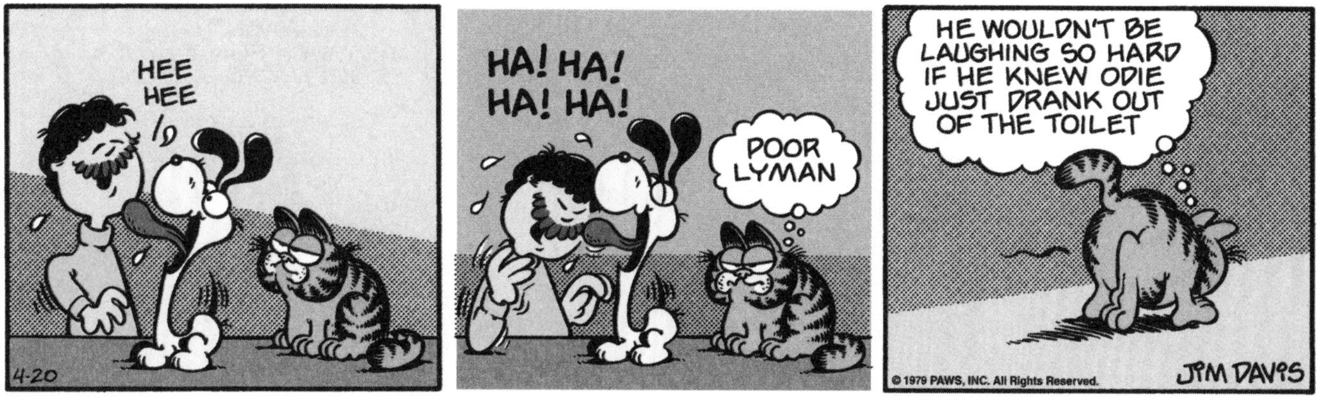
HEE HEE
4-20
HA! HA! HA! HA!
POOR LYMAN
HE WOULDN'T BE LAUGHING SO HARD IF HE KNEW ODIE JUST DRANK OUT OF THE TOILET
© 1979 PAWS, INC. All Rights Reserved.
JIM DAVIS

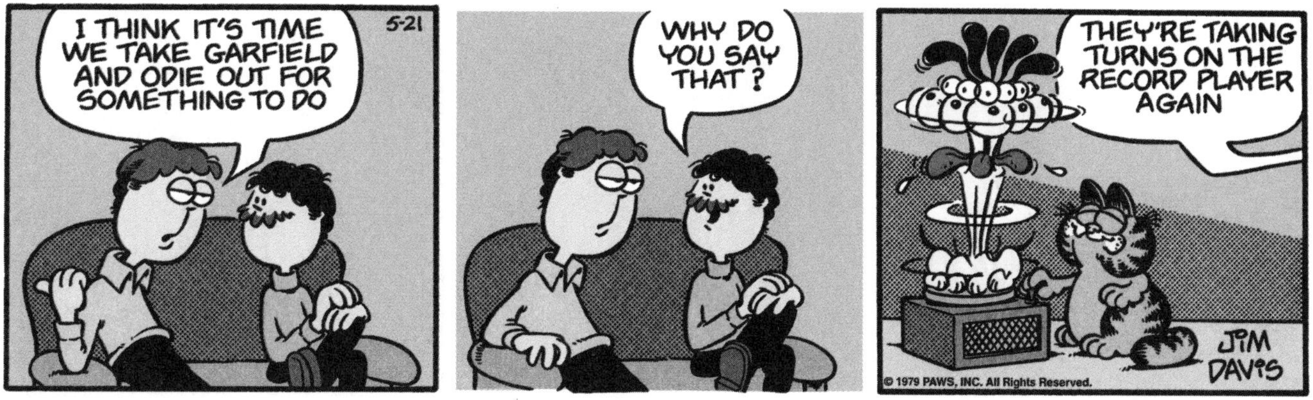
I THINK IT'S TIME WE TAKE GARFIELD AND ODIE OUT FOR SOMETHING TO DO
5-21
WHY DO YOU SAY THAT ?
THEY'RE TAKING TURNS ON THE RECORD PLAYER AGAIN
© 1979 PAWS, INC. All Rights Reserved.
JIM DAVIS

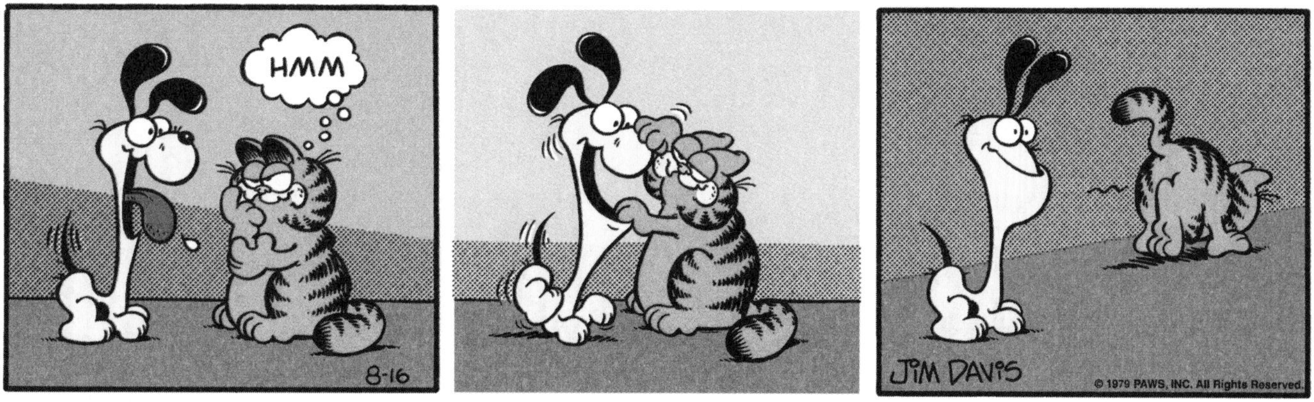
HMM
8-16
JIM DAVIS
© 1979 PAWS, INC. All Rights Reserved.

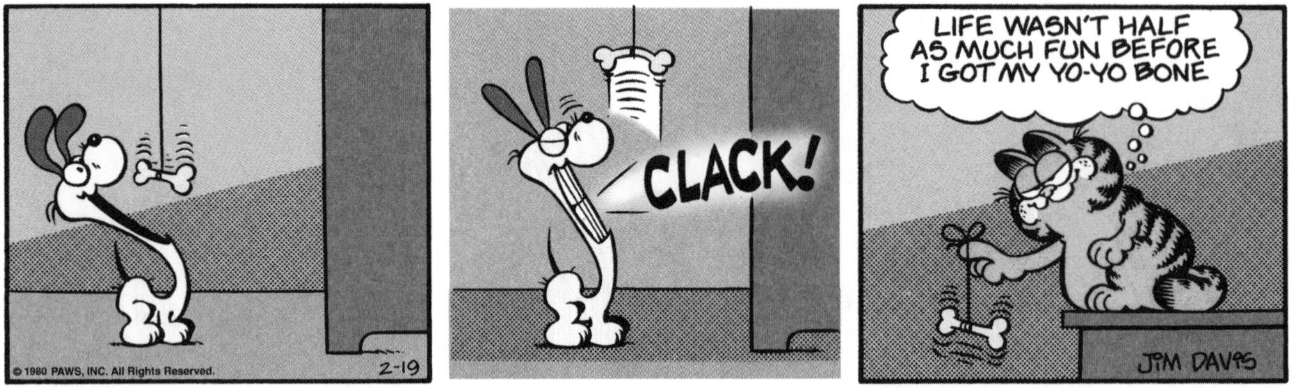
© 1980 PAWS, INC. All Rights Reserved.
2-19
CLACK!
LIFE WASN'T HALF AS MUCH FUN BEFORE I GOT MY YO-YO BONE
JIM DAVIS

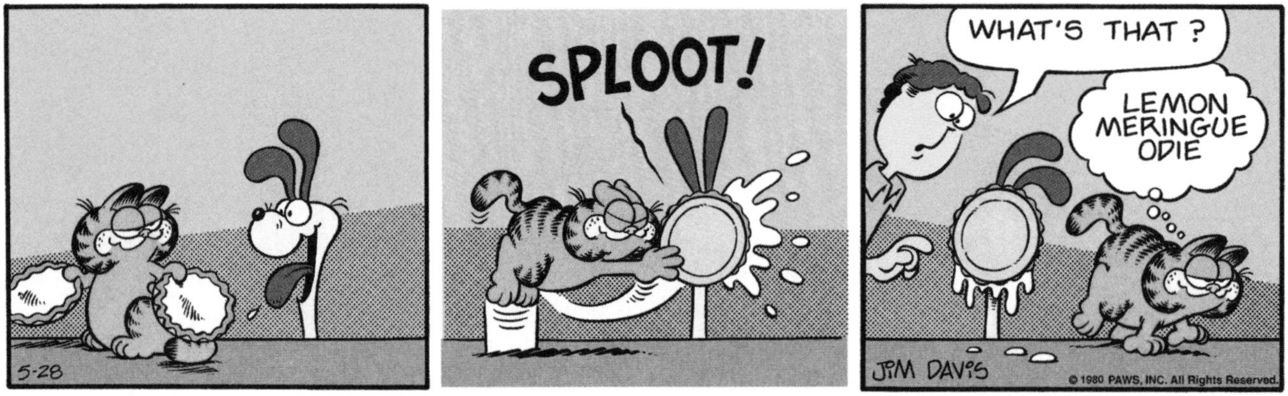
5-28
SPLOOT!
WHAT'S THAT ?
LEMON MERINGUE ODIE
JIM DAVIS
© 1980 PAWS, INC. All Rights Reserved.

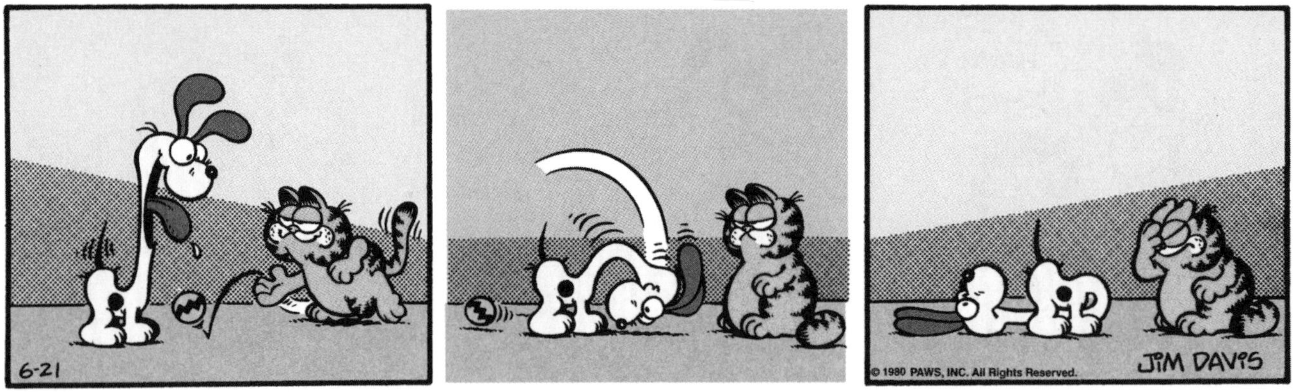
6-21
© 1980 PAWS, INC. All Rights Reserved.
JIM DAVIS

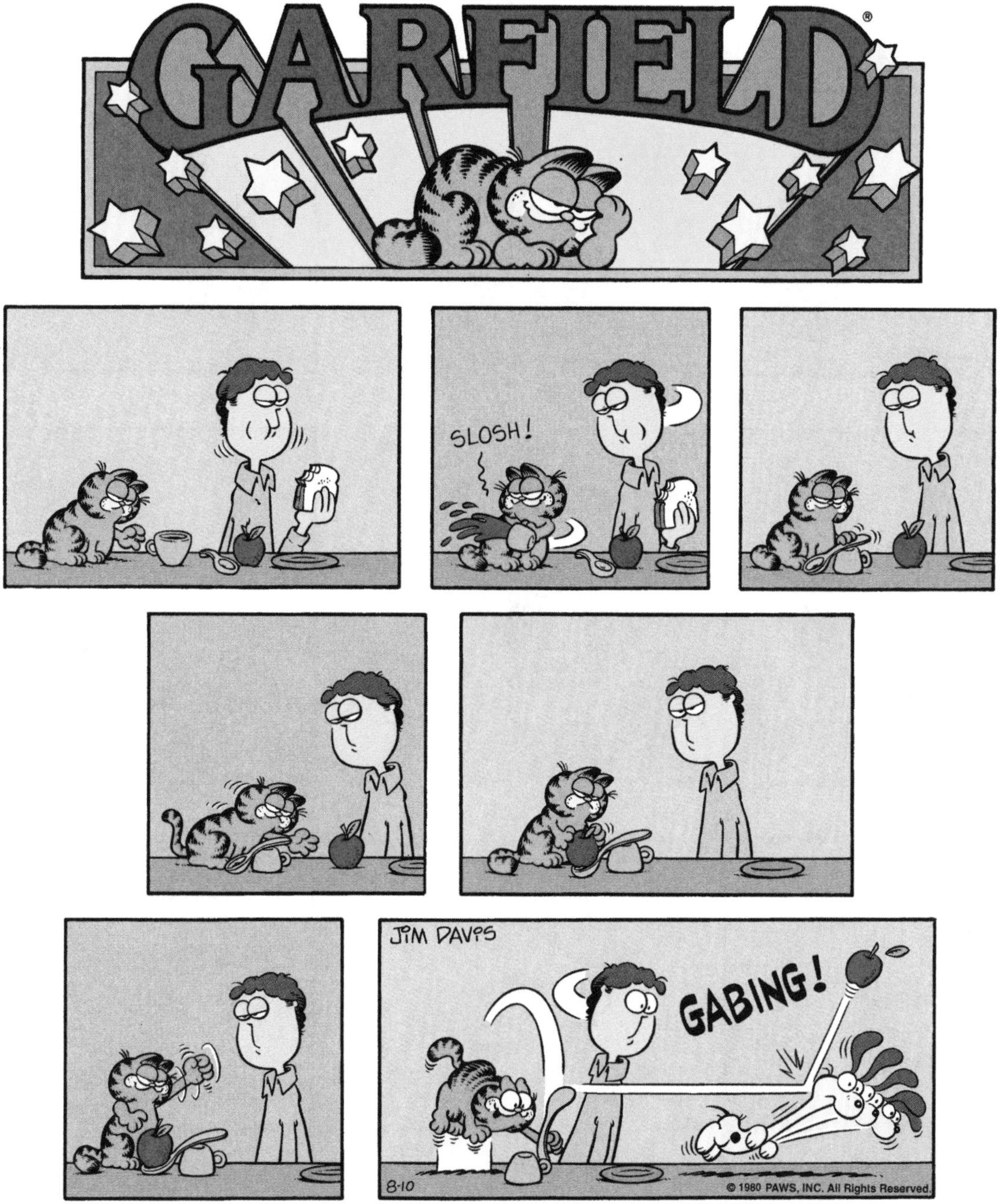
GARFIELD®
SLOSH!
JIM DAVIS
GABING!
8-10
© 1980 PAWS, INC. All Rights Reserved.

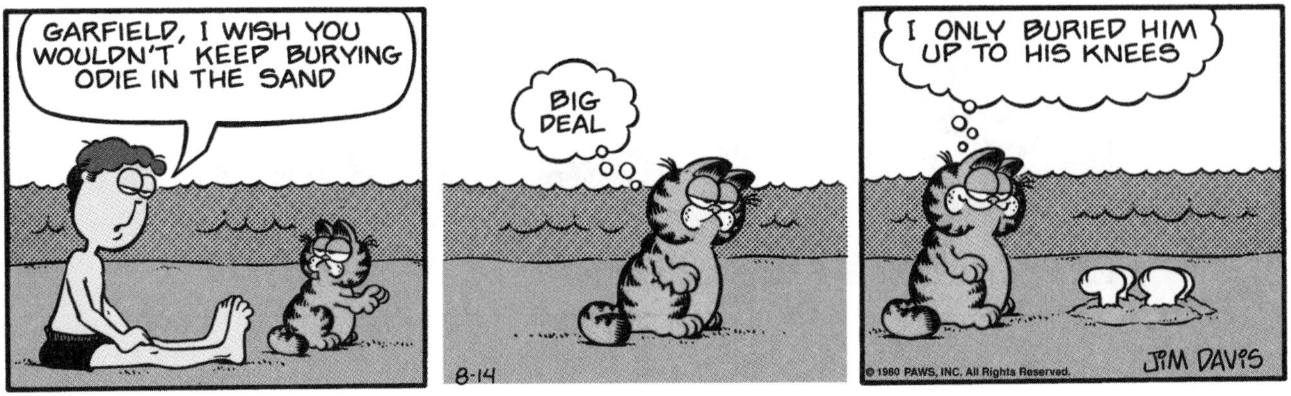
GARFIELD, I WISH YOU WOULDN'T KEEP BURYING ODIE IN THE SAND
BIG DEAL
8-14
I ONLY BURIED HIM UP TO HIS KNEES
© 1980 PAWS, INC. All Rights Reserved.
JIM DAVIS

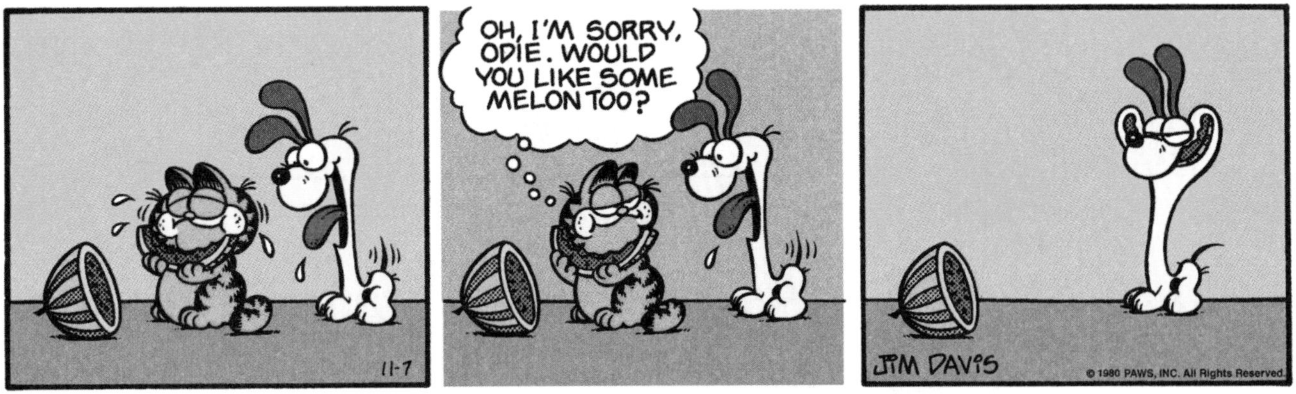
11-7
OH, I'M SORRY, ODIE. WOULD YOU LIKE SOME MELON TOO?
JIM DAVIS
© 1980 PAWS, INC. All Rights Reserved.

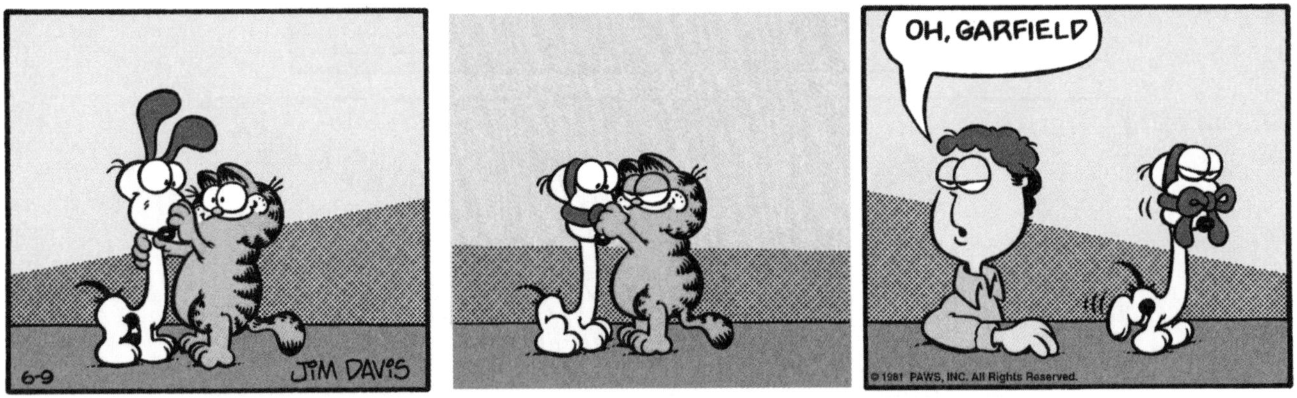
6-9
JIM DAVIS
OH, GARFIELD
© 1981 PAWS, INC. All Rights Reserved.

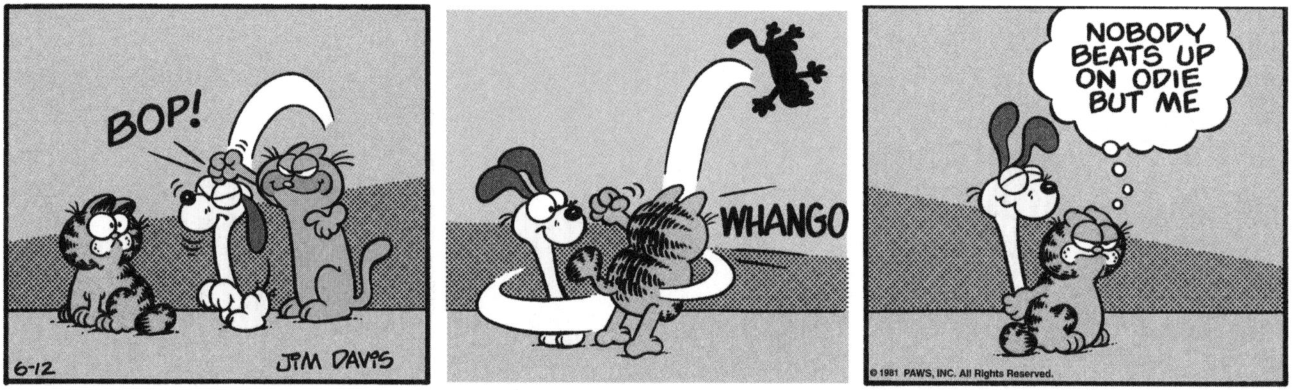
BOP!
6-12
JIM DAVIS
WHANGO
NOBODY BEATS UP ON ODIE BUT ME
© 1981 PAWS, INC. All Rights Reserved.

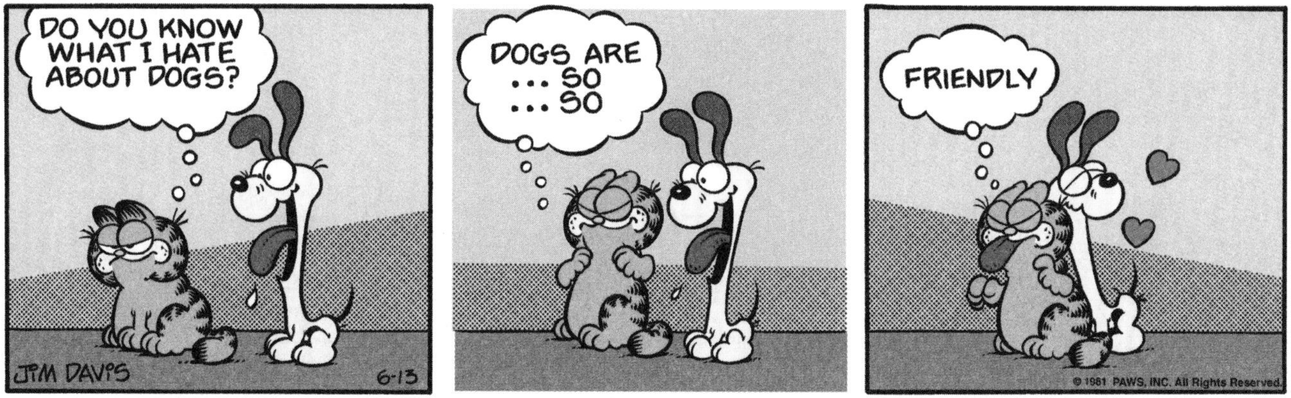
DO YOU KNOW WHAT I HATE ABOUT DOGS?
JIM DAVIS
6-13
DOGS ARE ... SO ... SO
FRIENDLY
© 1981 PAWS, INC. All Rights Reserved.

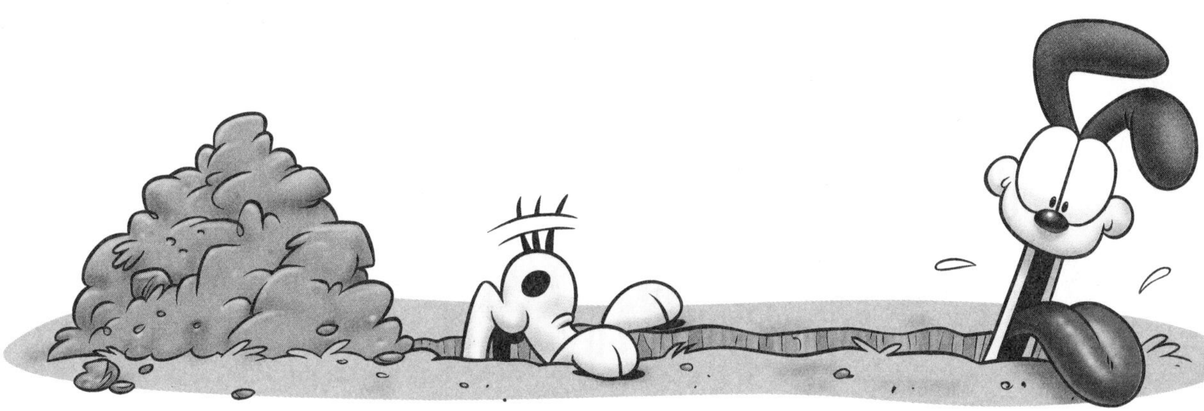

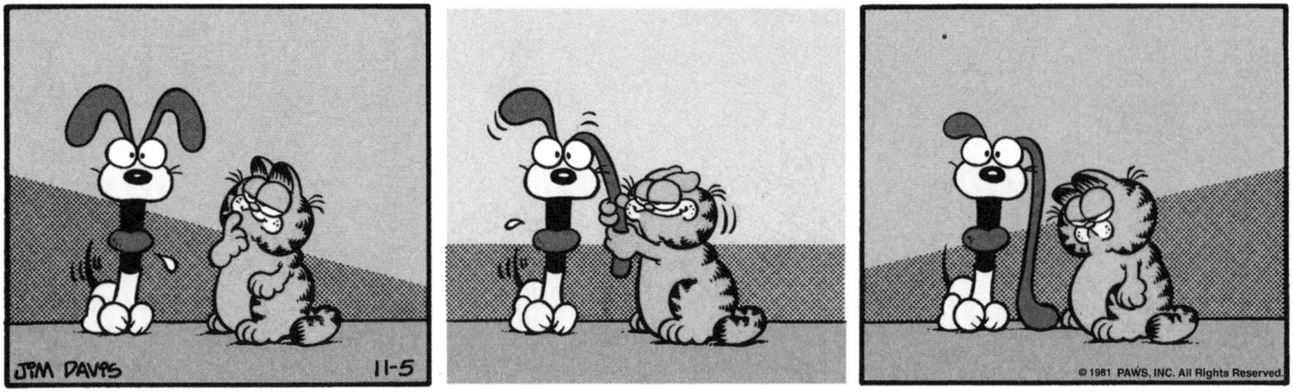
JIM DAVIS
11-5
© 1981 PAWS, INC. All Rights Reserved.

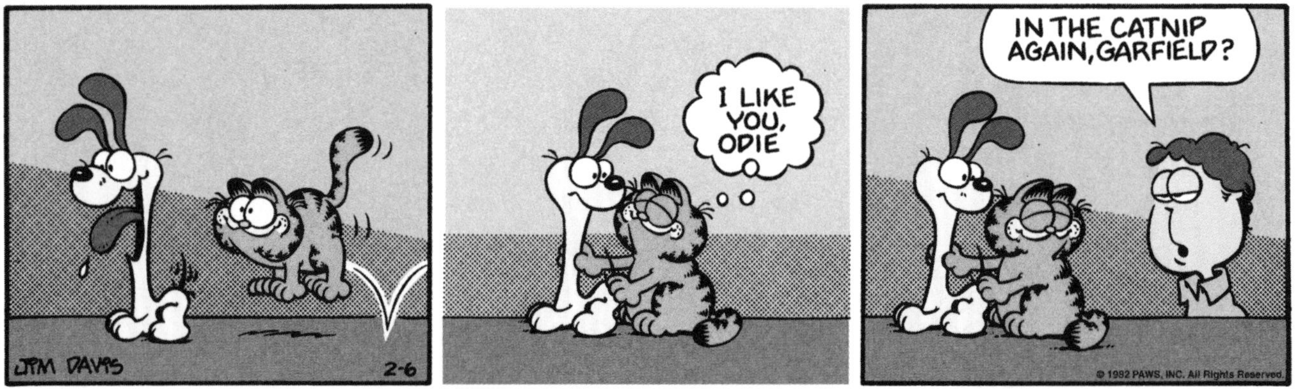
JIM DAVIS
2-6
I LIKE YOU, ODIE
IN THE CATNIP AGAIN, GARFIELD?
© 1982 PAWS, INC. All Rights Reserved.

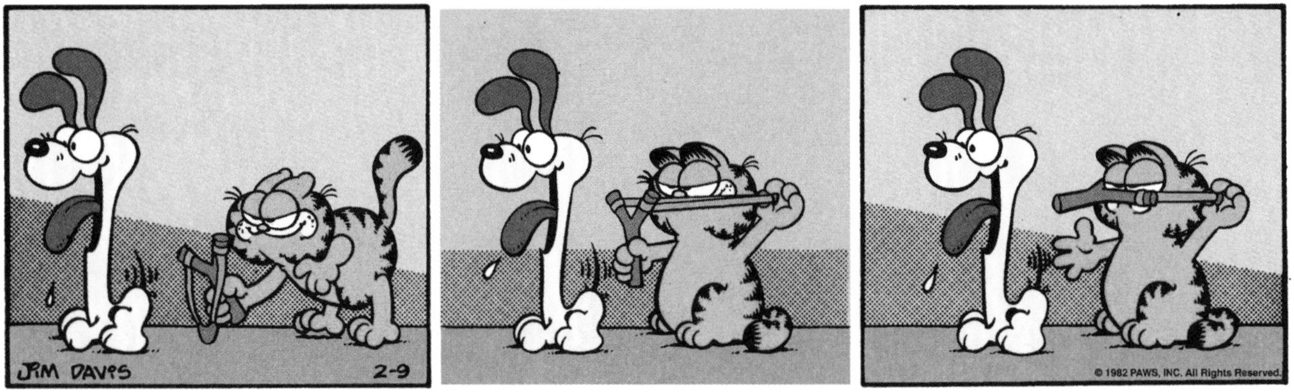
JIM DAVIS
2-9
© 1982 PAWS, INC. All Rights Reserved.

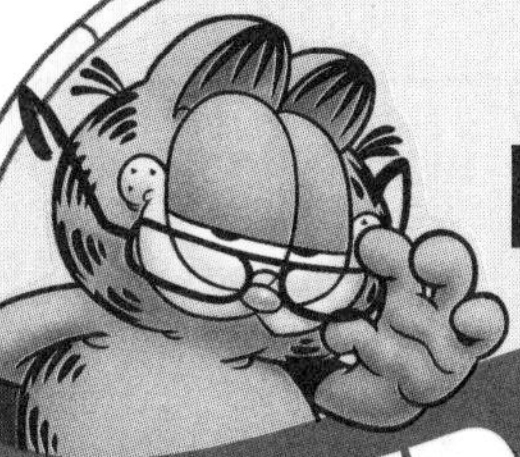

PROFESSOR GARFIELD'S NATURAL HISTORY OF DOGS

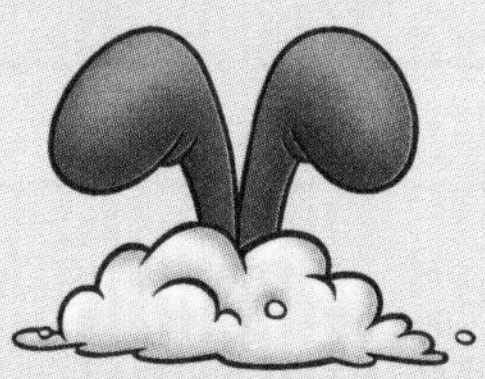

PROTO-DOG

A brainless slime dweller

DOGOSAUR 12 MILLION B.C.

Had the misfortune to live before trees and fire hydrants evolved; soon extinct.

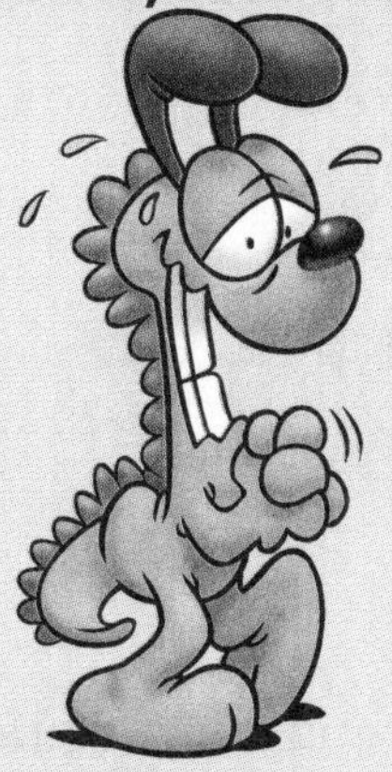

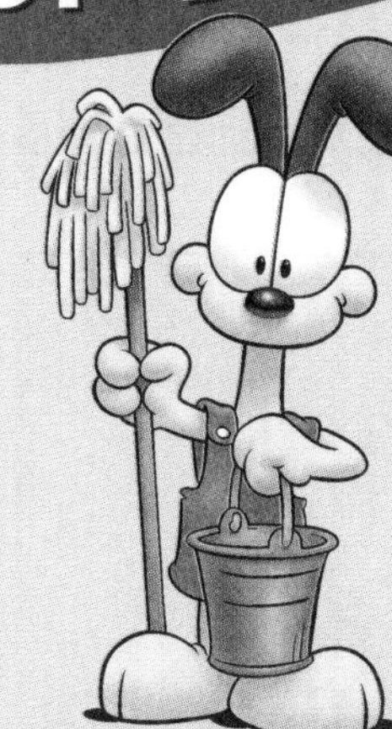

CRO-MAGNON DOG 10,000 B.C.

Domesticated, but still not housebroken.

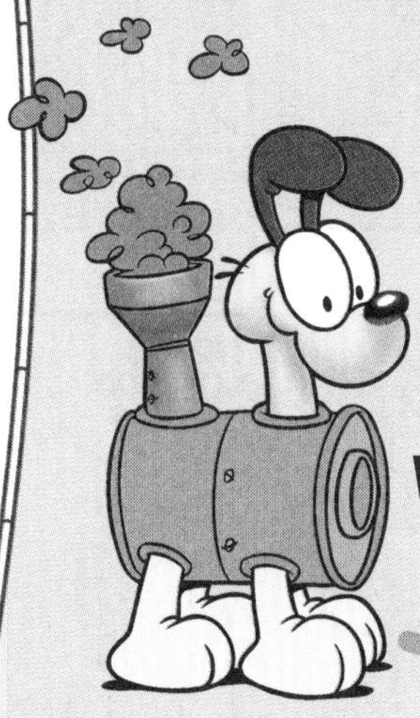

WOOD-BURNING DOG CA. 1850

Another mistake.

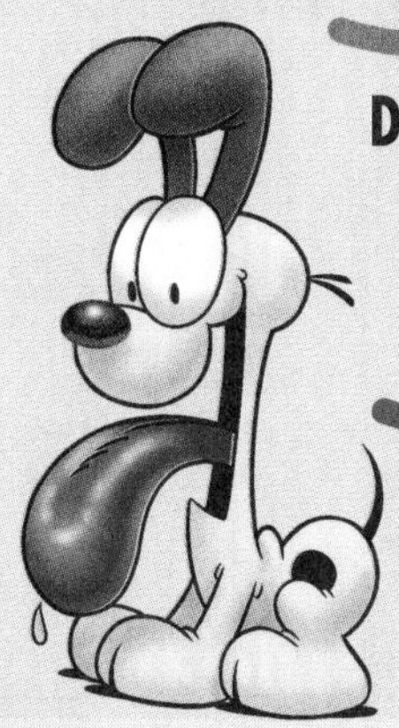

MODERN DOG

As you can see, not a lot of progress.

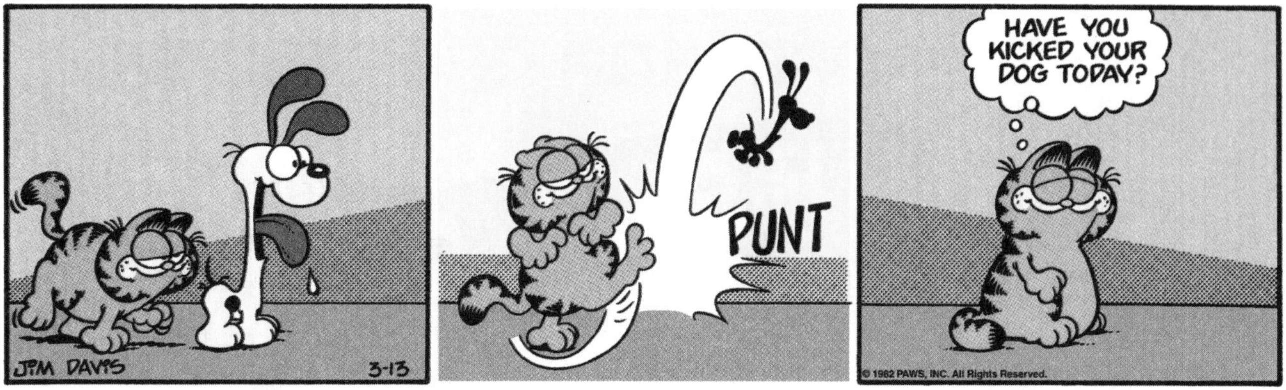
JIM DAVIS
3-13
PUNT
HAVE YOU KICKED YOUR DOG TODAY?
© 1982 PAWS, INC. All Rights Reserved.

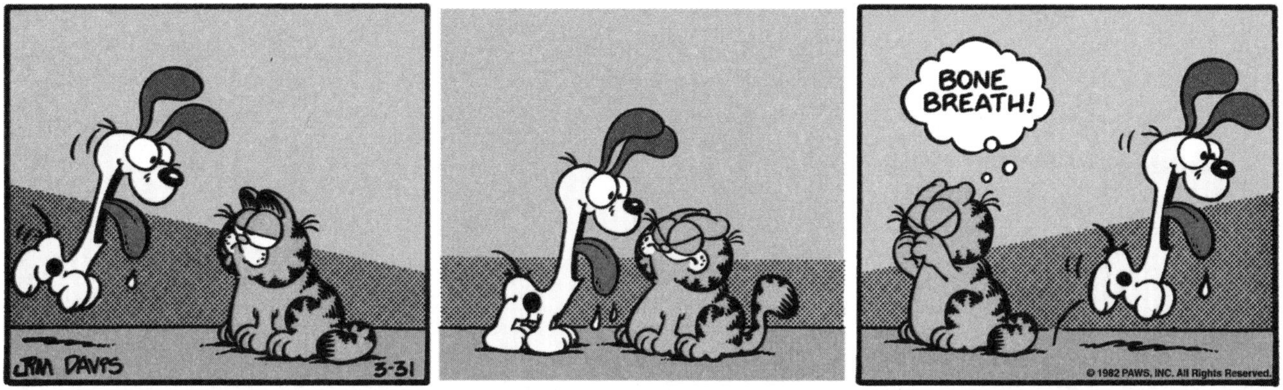
JIM DAVIS
3-31
BONE BREATH!
© 1982 PAWS, INC. All Rights Reserved.

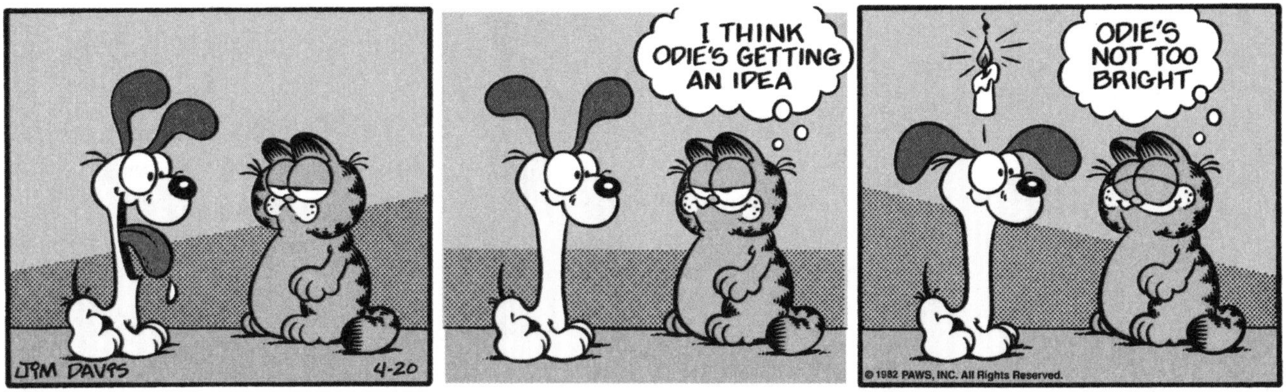
JIM DAVIS
4-20
I THINK ODIE'S GETTING AN IDEA
ODIE'S NOT TOO BRIGHT
© 1982 PAWS, INC. All Rights Reserved.

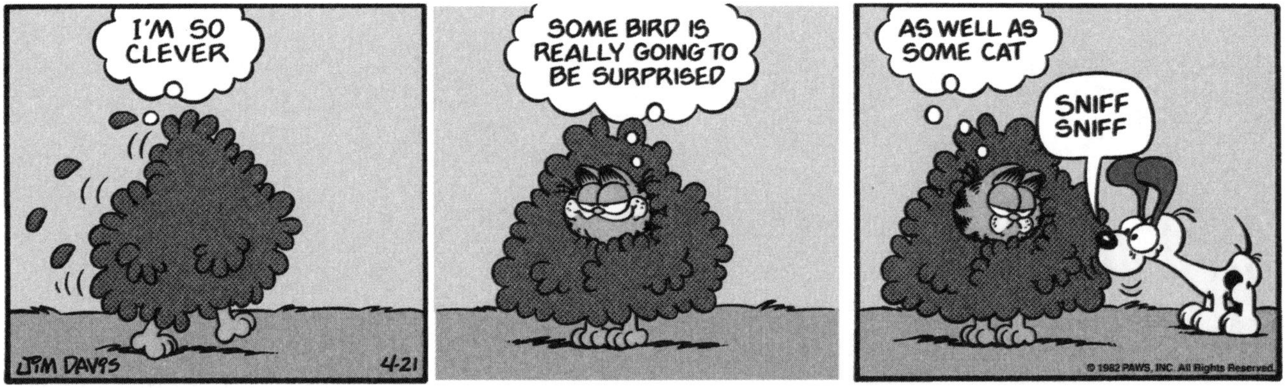
I'M SO CLEVER
JIM DAVIS
4-21
SOME BIRD IS REALLY GOING TO BE SURPRISED
AS WELL AS SOME CAT
SNIFF SNIFF
© 1982 PAWS, INC. All Rights Reserved.

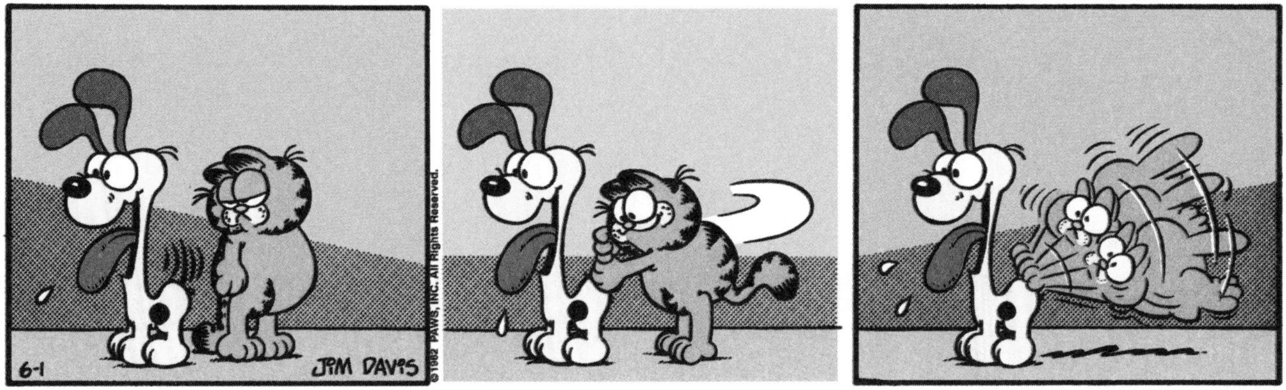
6-1
JIM DAVIS
© 1982 PAWS, INC. All Rights Reserved.

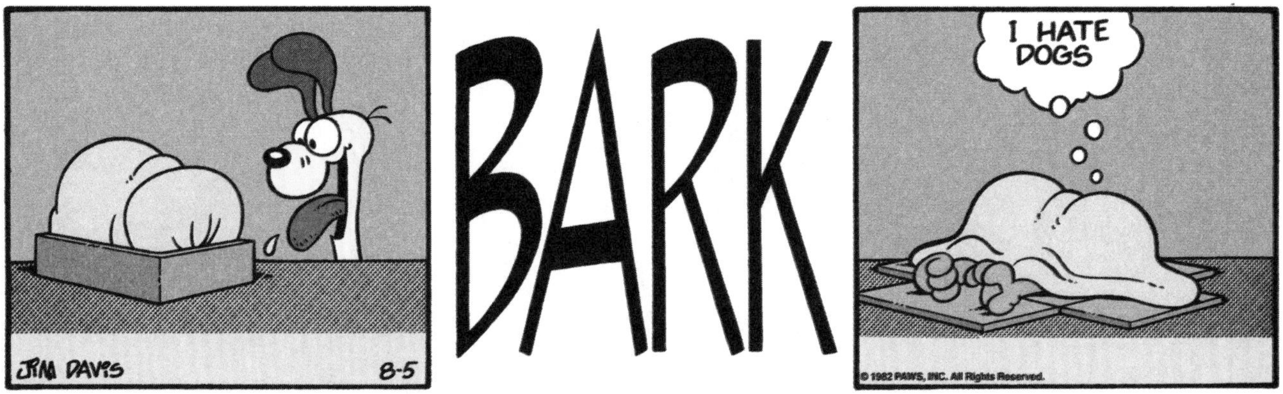
JIM DAVIS
8-5
BARK
I HATE DOGS
© 1982 PAWS, INC. All Rights Reserved.

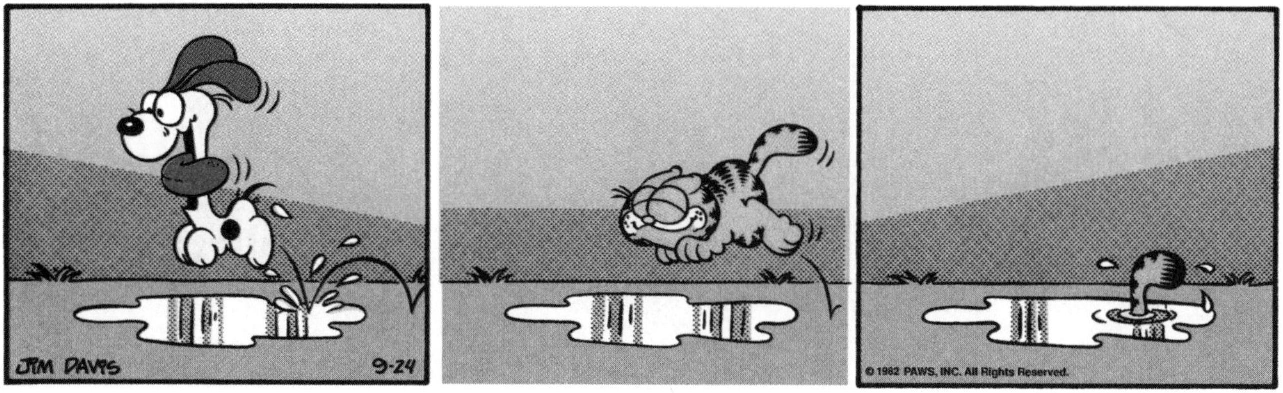
JIM DAVIS
9-24
© 1982 PAWS, INC. All Rights Reserved.

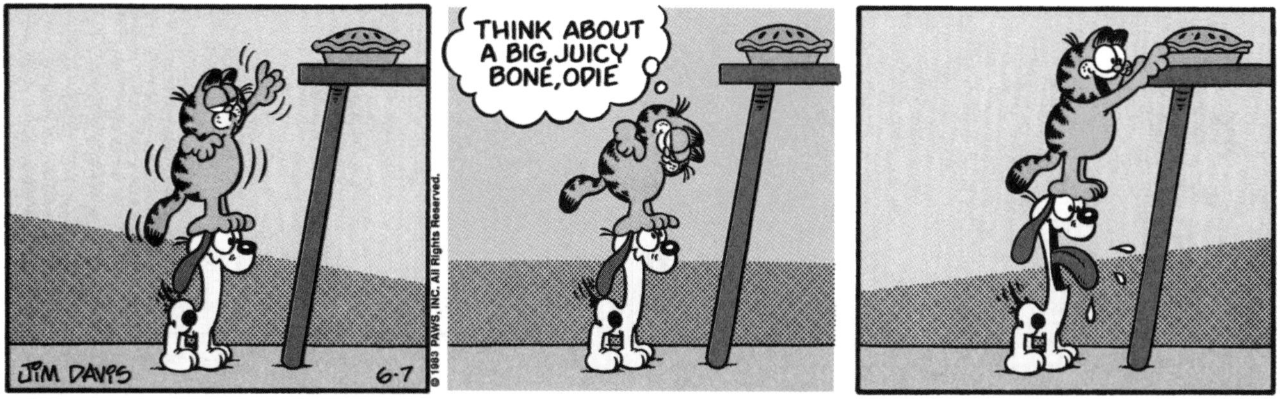
JIM DAVIS
6-7
© 1983 PAWS, INC. All Rights Reserved.
THINK ABOUT A BIG, JUICY BONE, ODIE

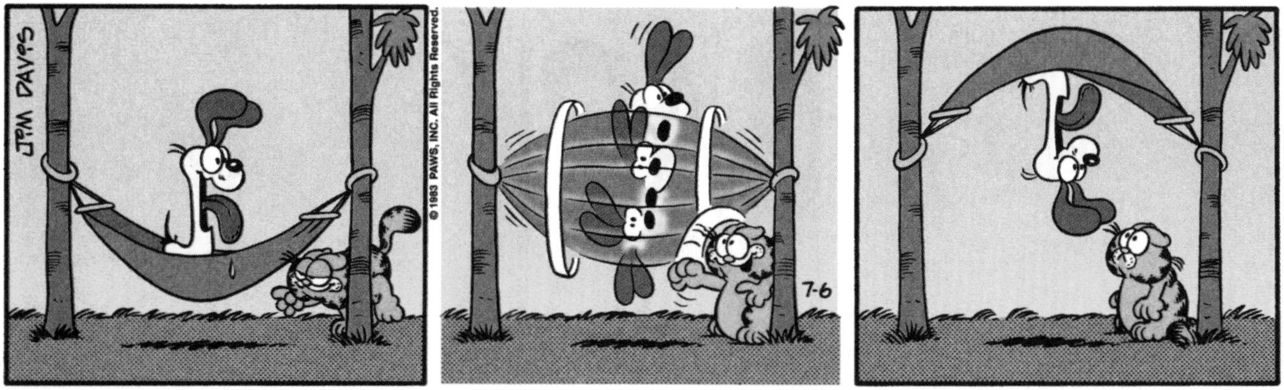
JIM DAVIS
© 1983 PAWS, INC. All Rights Reserved.
7-6

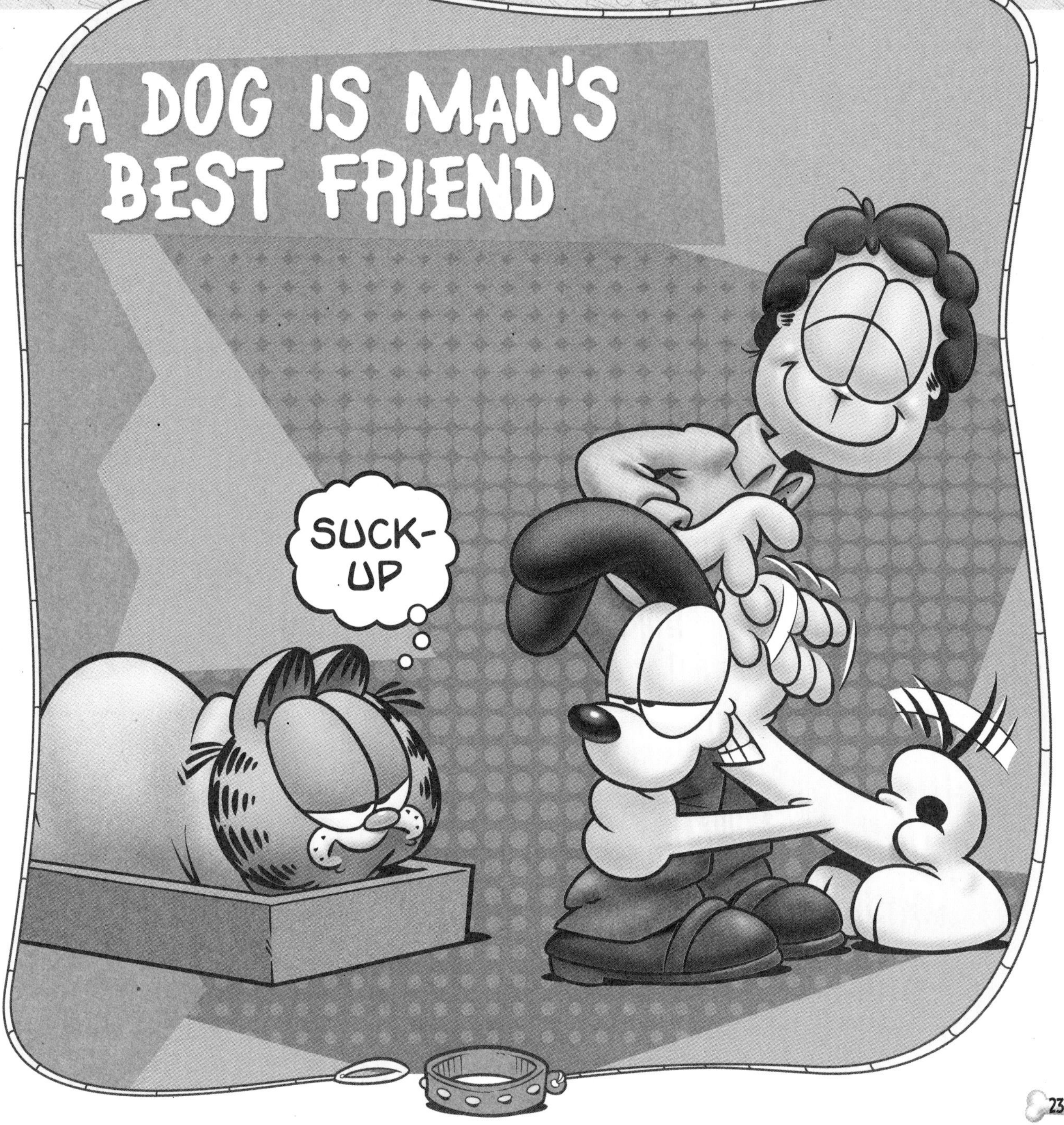
A DOG IS MAN'S BEST FRIEND
SUCK-UP

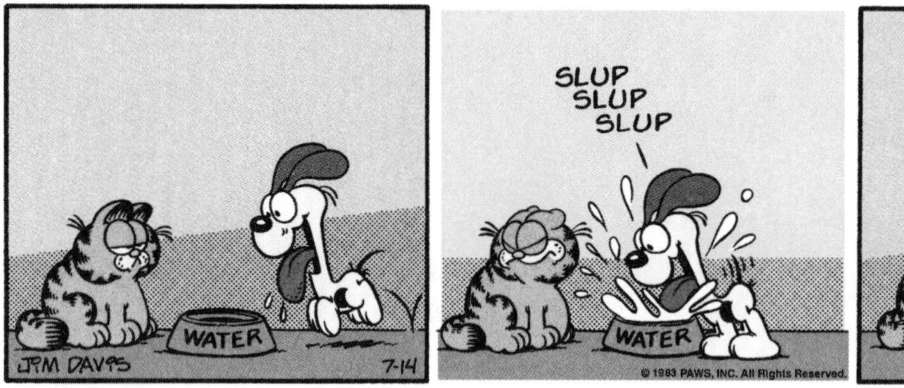
WATER
JIM DAVIS
7-14
SLUP
SLUP
SLUP
WATER
© 1983 PAWS, INC. All Rights Reserved.
DROOL
FUEL
WATER

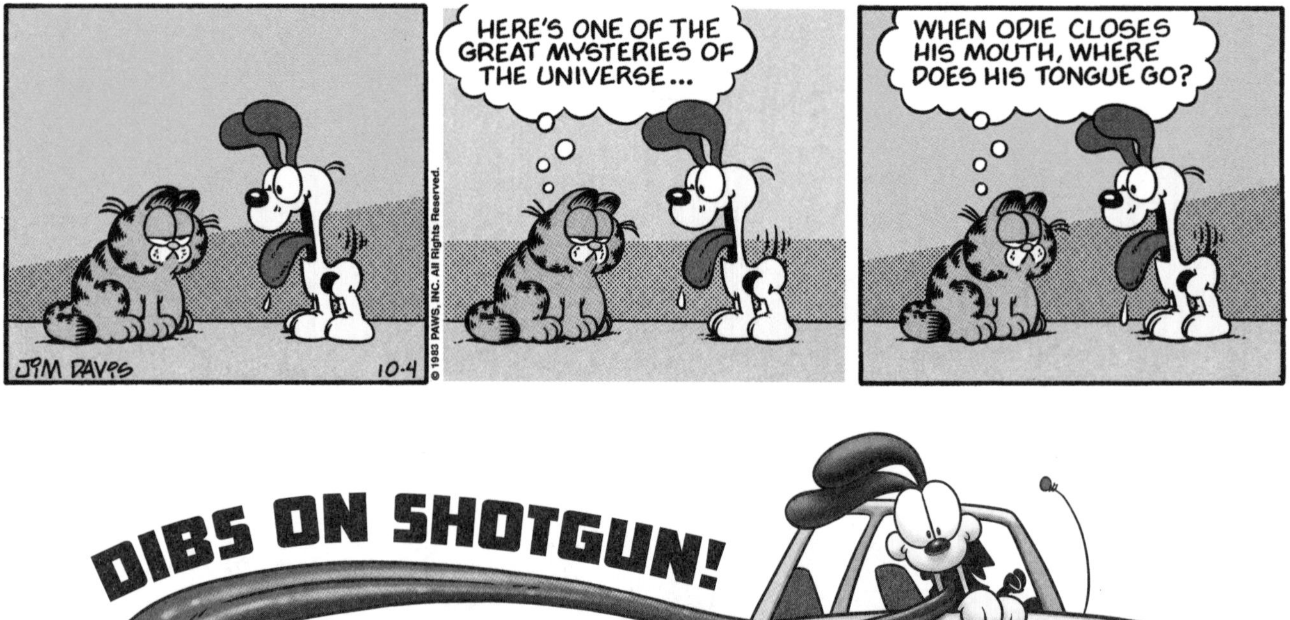
JIM DAVIS
10-4
© 1983 PAWS, INC. All Rights Reserved.
HERE'S ONE OF THE GREAT MYSTERIES OF THE UNIVERSE...
WHEN ODIE CLOSES HIS MOUTH, WHERE DOES HIS TONGUE GO?

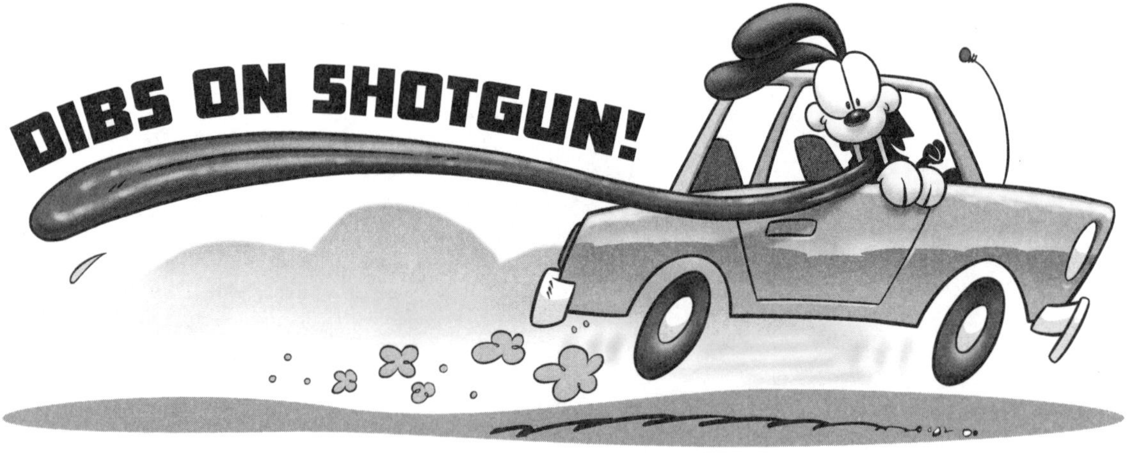
DIBS ON SHOTGUN!

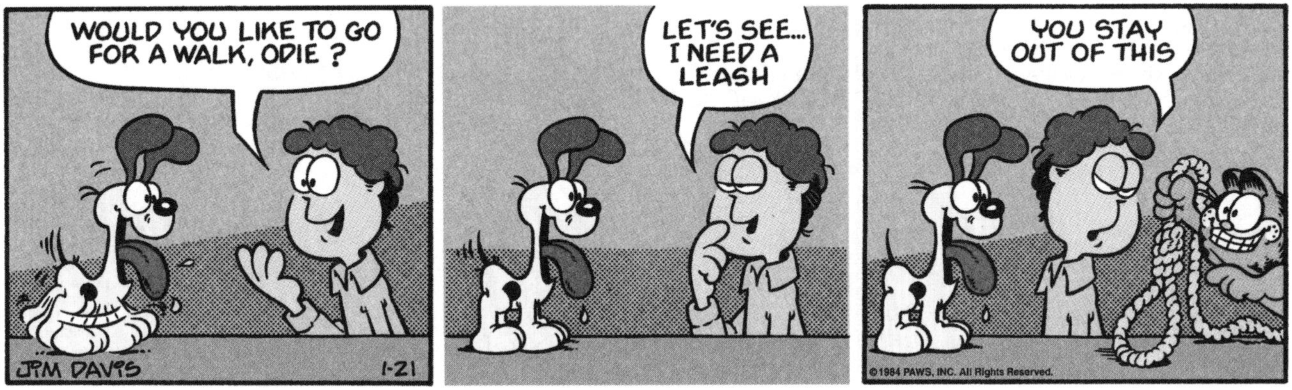
WOULD YOU LIKE TO GO FOR A WALK, ODIE ?
JIM DAVIS 1-21
LET'S SEE... I NEED A LEASH
YOU STAY OUT OF THIS
©1984 PAWS, INC. All Rights Reserved.

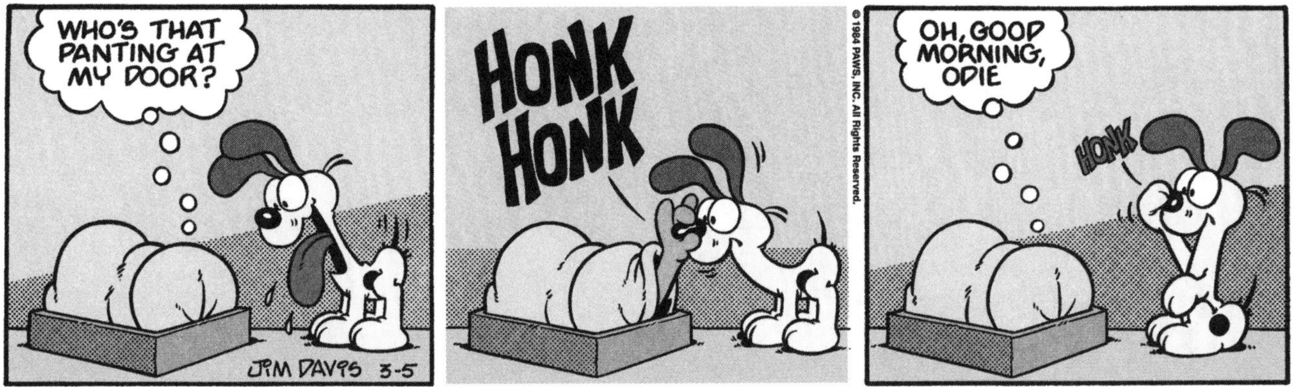
WHO'S THAT PANTING AT MY DOOR?
JIM DAVIS 3-5
HONK HONK
© 1984 PAWS, INC. All Rights Reserved.
OH, GOOD MORNING, ODIE
HONK

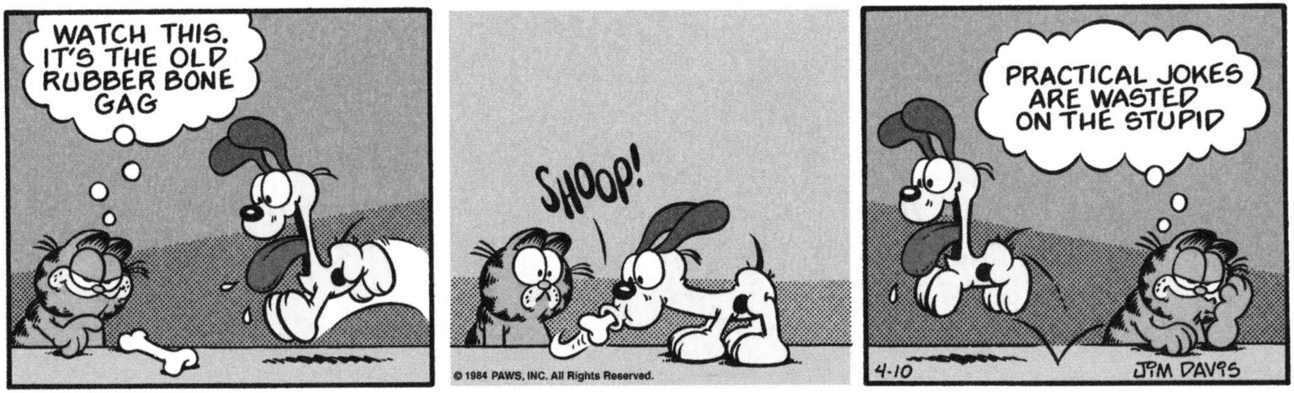
WATCH THIS. IT'S THE OLD RUBBER BONE GAG
SHOOP!
© 1984 PAWS, INC. All Rights Reserved.
PRACTICAL JOKES ARE WASTED ON THE STUPID
4-10
JIM DAVIS

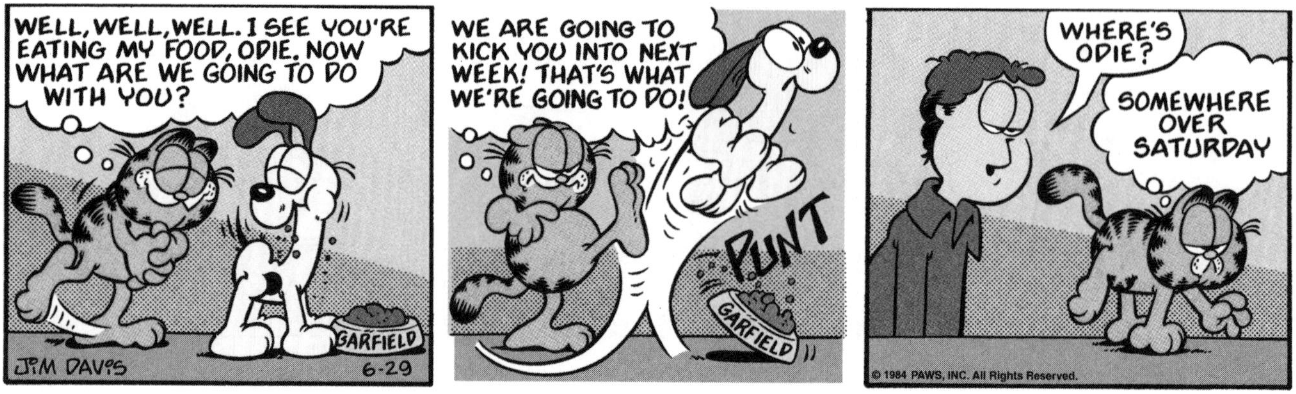
WELL, WELL, WELL. I SEE YOU'RE EATING MY FOOD, ODIE. NOW WHAT ARE WE GOING TO DO WITH YOU?
GARFIELD
JIM DAVIS
6-29
WE ARE GOING TO KICK YOU INTO NEXT WEEK! THAT'S WHAT WE'RE GOING TO DO!
PUNT
GARFIELD
WHERE'S ODIE?
SOMEWHERE OVER SATURDAY
© 1984 PAWS, INC. All Rights Reserved.

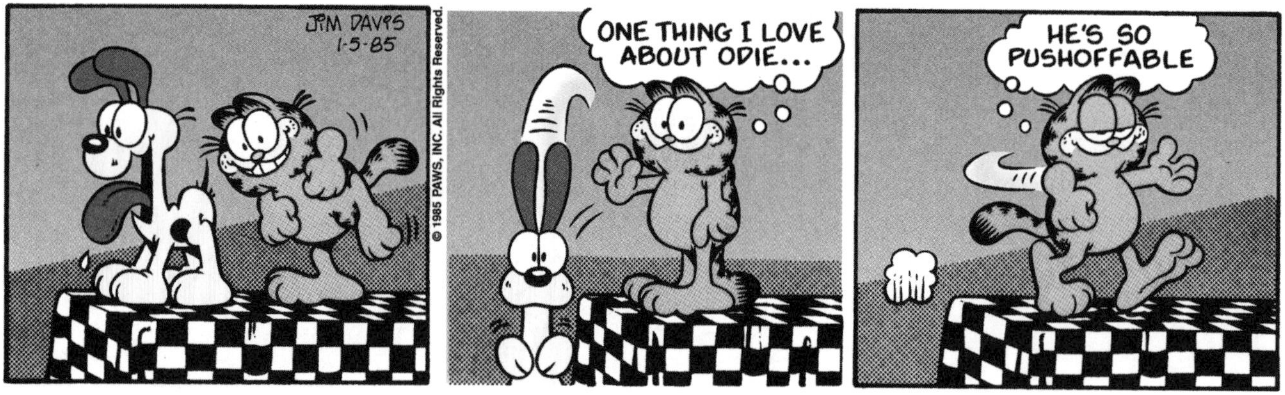
JIM DAVIS
1-5-85
© 1985 PAWS, INC. All Rights Reserved.
ONE THING I LOVE ABOUT ODIE...
HE'S SO PUSHOFFABLE

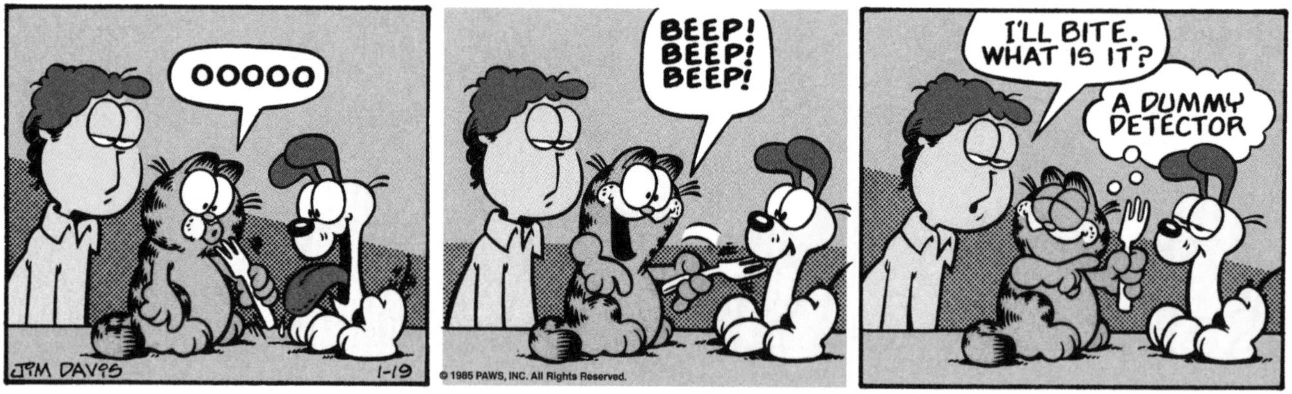
OOOOO
JIM DAVIS
1-19
BEEP! BEEP! BEEP!
© 1985 PAWS, INC. All Rights Reserved.
I'LL BITE. WHAT IS IT?
A DUMMY DETECTOR

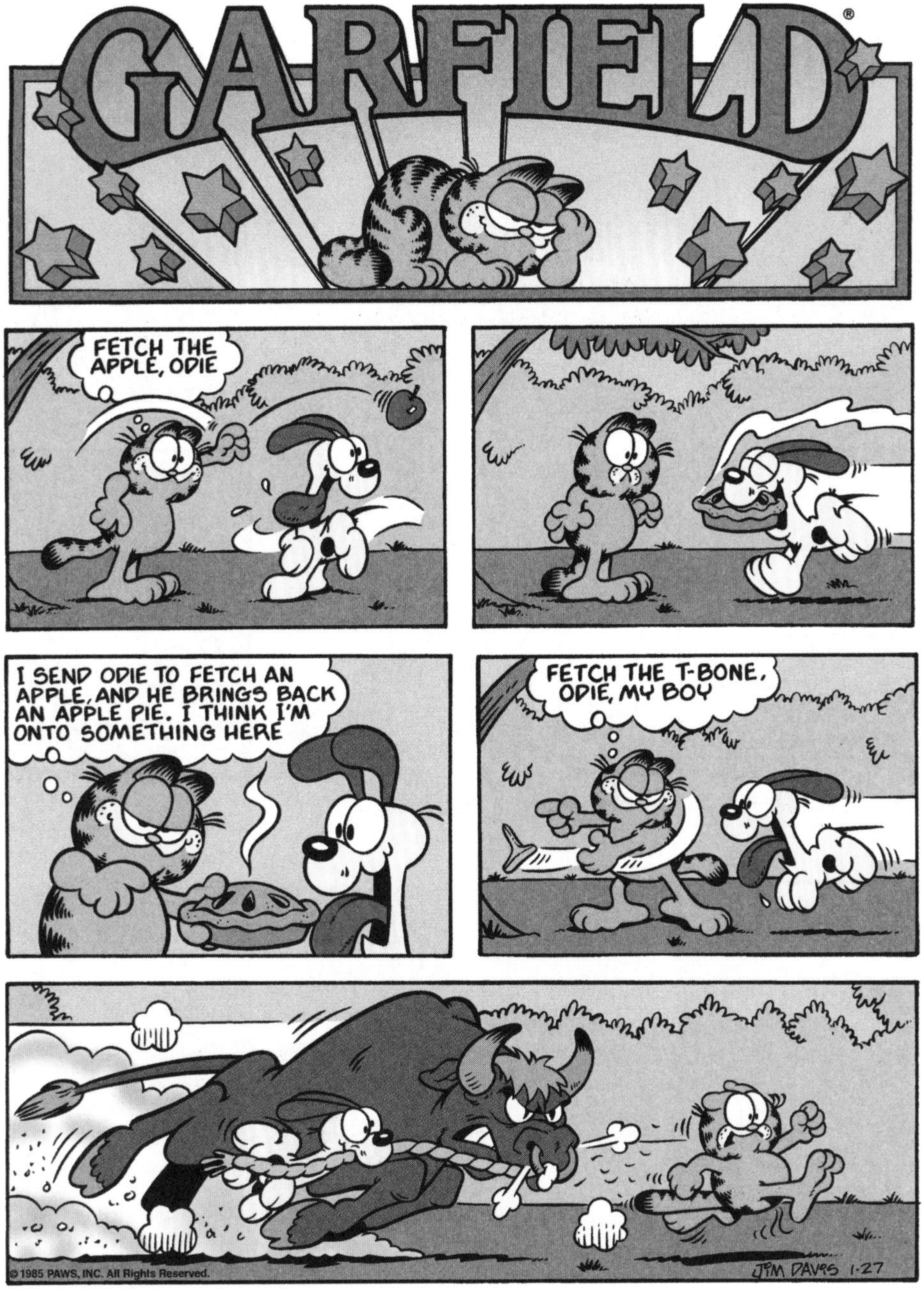
GARFIELD®
FETCH THE APPLE, ODIE
I SEND ODIE TO FETCH AN APPLE, AND HE BRINGS BACK AN APPLE PIE. I THINK I'M ONTO SOMETHING HERE
FETCH THE T-BONE, ODIE, MY BOY
© 1985 PAWS, INC. All Rights Reserved.
JIM DAVIS 1-27

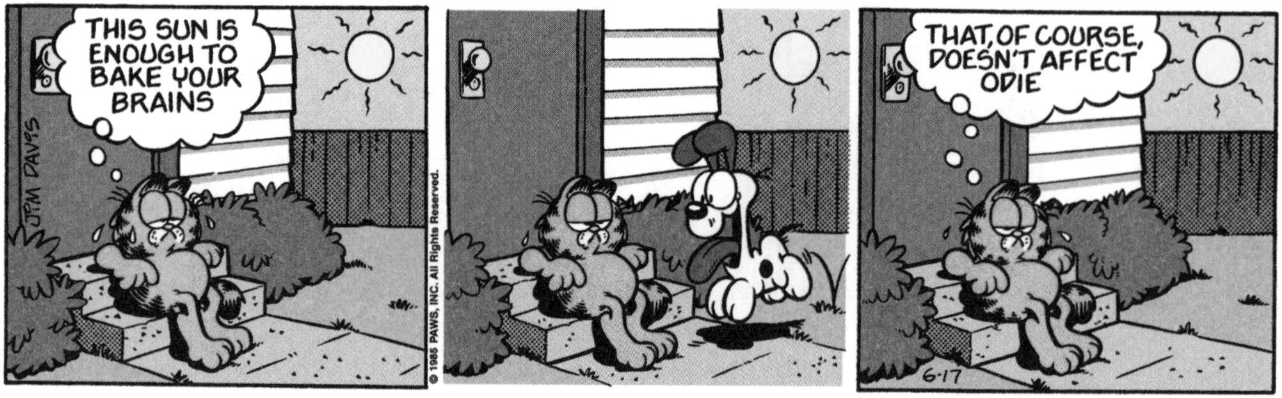
THIS SUN IS ENOUGH TO BAKE YOUR BRAINS
JIM DAVIS
© 1985 PAWS, INC. All Rights Reserved.
THAT, OF COURSE, DOESN'T AFFECT ODIE
6-17

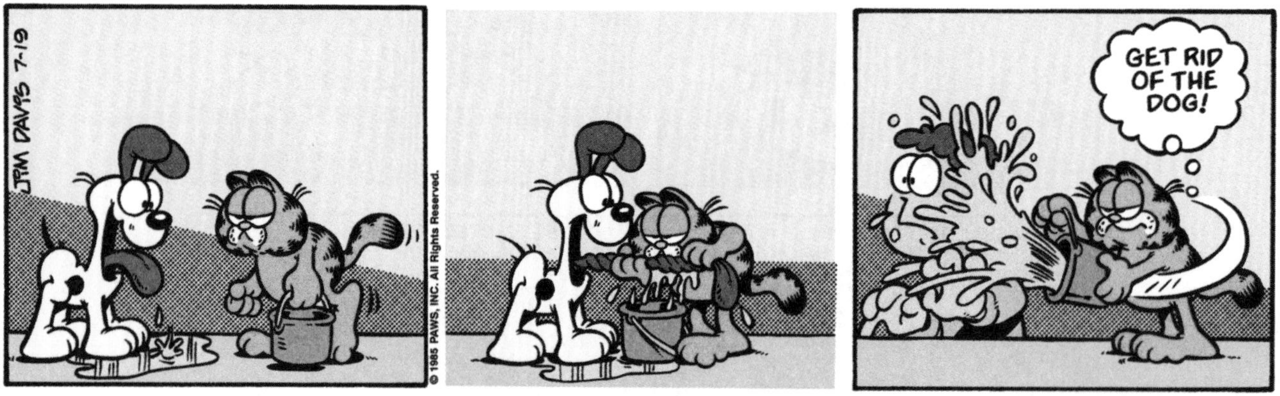
JIM DAVIS 7-19
© 1985 PAWS, INC. All Rights Reserved.
GET RID OF THE DOG!

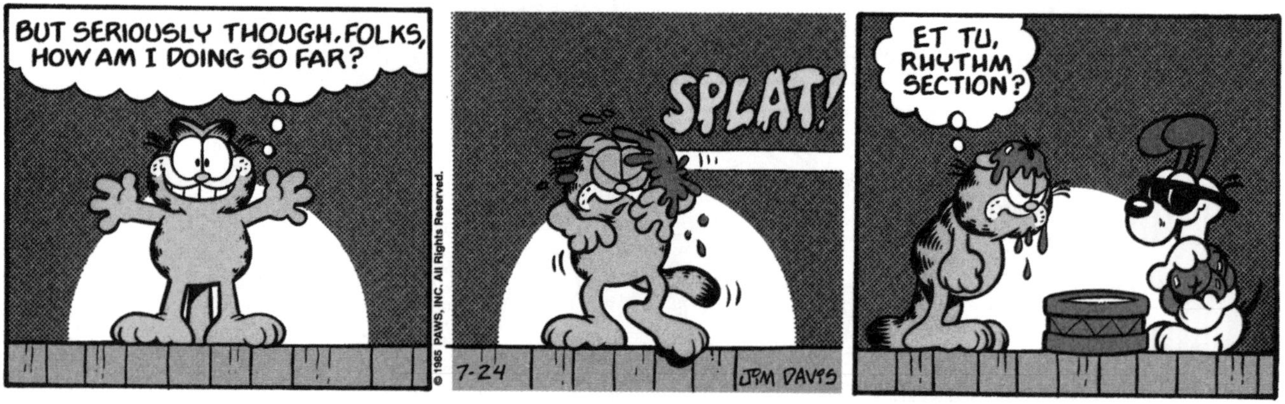
BUT SERIOUSLY THOUGH, FOLKS, HOW AM I DOING SO FAR?
© 1985 PAWS, INC. All Rights Reserved.
SPLAT!
7-24
JIM DAVIS
ET TU, RHYTHM SECTION?

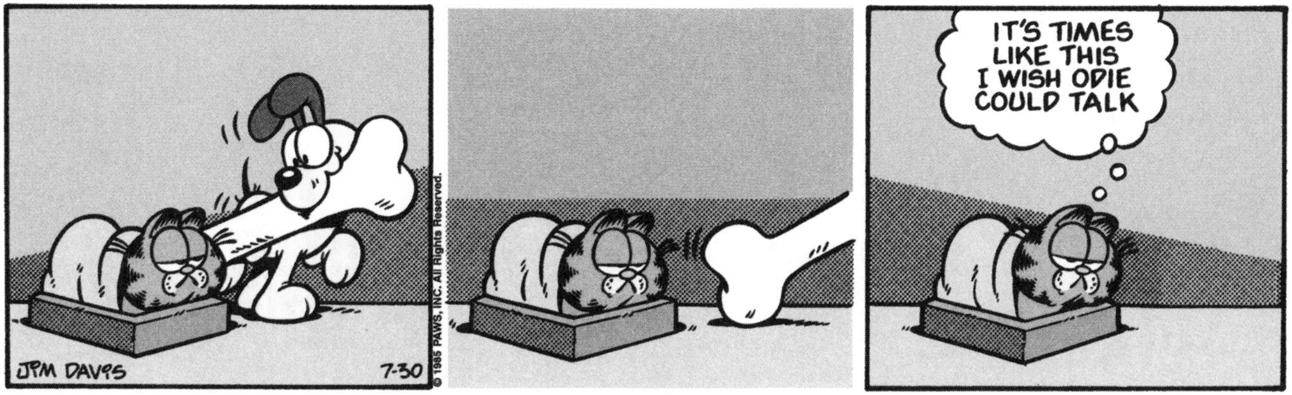
JIM DAVIS
7-30
© 1985 PAWS, INC. All Rights Reserved.
IT'S TIMES LIKE THIS I WISH ODIE COULD TALK

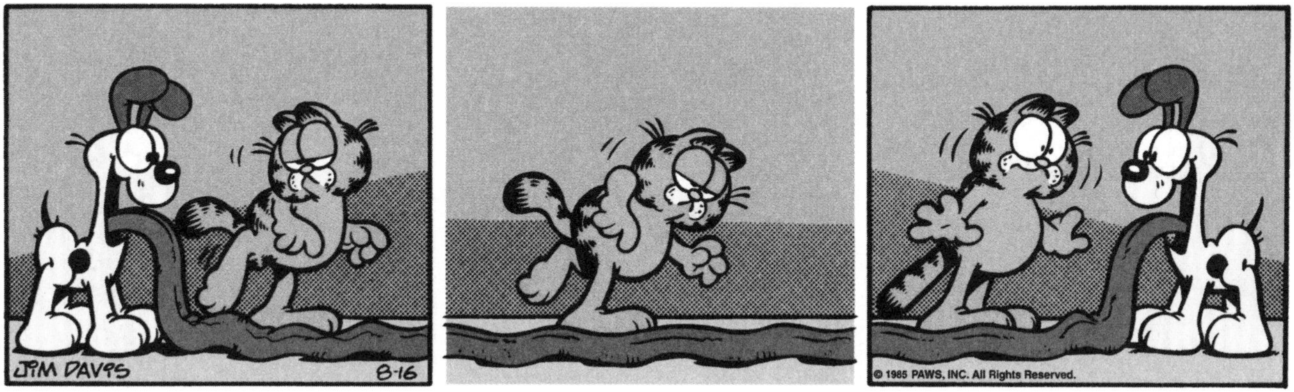
JIM DAVIS
8-16
© 1985 PAWS, INC. All Rights Reserved.

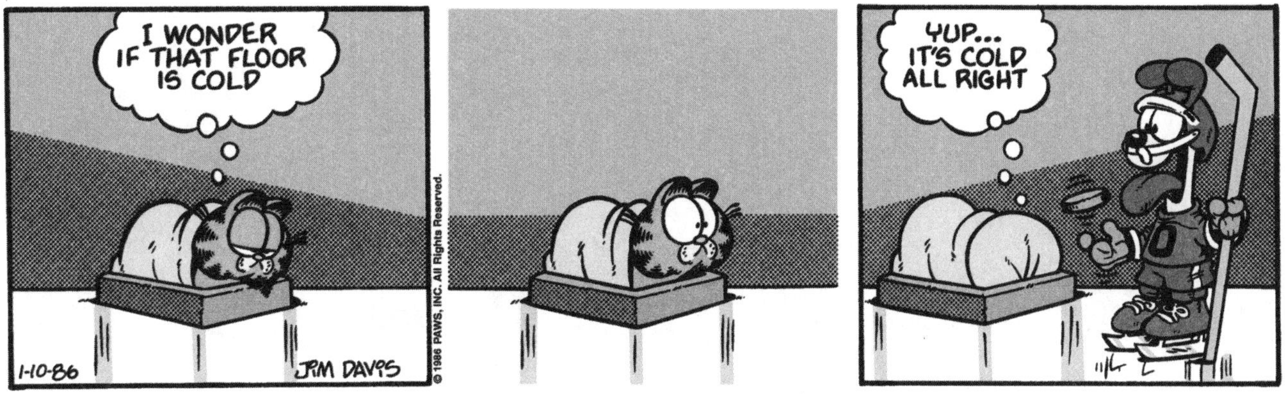
I WONDER IF THAT FLOOR IS COLD
1-10-86
JIM DAVIS
© 1986 PAWS, INC. All Rights Reserved.
YUP... IT'S COLD ALL RIGHT

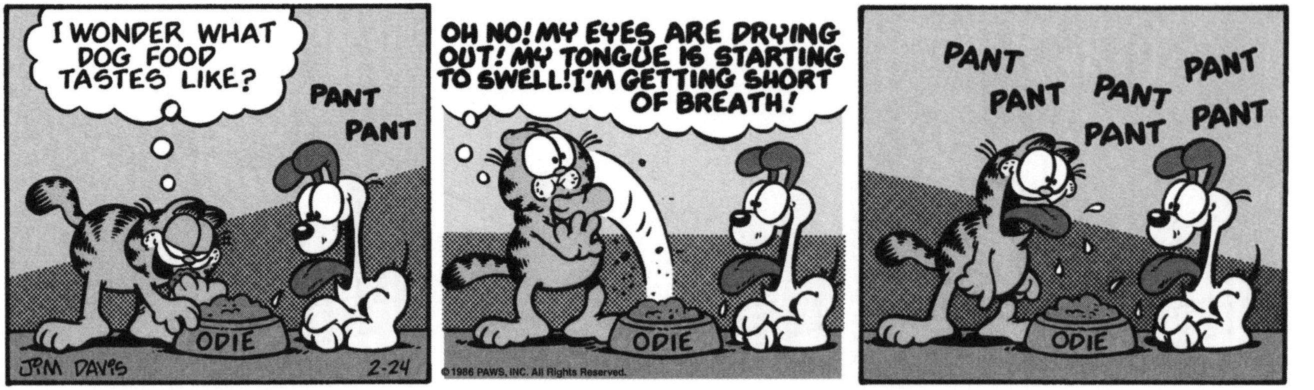
I WONDER WHAT DOG FOOD TASTES LIKE?
PANT PANT
JIM DAVIS 2-24
OH NO! MY EYES ARE DRYING OUT! MY TONGUE IS STARTING TO SWELL! I'M GETTING SHORT OF BREATH!
© 1986 PAWS, INC. All Rights Reserved.
PANT PANT PANT PANT PANT PANT
ODIE

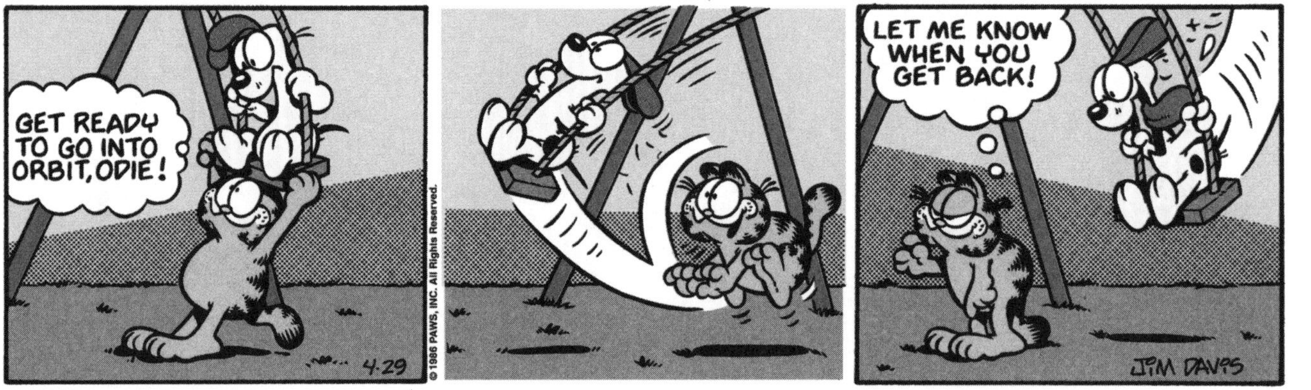
GET READY TO GO INTO ORBIT, ODIE!
4-29
© 1986 PAWS, INC. All Rights Reserved.
LET ME KNOW WHEN YOU GET BACK!
JIM DAVIS

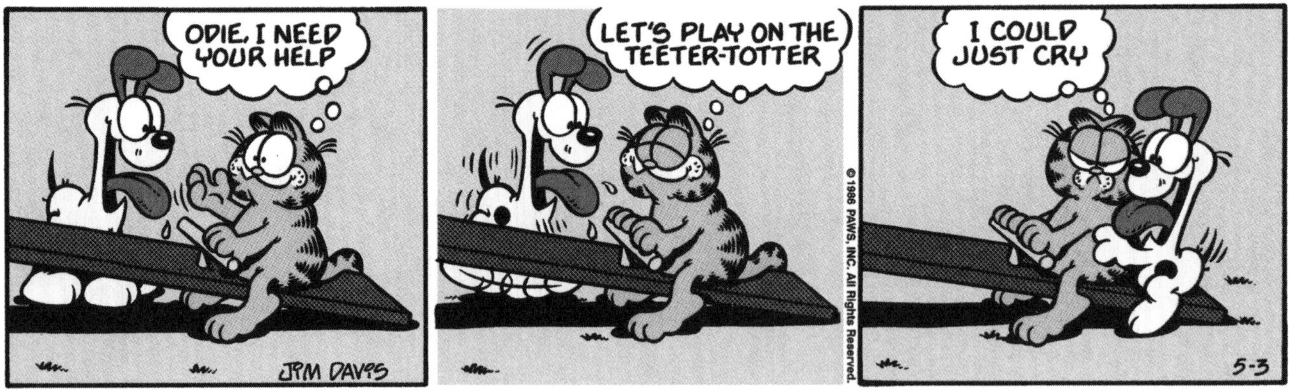
ODIE, I NEED YOUR HELP
JIM DAVIS
LET'S PLAY ON THE TEETER-TOTTER
© 1986 PAWS, INC. All Rights Reserved.
I COULD JUST CRY
5-3

ODIE'S PAST LIVES
BARK TWAIN
DROOLIUS CAESAR
A ROCK
BOOB RUTH

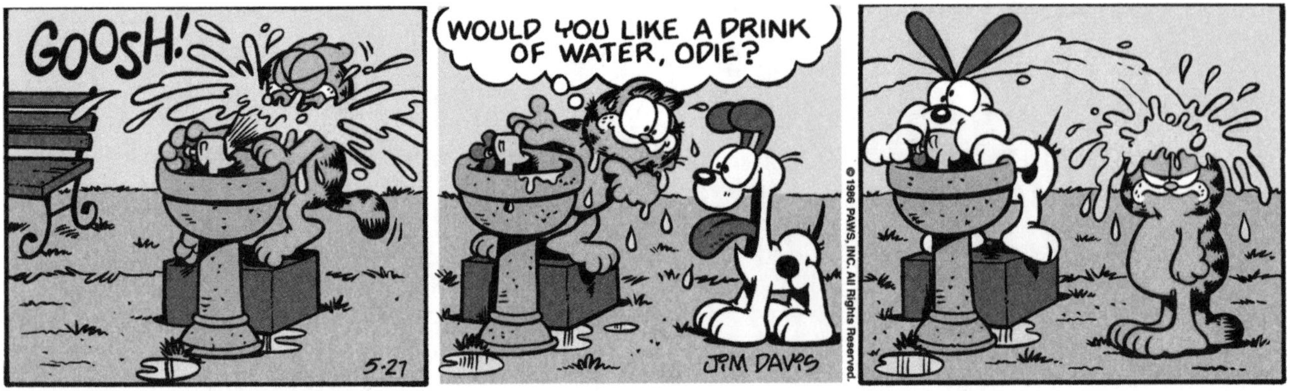
GOOSH!
5-27
WOULD YOU LIKE A DRINK OF WATER, ODIE?
JIM DAVIS
© 1986 PAWS, INC. All Rights Reserved.

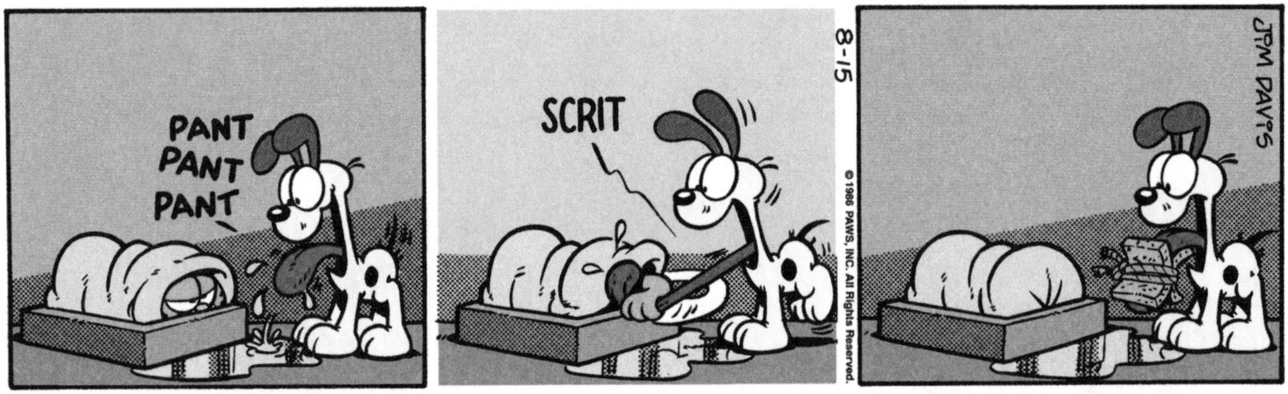
PANT
PANT
PANT
SCRIT
8-15
© 1986 PAWS, INC. All Rights Reserved.
JIM DAVIS

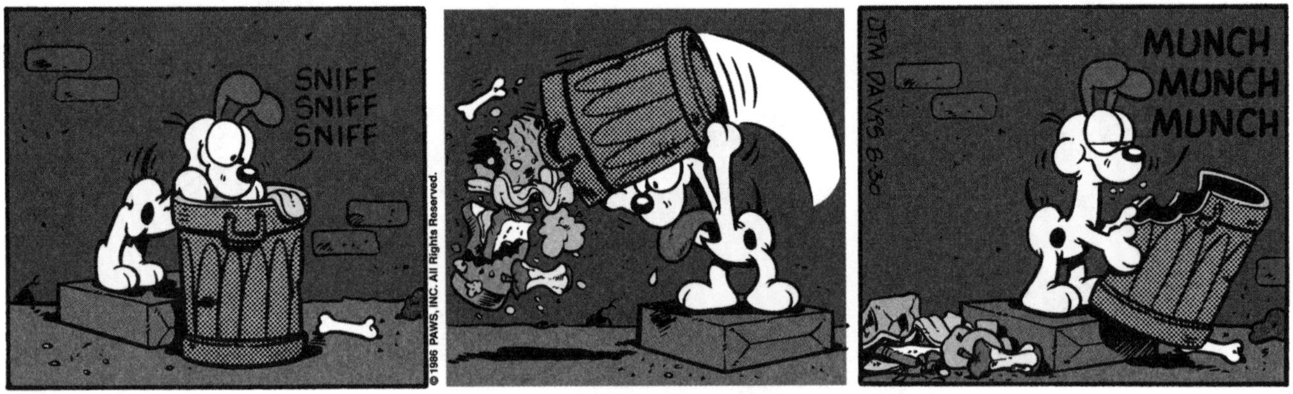
SNIFF
SNIFF
SNIFF
© 1986 PAWS, INC. All Rights Reserved.
JIM DAVIS 8-30
MUNCH
MUNCH
MUNCH

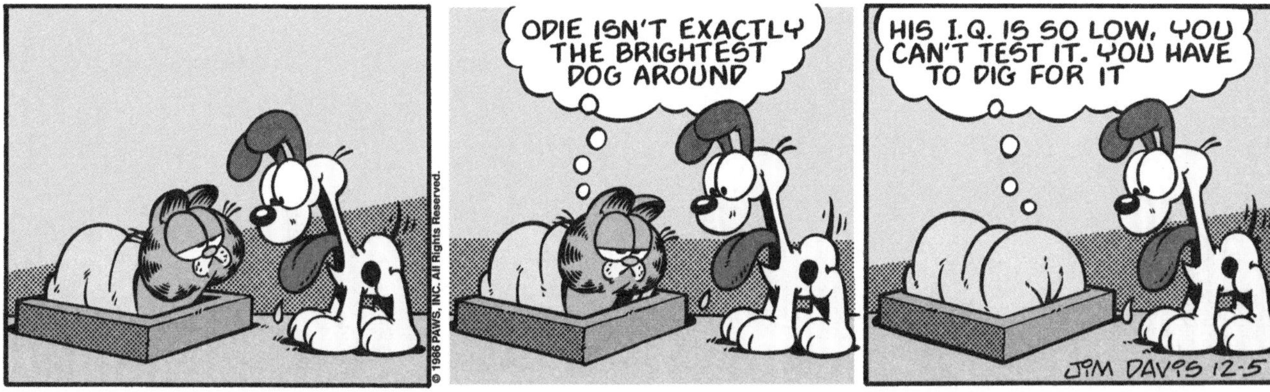
© 1986 PAWS, INC. All Rights Reserved.
ODIE ISN'T EXACTLY THE BRIGHTEST DOG AROUND
HIS I.Q. IS SO LOW, YOU CAN'T TEST IT. YOU HAVE TO DIG FOR IT
JIM DAVIS 12-5

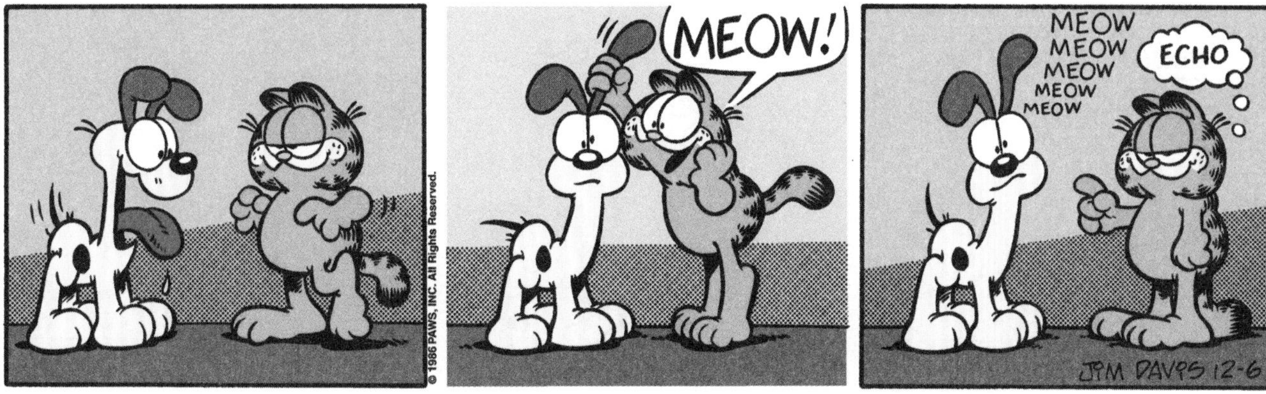
© 1986 PAWS, INC. All Rights Reserved.
MEOW!
MEOW MEOW MEOW MEOW MEOW
ECHO
JIM DAVIS 12-6

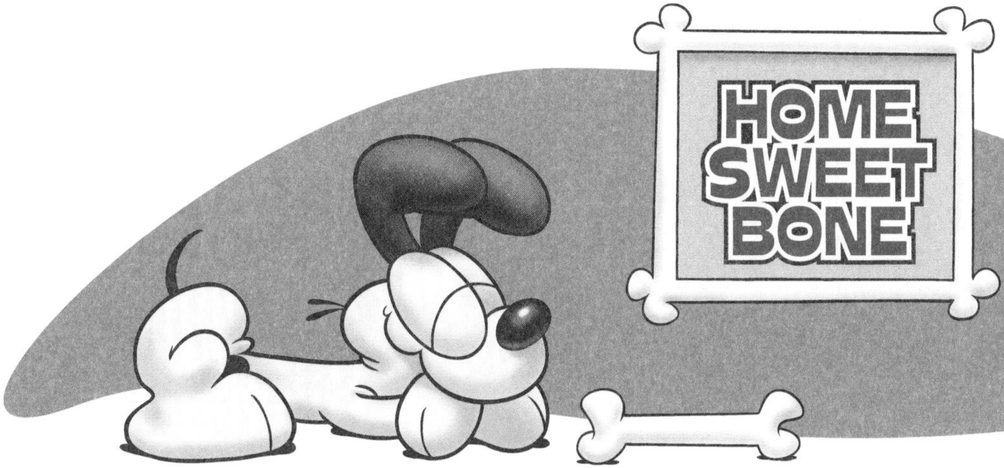
HOME SWEET BONE

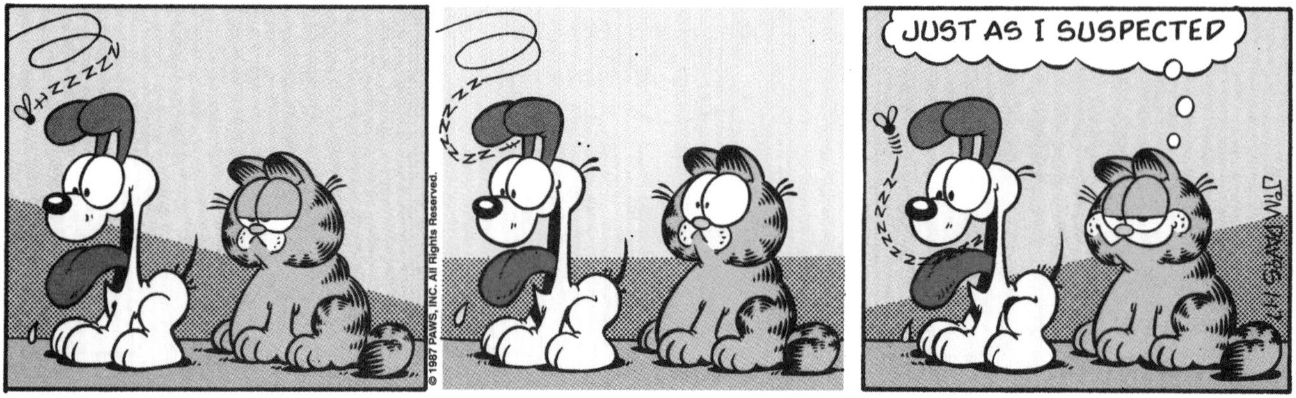
ZZZZZ
ZZZZZ
© 1987 PAWS, INC. All Rights Reserved.
JUST AS I SUSPECTED
ZZZZZZZ
JIM DAVIS 2-17

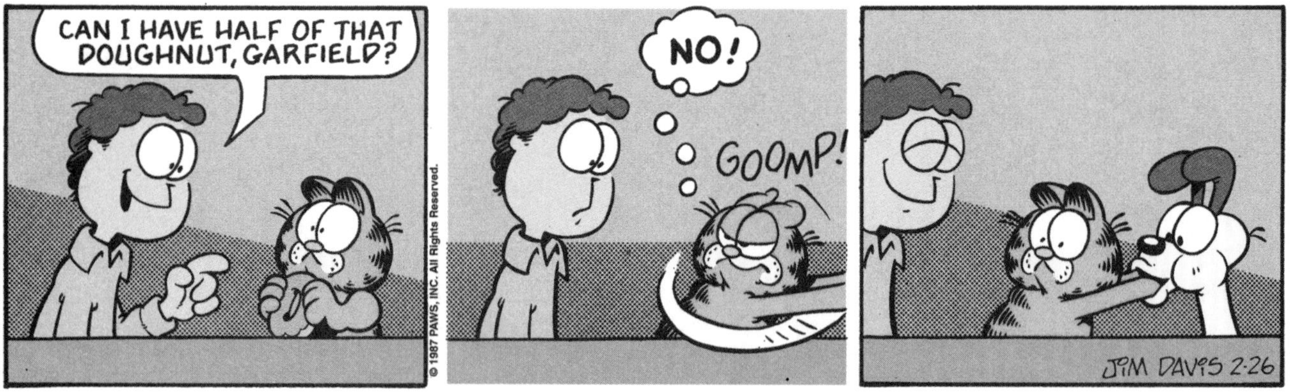
CAN I HAVE HALF OF THAT DOUGHNUT, GARFIELD?
© 1987 PAWS, INC. All Rights Reserved.
NO!
GOOMP!
JIM DAVIS 2-26

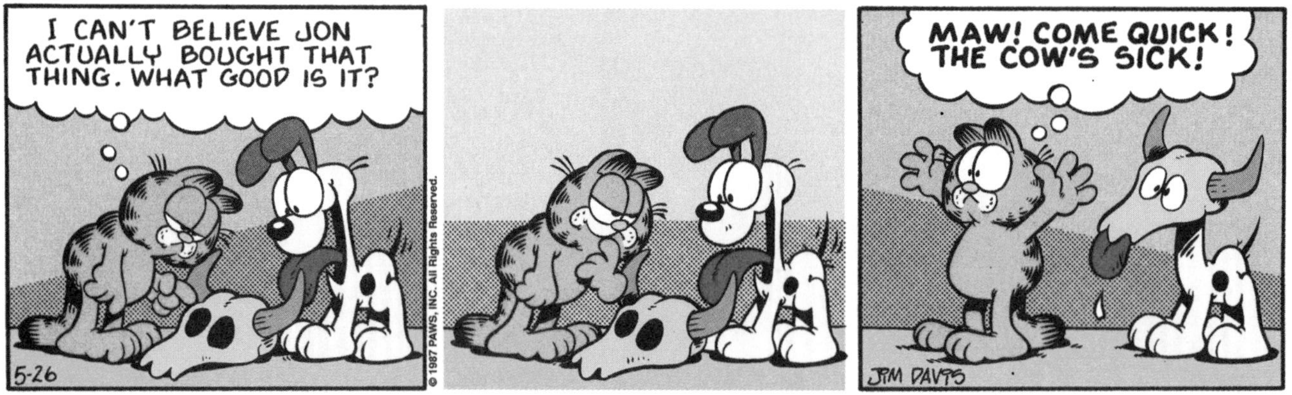
I CAN'T BELIEVE JON ACTUALLY BOUGHT THAT THING. WHAT GOOD IS IT?
5-26
© 1987 PAWS, INC. All Rights Reserved.
MAW! COME QUICK! THE COW'S SICK!
JIM DAVIS

GARFIELD'S favorite games to play with Odie

Traffic Twister

Volley Dog

Spin the Beagle

Fetch the Ham

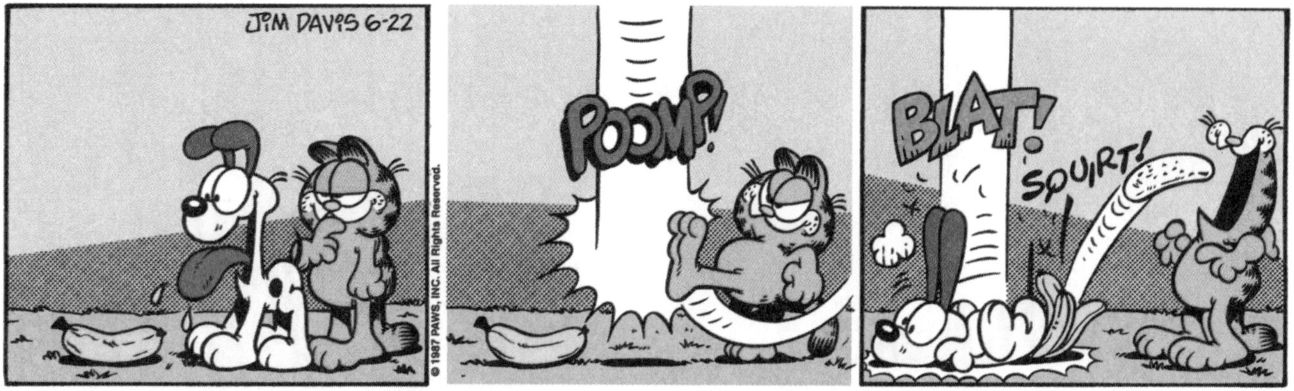
JIM DAVIS 6-22
© 1987 PAWS, INC. All Rights Reserved.
POOMP!
BLAT!
SQUIRT!

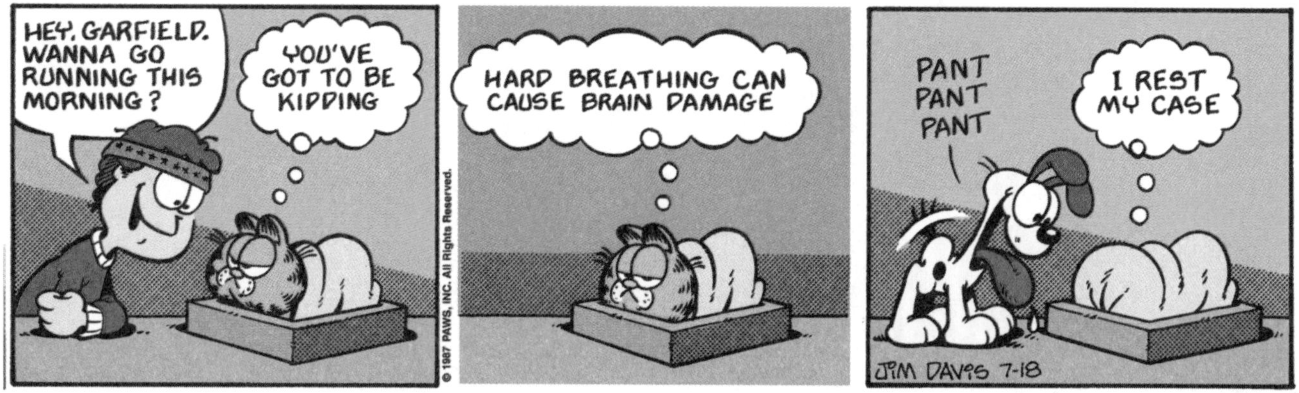
HEY, GARFIELD. WANNA GO RUNNING THIS MORNING?
YOU'VE GOT TO BE KIDDING
© 1987 PAWS, INC. All Rights Reserved.
HARD BREATHING CAN CAUSE BRAIN DAMAGE
PANT PANT PANT
I REST MY CASE
JIM DAVIS 7-18

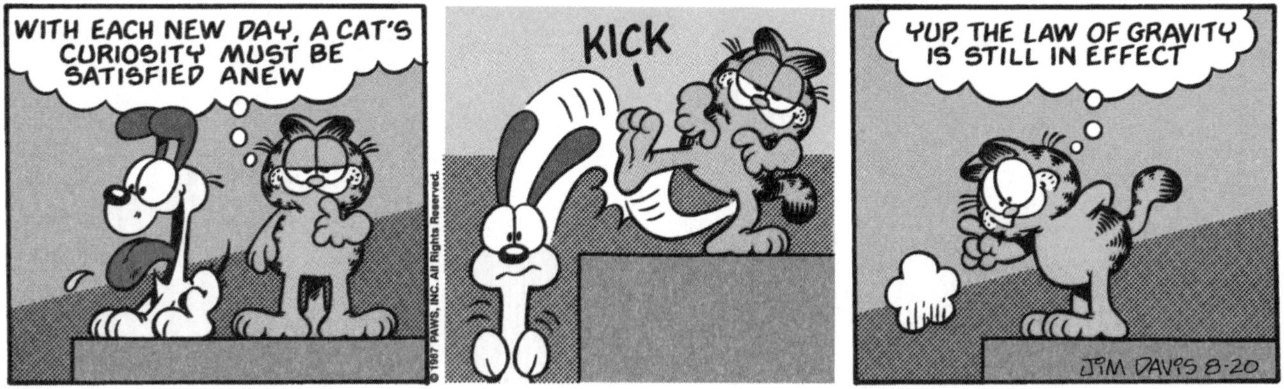
WITH EACH NEW DAY, A CAT'S CURIOSITY MUST BE SATISFIED ANEW
© 1987 PAWS, INC. All Rights Reserved.
KICK
YUP, THE LAW OF GRAVITY IS STILL IN EFFECT
JIM DAVIS 8-20

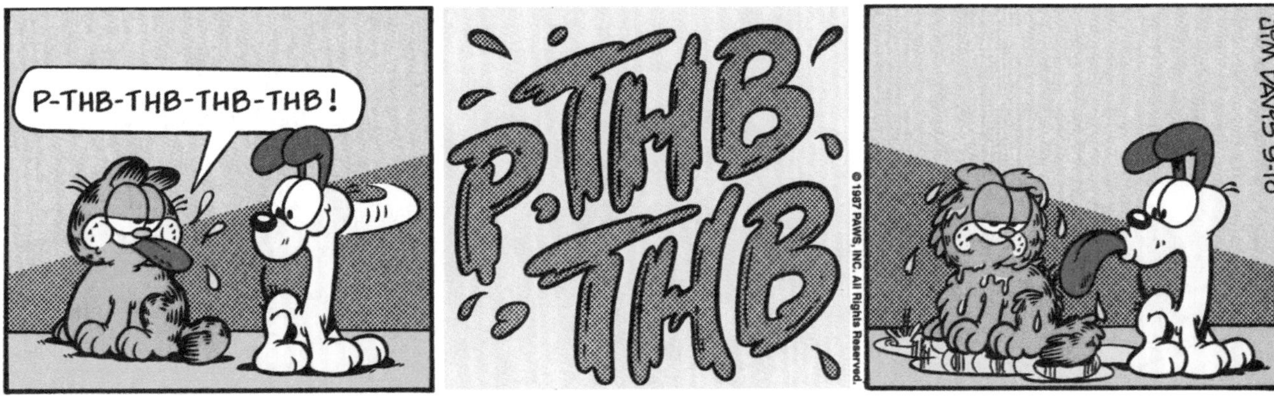
P-THB-THB-THB-THB!
P-THB THB
© 1987 PAWS, INC. All Rights Reserved.
JIM DAVIS 9-10

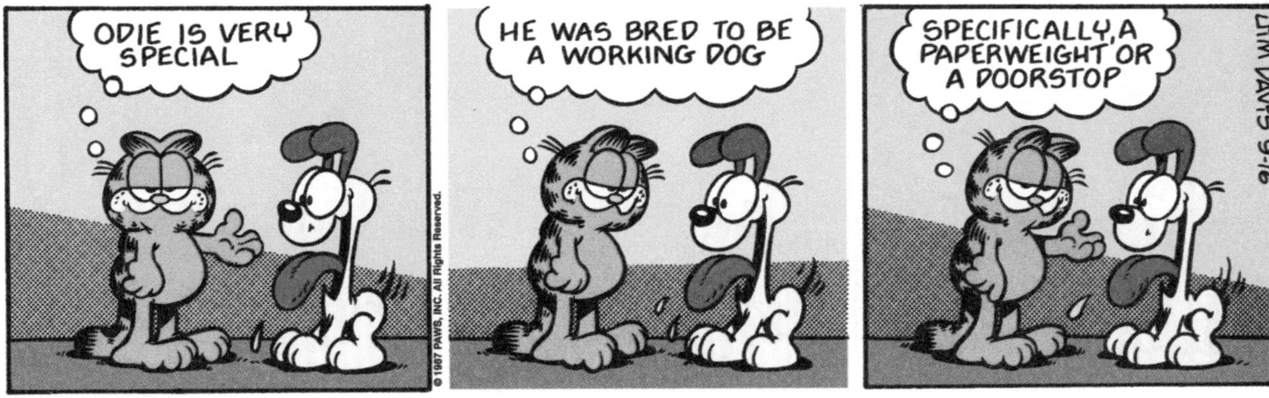
ODIE IS VERY SPECIAL
© 1987 PAWS, INC. All Rights Reserved.
HE WAS BRED TO BE A WORKING DOG
SPECIFICALLY, A PAPERWEIGHT OR A DOORSTOP
JIM DAVIS 9-16

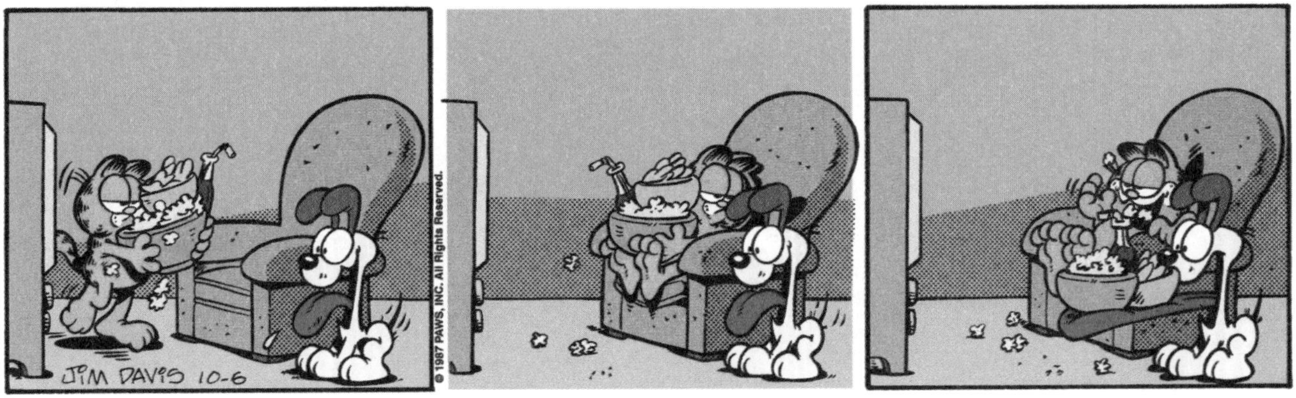
JIM DAVIS 10-6
© 1987 PAWS, INC. All Rights Reserved.

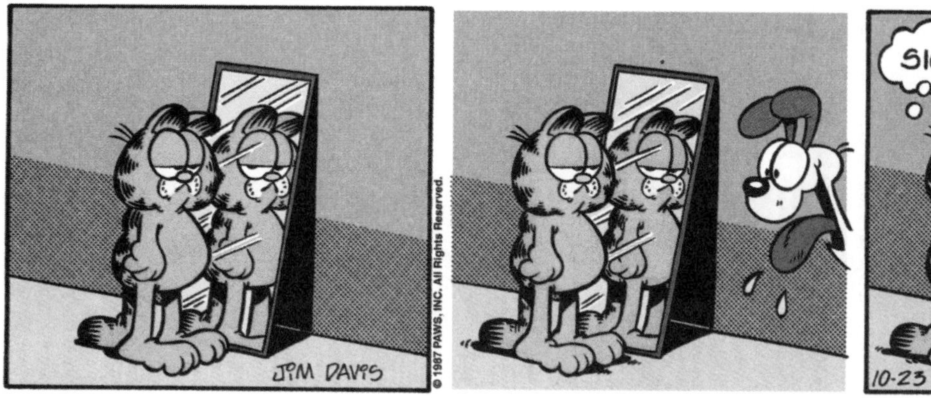
JIM DAVIS
© 1987 PAWS, INC. All Rights Reserved.
SIGH
10-23

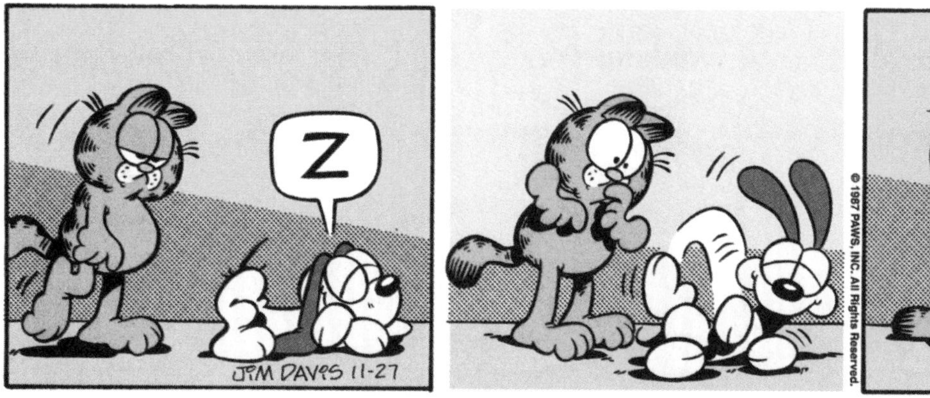
Z
JIM DAVIS 11-27
© 1987 PAWS, INC. All Rights Reserved.
N

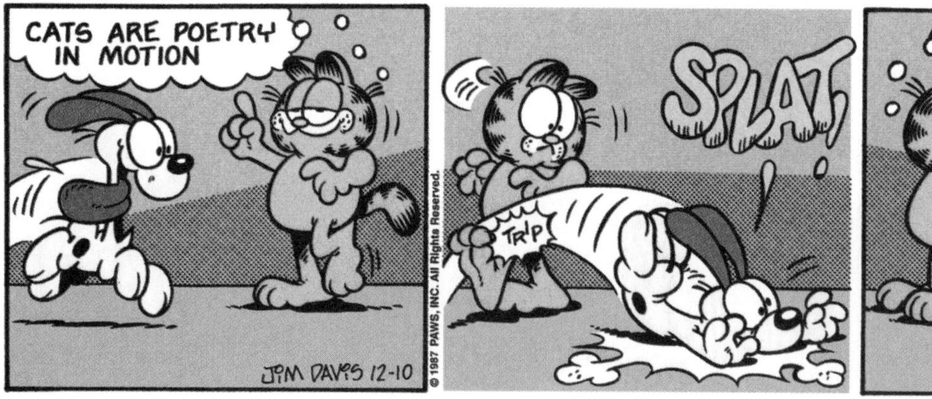
CATS ARE POETRY IN MOTION
JIM DAVIS 12-10
© 1987 PAWS, INC. All Rights Reserved.
SPLAT
TRIP
DOGS ARE GIBBERISH IN NEUTRAL

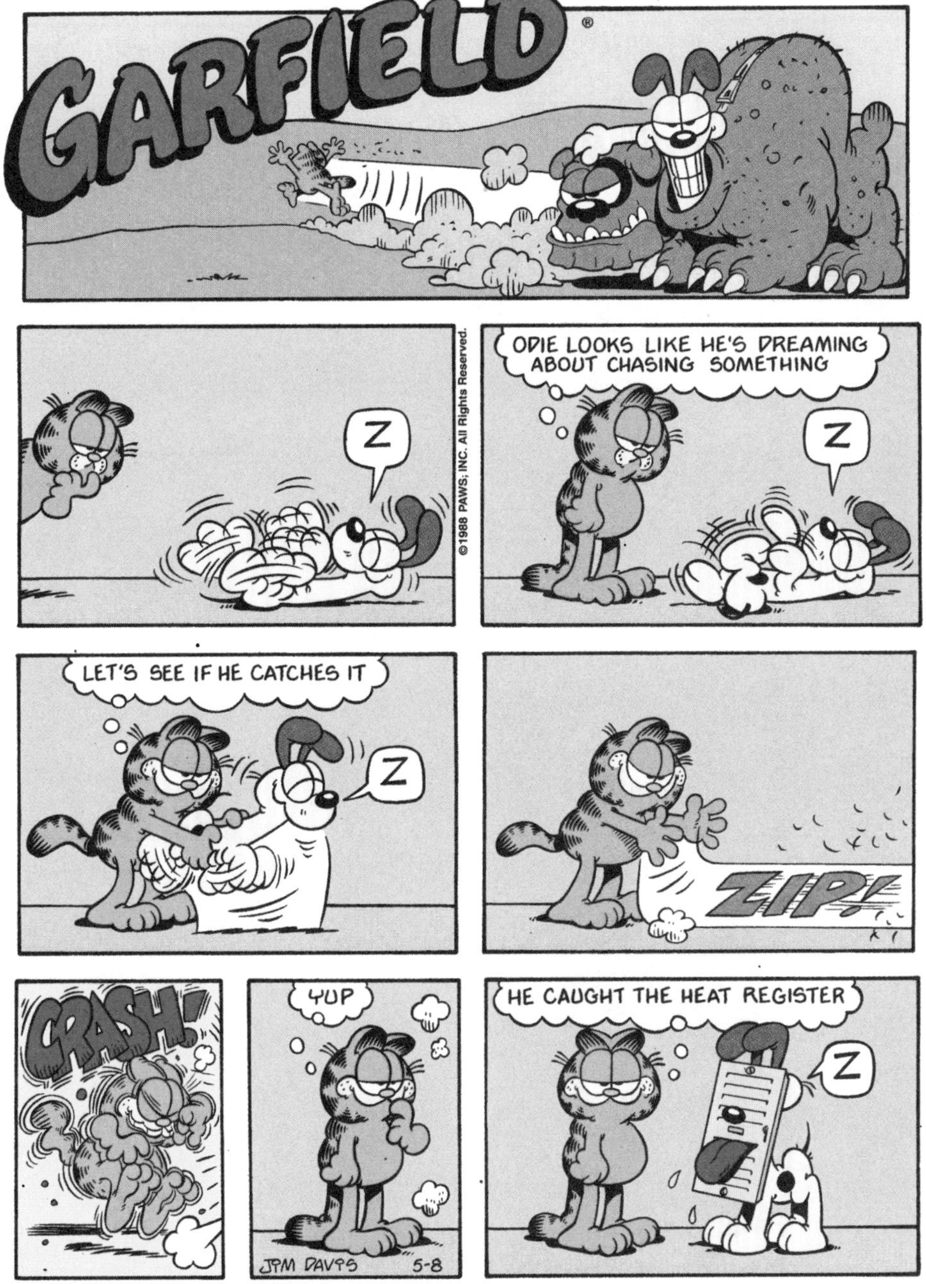
GARFIELD®
Z
©1988 PAWS, INC. All Rights Reserved.
ODIE LOOKS LIKE HE'S DREAMING ABOUT CHASING SOMETHING
Z
LET'S SEE IF HE CATCHES IT
Z
ZIP!
CRASH!
YUP
JIM DAVIS 5-8
HE CAUGHT THE HEAT REGISTER
Z

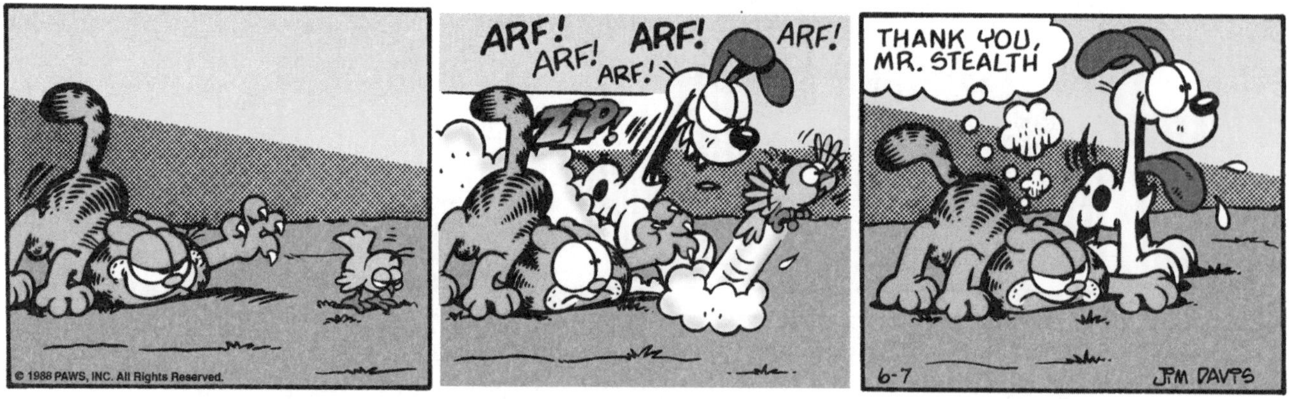
© 1988 PAWS, INC. All Rights Reserved.
ARF! ARF! ARF! ARF! ARF!
ZIP!
THANK YOU, MR. STEALTH
6-7
JIM DAVIS

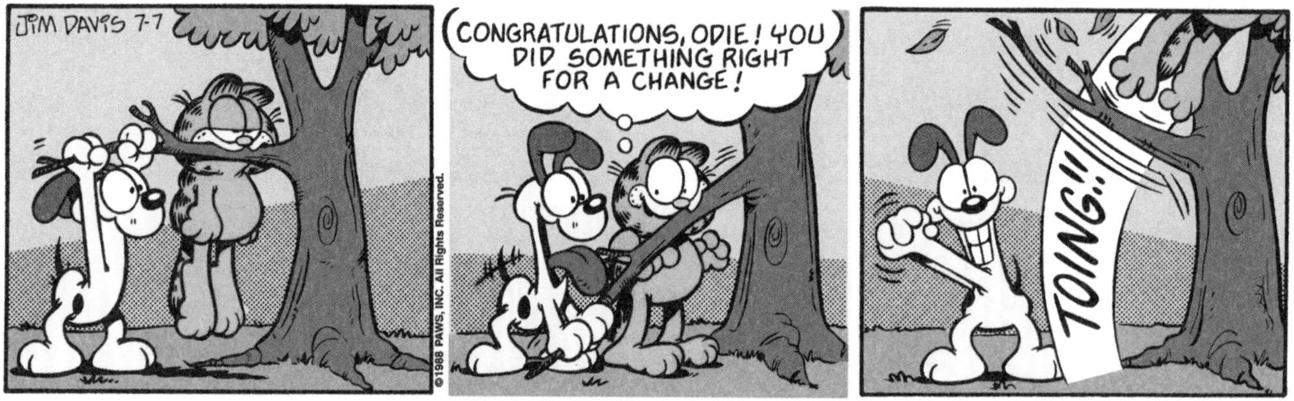
JIM DAVIS 7-7
© 1988 PAWS, INC. All Rights Reserved.
CONGRATULATIONS, ODIE! YOU DID SOMETHING RIGHT FOR A CHANGE!
TOING!!

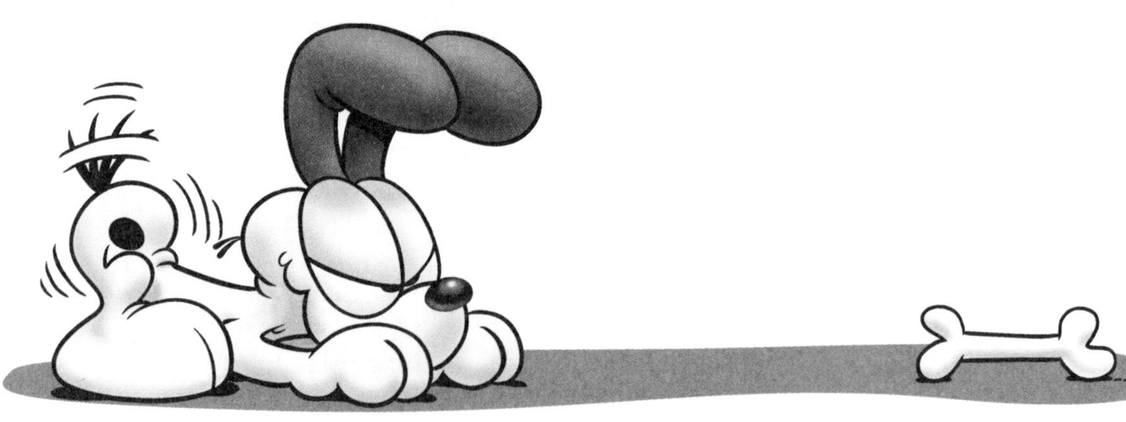

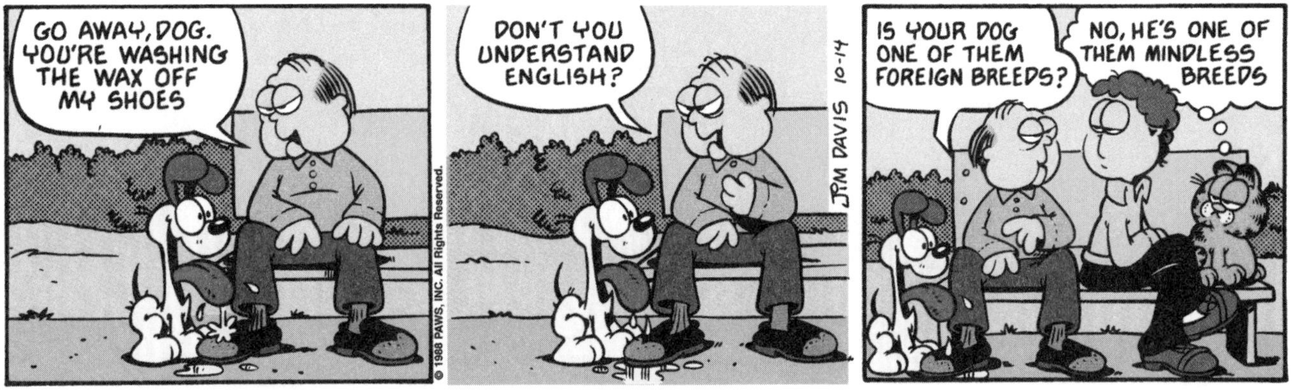
GO AWAY, DOG. YOU'RE WASHING THE WAX OFF MY SHOES
© 1988 PAWS, INC. All Rights Reserved.
DON'T YOU UNDERSTAND ENGLISH?
JIM DAVIS 10-14
IS YOUR DOG ONE OF THEM FOREIGN BREEDS?
NO, HE'S ONE OF THEM MINDLESS BREEDS

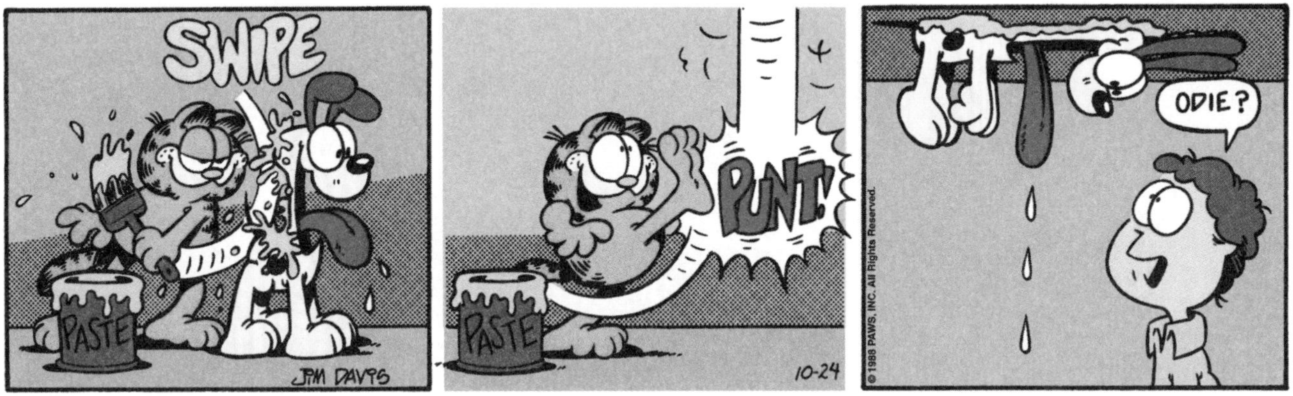
SWIPE
PASTE
JIM DAVIS
PUNT!
PASTE
10-24
© 1988 PAWS, INC. All Rights Reserved.
ODIE?

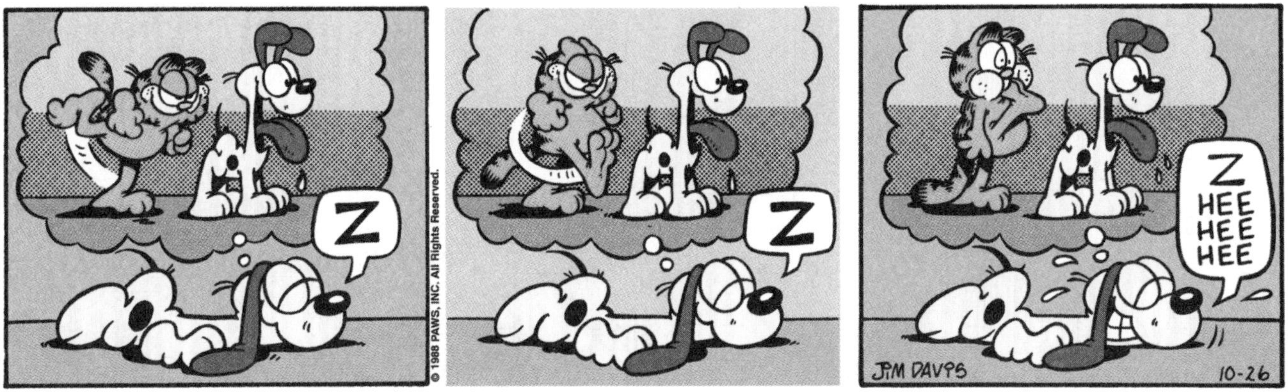
Z
© 1988 PAWS, INC. All Rights Reserved.
Z
Z HEE HEE HEE
JIM DAVIS
10-26

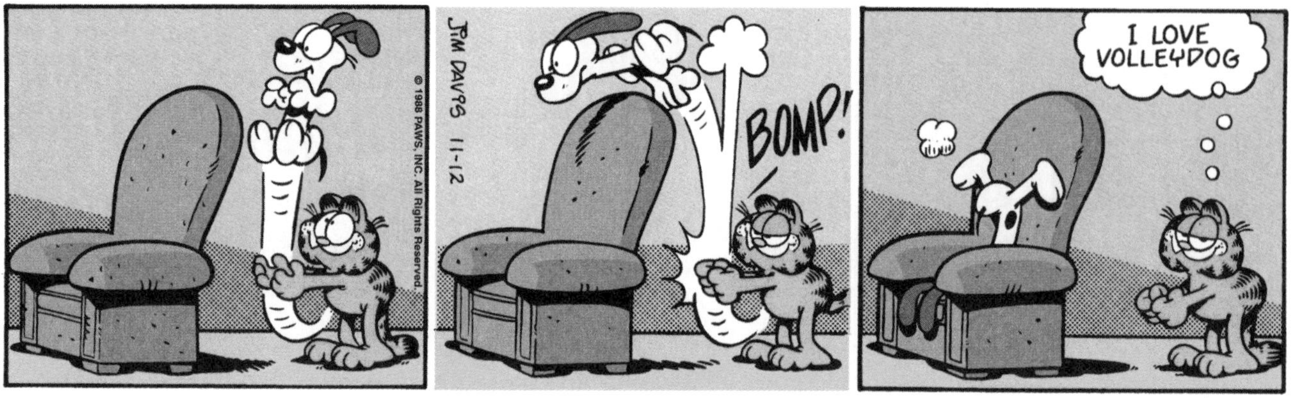
© 1988 PAWS, INC. All Rights Reserved.
JIM DAVIS 11-12
BOMP!
I LOVE VOLLEYDOG

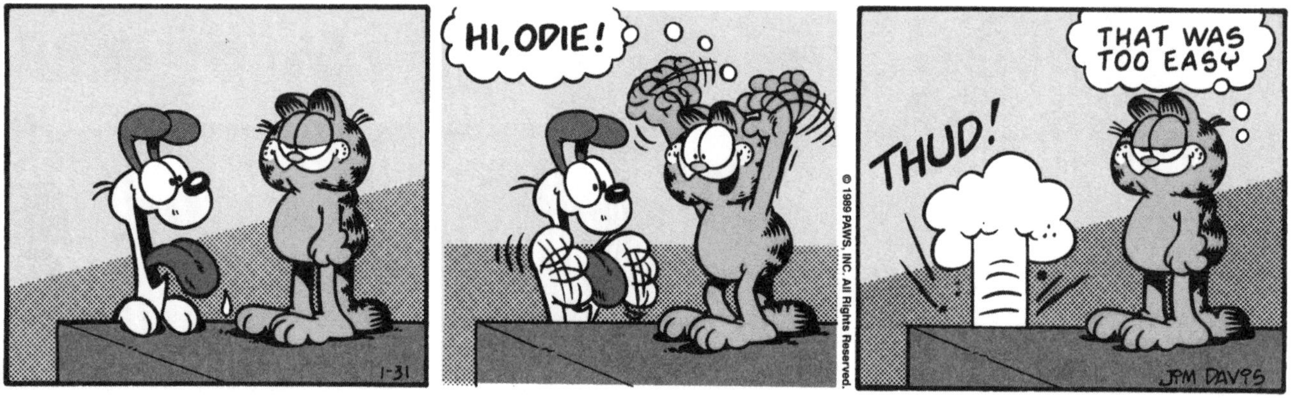
1-31
HI, ODIE!
© 1989 PAWS, INC. All Rights Reserved.
THUD!
THAT WAS TOO EASY
JIM DAVIS

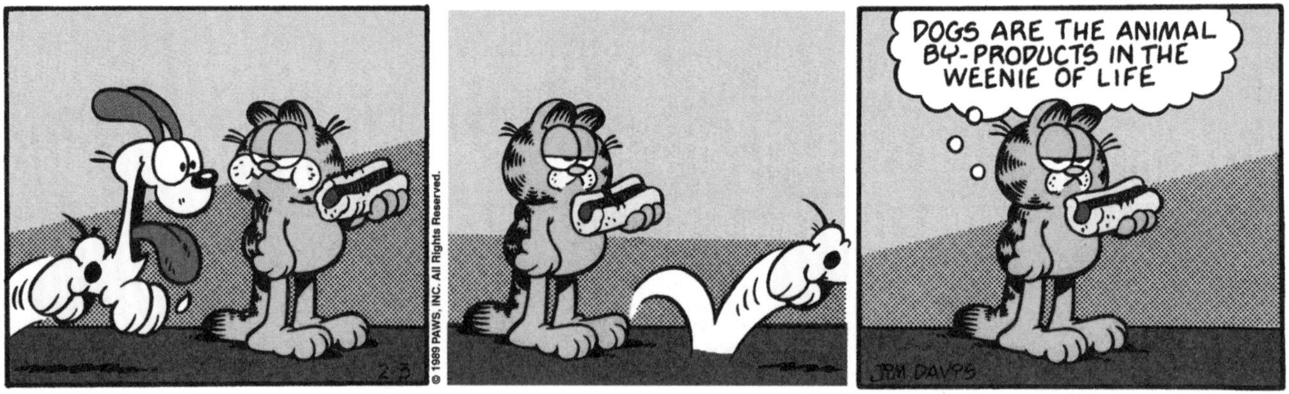
2-3
© 1989 PAWS, INC. All Rights Reserved.
DOGS ARE THE ANIMAL BY-PRODUCTS IN THE WEENIE OF LIFE
JIM DAVIS

TOP TEN REASONS WHY ODIE CAN'T READ

10 Had a tough time just learning to breathe

9 Illiterate Marmaduke a bad influence

8 Didn't want to learn from teacher; just wanted to lick her face

7 Poor curriculum: too much *Beowulf,* not enough *Huckleberry Hound*

6 Was sick that day

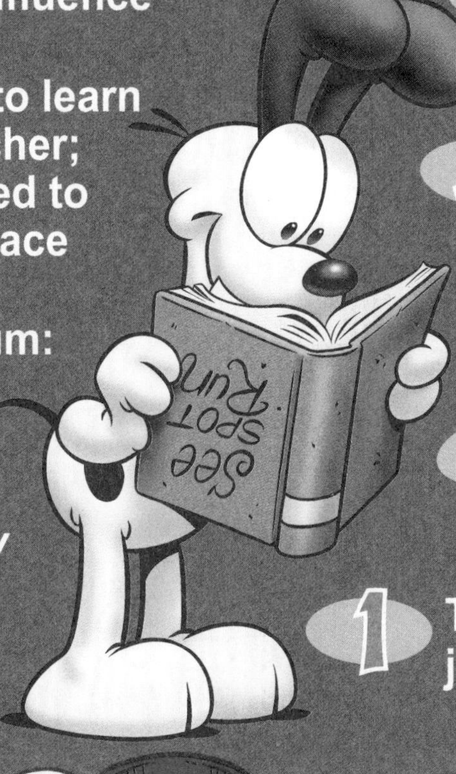
See Spot Run

5 Paper-training gave him a low opinion of printed matter

4 Television

3 Came from one of those "jock" pet shops

2 Tough to decipher drool-soaked pages

1 Three words: just plain stupid!

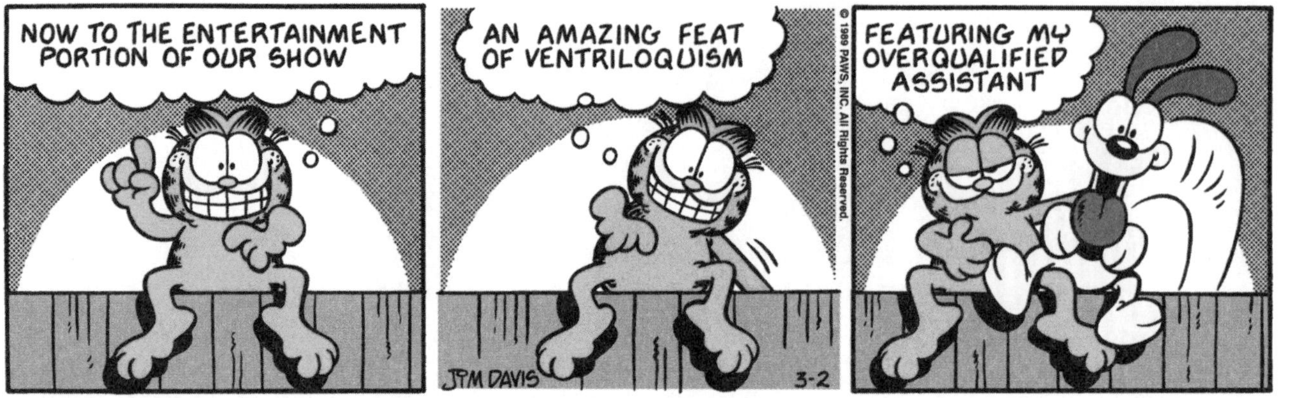
NOW TO THE ENTERTAINMENT PORTION OF OUR SHOW
AN AMAZING FEAT OF VENTRILOQUISM
© 1989 PAWS, INC. All Rights Reserved.
JIM DAVIS
3-2
FEATURING MY OVERQUALIFIED ASSISTANT

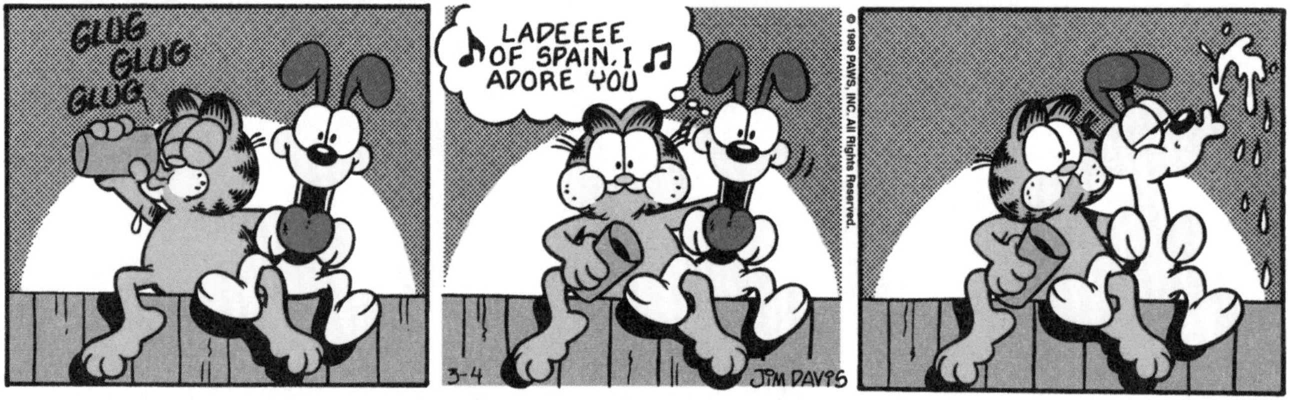
GLUG GLUG GLUG
LADEEEE OF SPAIN, I ADORE YOU
© 1989 PAWS, INC. All Rights Reserved.
3-4
JIM DAVIS

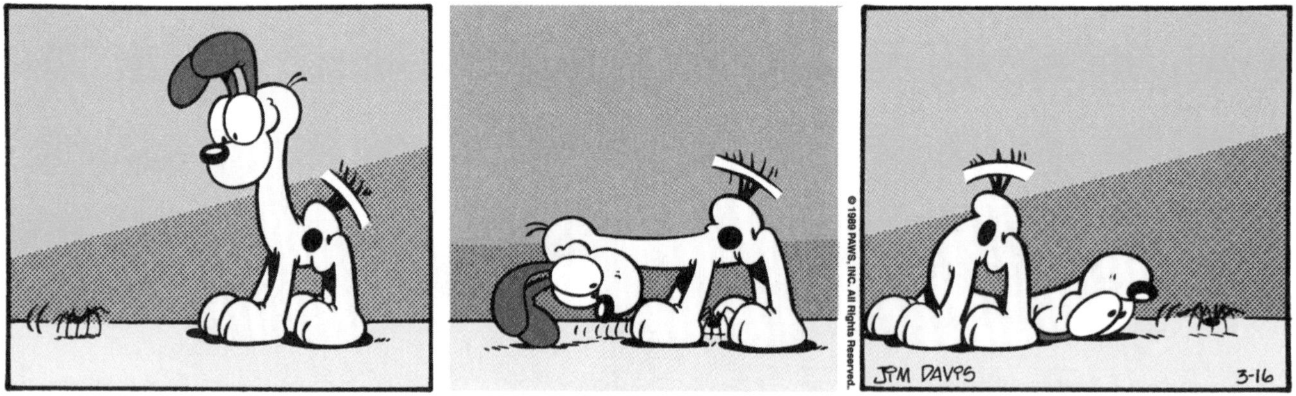
© 1989 PAWS, INC. All Rights Reserved.
JIM DAVIS
3-16

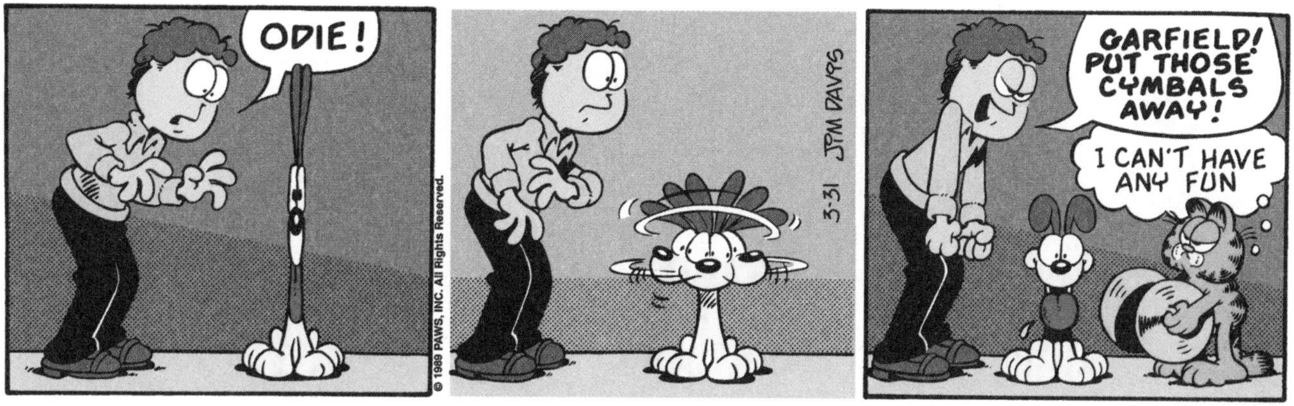
ODIE!
© 1989 PAWS, INC. All Rights Reserved.
3-31 JIM DAVIS
GARFIELD! PUT THOSE CYMBALS AWAY!
I CAN'T HAVE ANY FUN

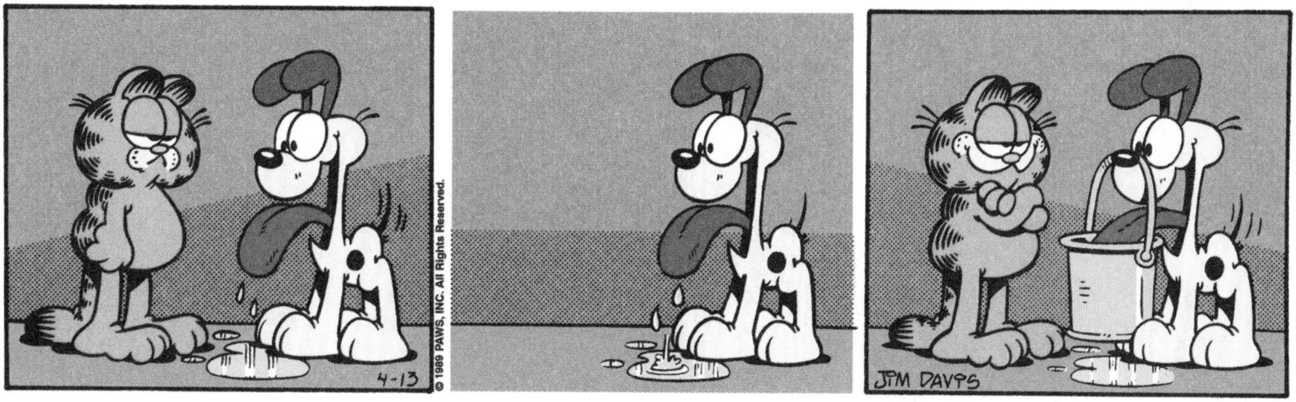
4-13
© 1989 PAWS, INC. All Rights Reserved.
JIM DAVIS

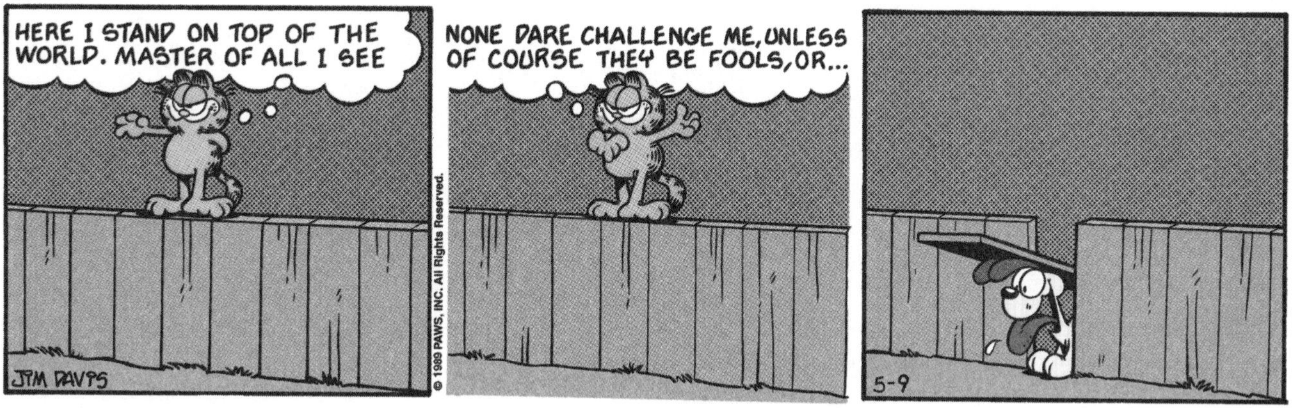
HERE I STAND ON TOP OF THE WORLD. MASTER OF ALL I SEE
JIM DAVIS
© 1989 PAWS, INC. All Rights Reserved.
NONE DARE CHALLENGE ME, UNLESS OF COURSE THEY BE FOOLS, OR...
5-9

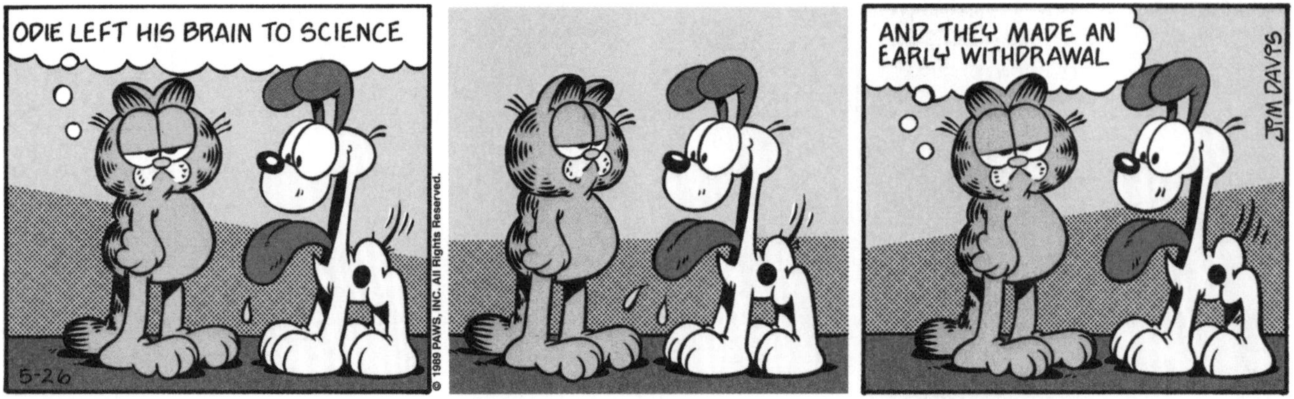
ODIE LEFT HIS BRAIN TO SCIENCE
5-26
© 1989 PAWS, INC. All Rights Reserved.
AND THEY MADE AN EARLY WITHDRAWAL
JIM DAVIS

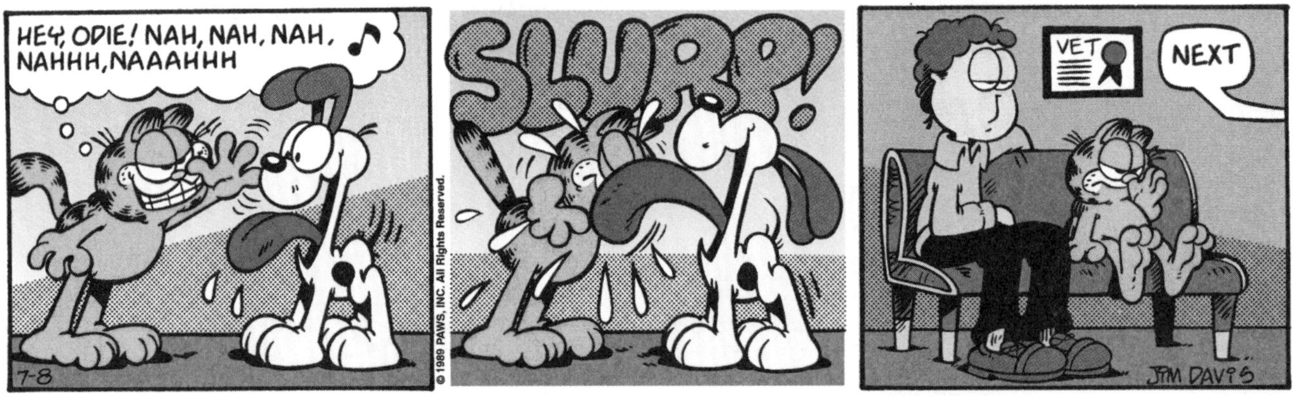
HEY, ODIE! NAH, NAH, NAH, NAHHH, NAAAHHH ♪
7-8
© 1989 PAWS, INC. All Rights Reserved.
SLURP!
VET
NEXT
JIM DAVIS

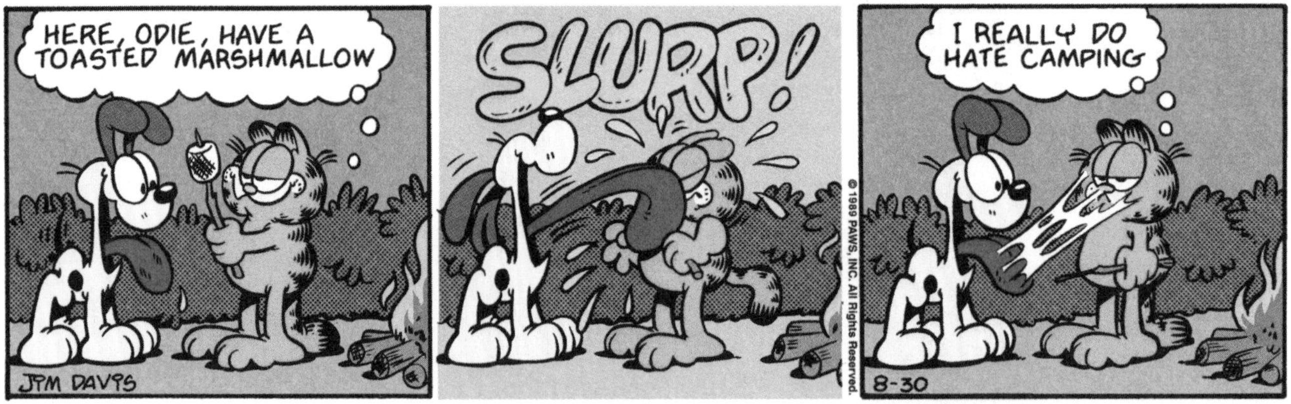
HERE, ODIE, HAVE A TOASTED MARSHMALLOW
JIM DAVIS
SLURP!
© 1989 PAWS, INC. All Rights Reserved.
I REALLY DO HATE CAMPING
8-30

A DOG's bARK iS WorSe ThAn hiS BiTe
BUT NOT WORSE THAN HIS BREATH

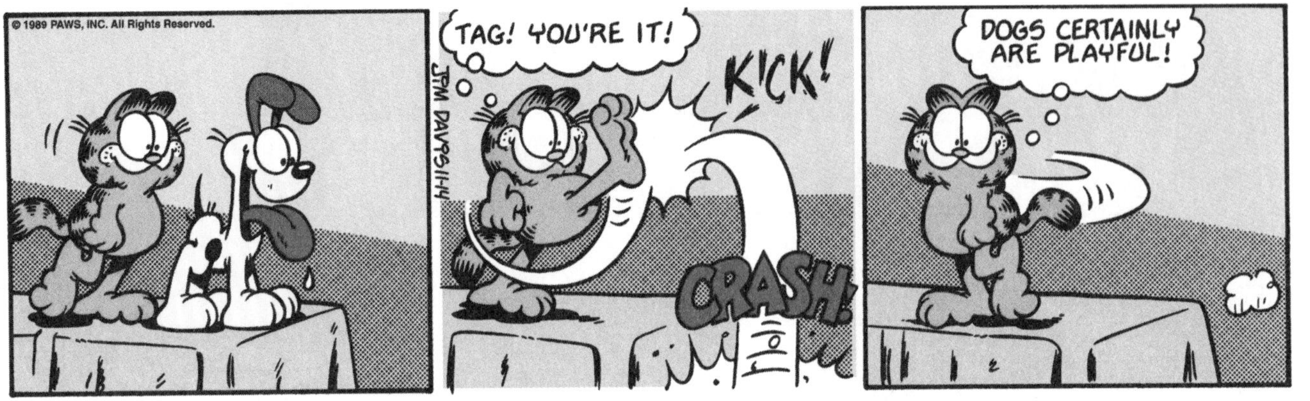
© 1989 PAWS, INC. All Rights Reserved.
TAG! YOU'RE IT!
KICK!
CRASH!
DOGS CERTAINLY ARE PLAYFUL!

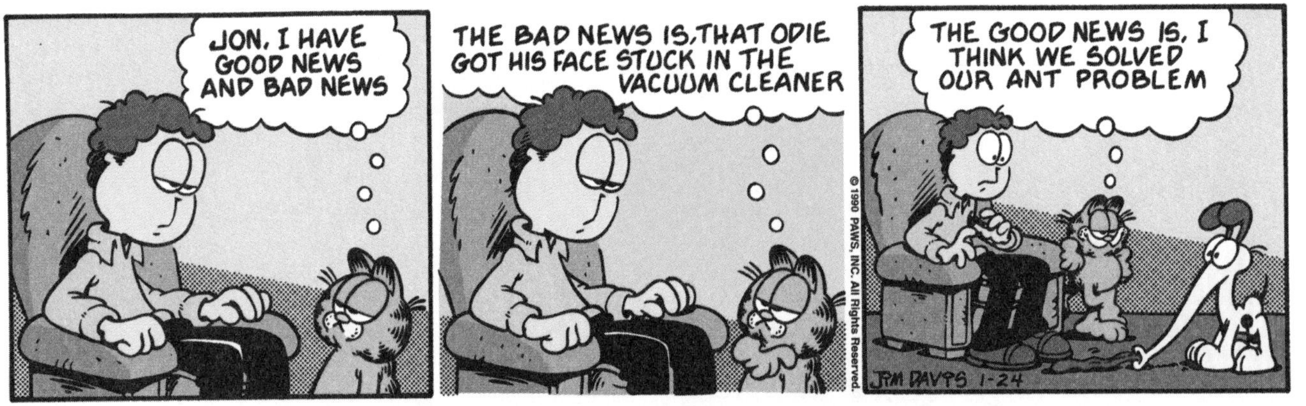
JON, I HAVE GOOD NEWS AND BAD NEWS
THE BAD NEWS IS, THAT ODIE GOT HIS FACE STUCK IN THE VACUUM CLEANER
THE GOOD NEWS IS, I THINK WE SOLVED OUR ANT PROBLEM
© 1990 PAWS, INC. All Rights Reserved.

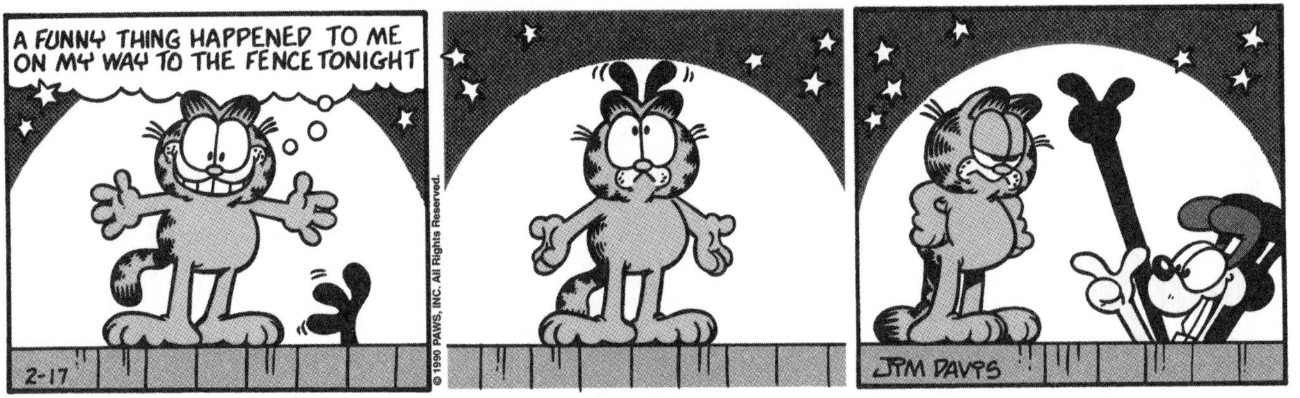
A FUNNY THING HAPPENED TO ME ON MY WAY TO THE FENCE TONIGHT
© 1990 PAWS, INC. All Rights Reserved.

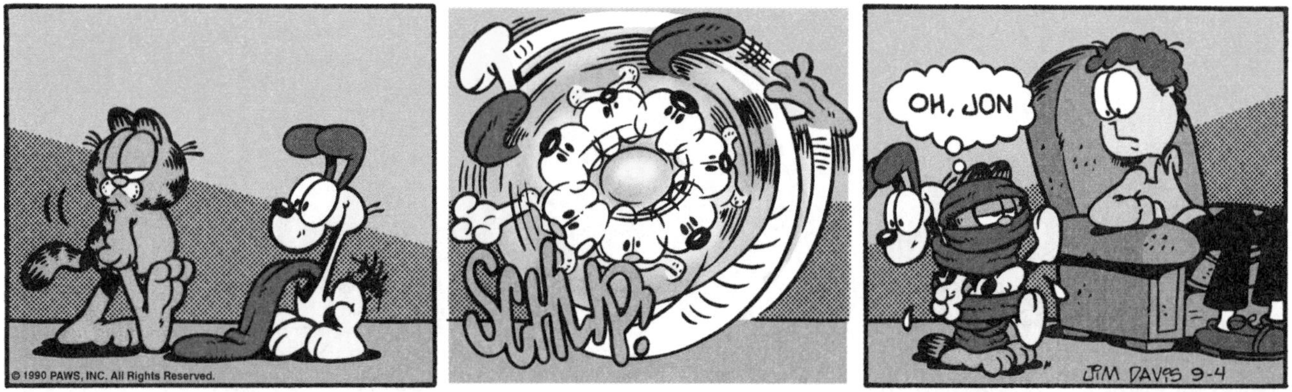
© 1990 PAWS, INC. All Rights Reserved.
SCHLUP!
OH, JON
JIM DAVIS 9-4

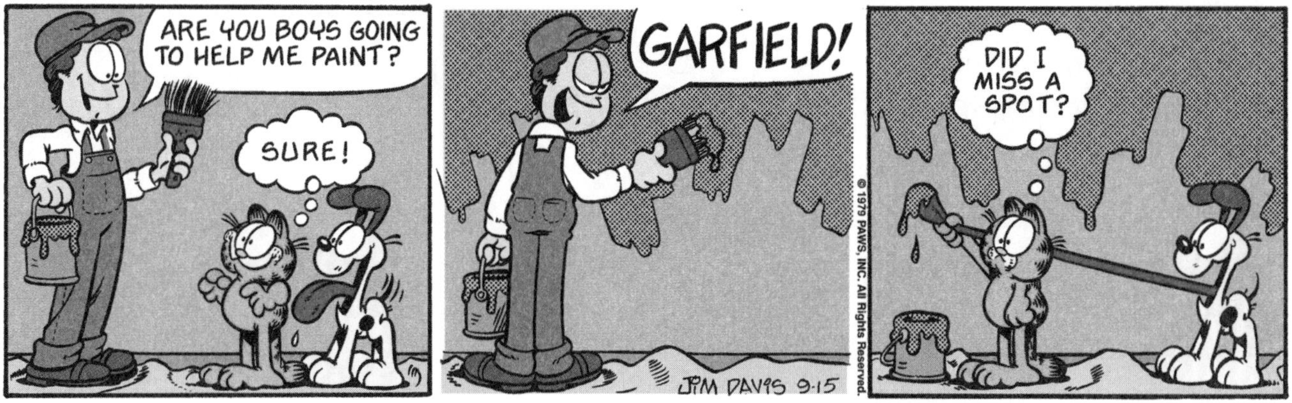
ARE YOU BOYS GOING TO HELP ME PAINT?
SURE!
GARFIELD!
JIM DAVIS 9-15
© 1979 PAWS, INC. All Rights Reserved.
DID I MISS A SPOT?

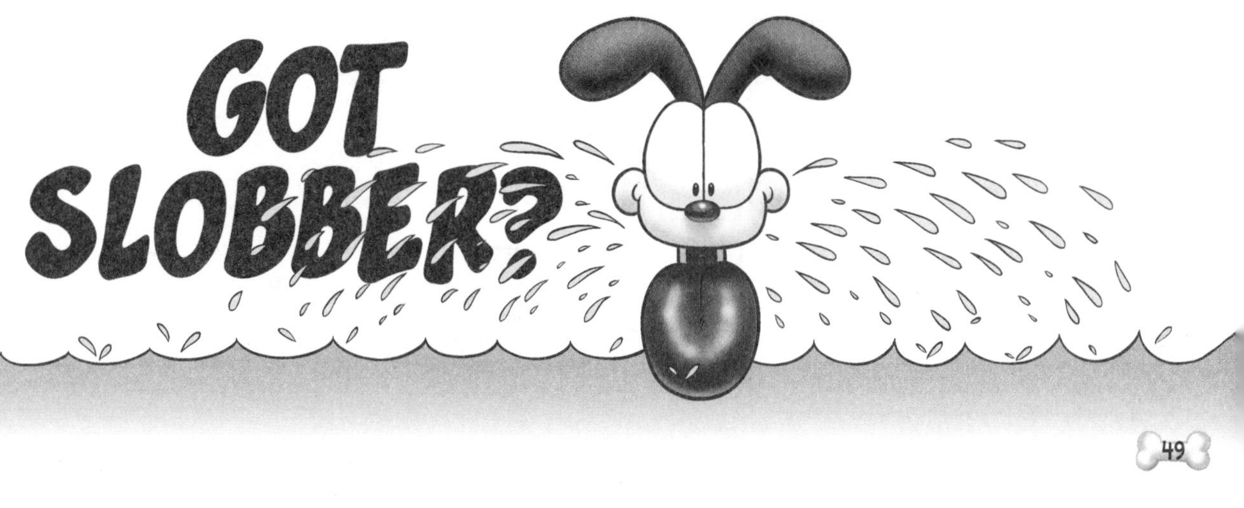
GOT SLOBBER?

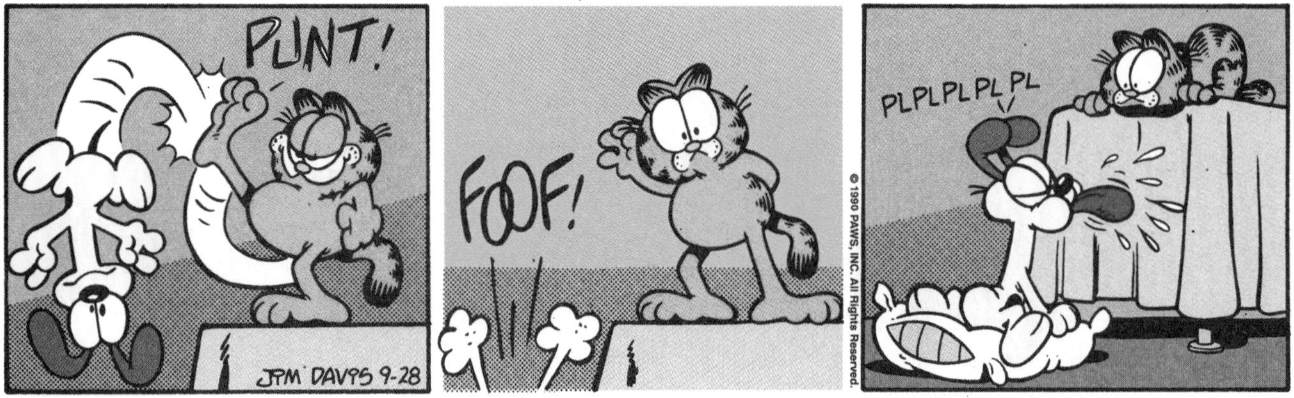
PUNT!
JIM DAVIS 9-28
FOOF!
PLPLPLPLPL

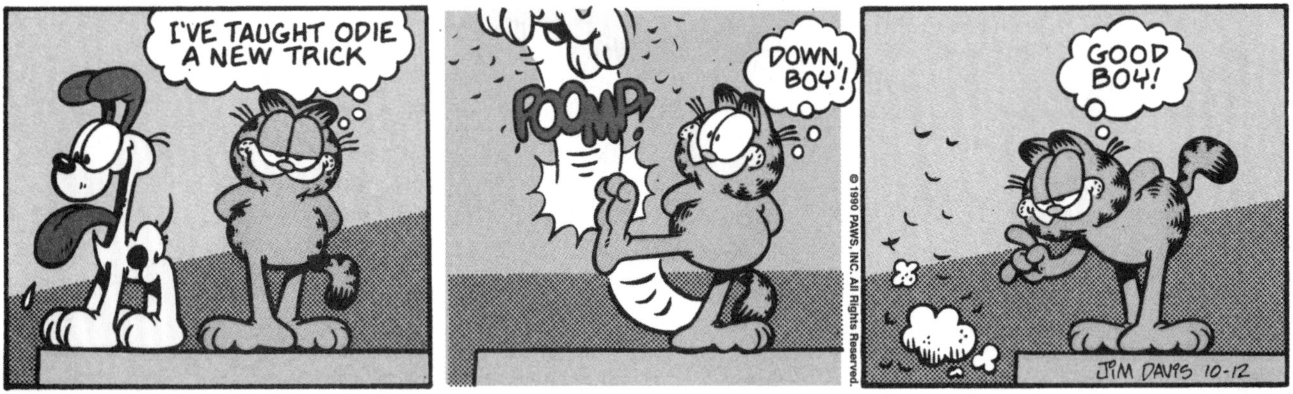
I'VE TAUGHT ODIE A NEW TRICK
POOMP!
DOWN, BOY!
GOOD BOY!
JIM DAVIS 10-12

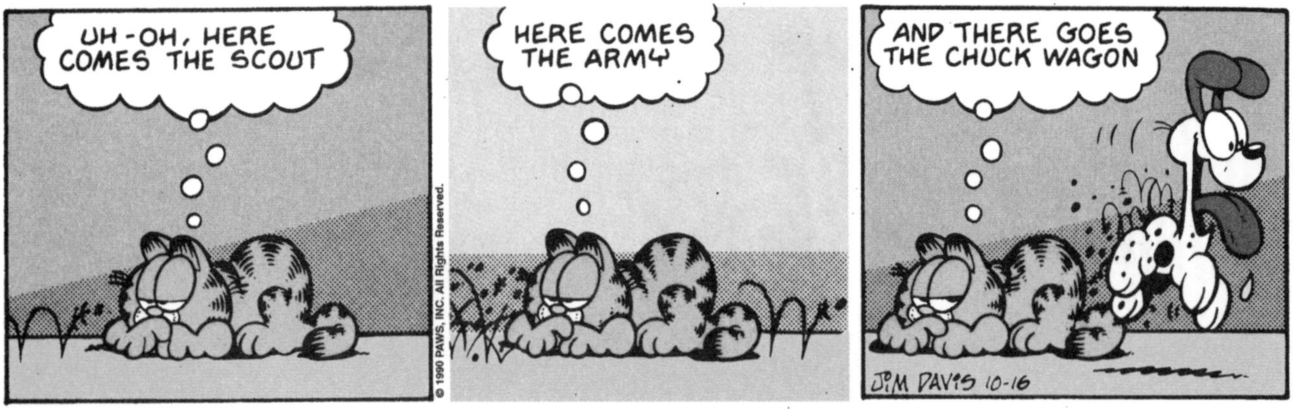
UH-OH, HERE COMES THE SCOUT
HERE COMES THE ARMY
AND THERE GOES THE CHUCK WAGON
JIM DAVIS 10-16

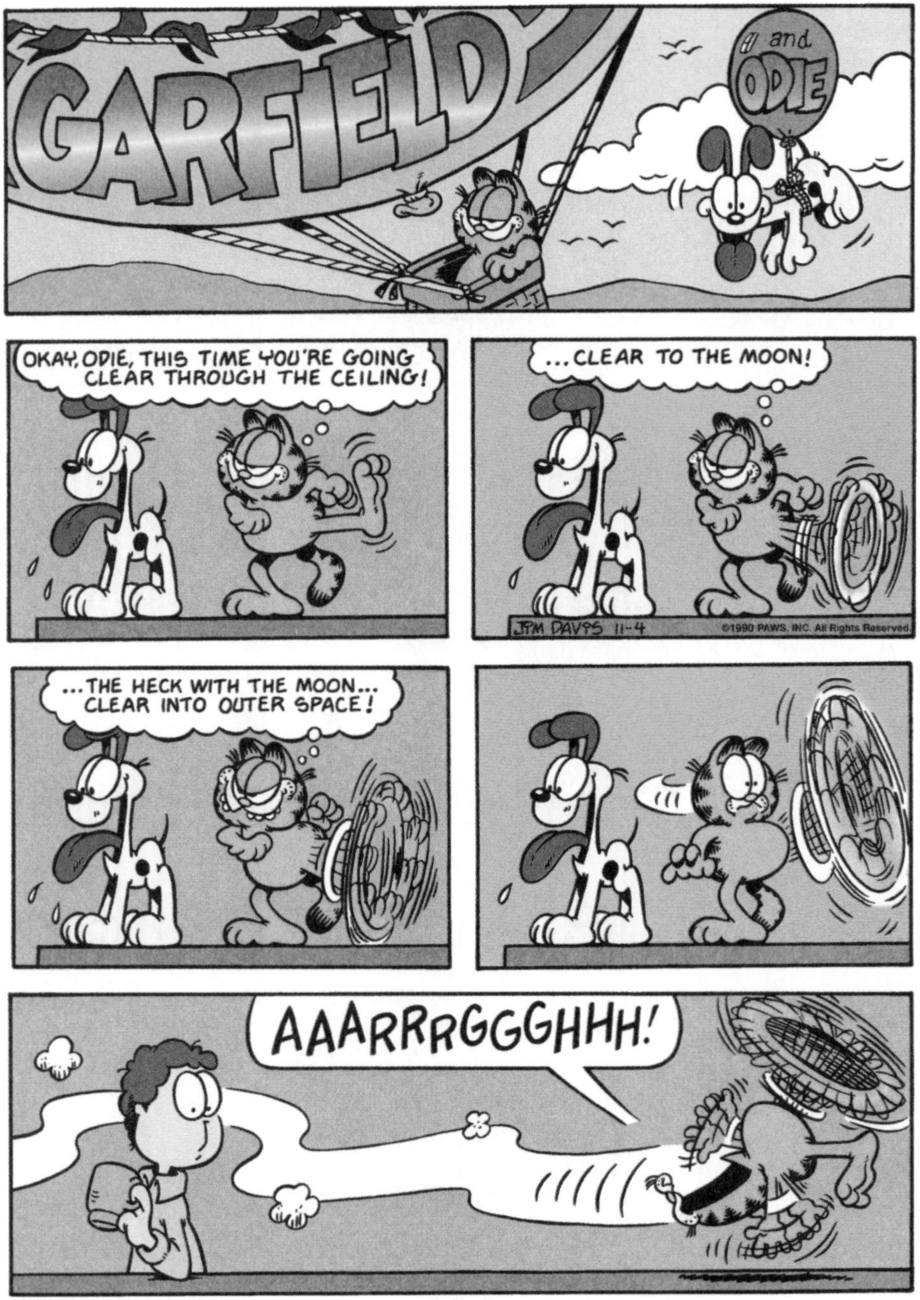
GARFIELD
and ODIE
OKAY, ODIE, THIS TIME YOU'RE GOING CLEAR THROUGH THE CEILING!
...CLEAR TO THE MOON!
JPM DAVIS 11-4
©1990 PAWS, INC. All Rights Reserved.
...THE HECK WITH THE MOON... CLEAR INTO OUTER SPACE!
AAARRRGGGHHH!

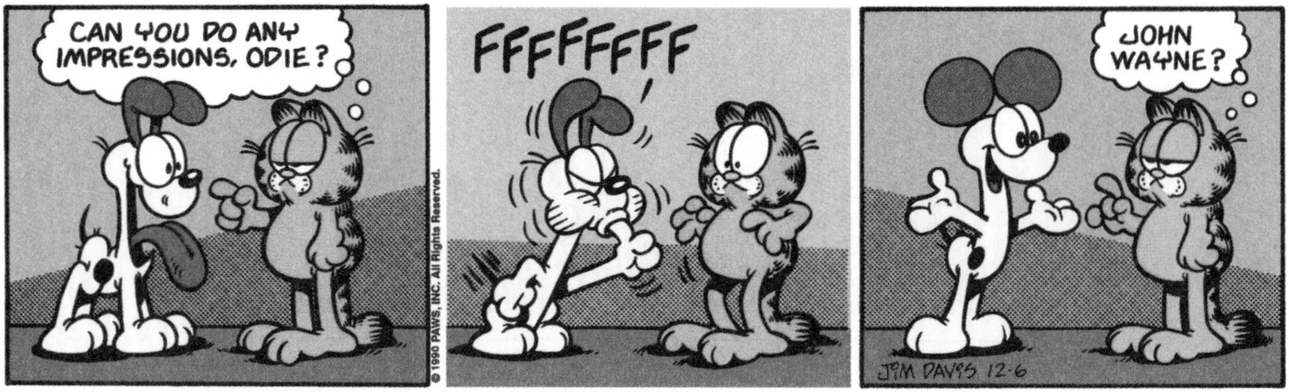
CAN YOU DO ANY IMPRESSIONS, ODIE?
FFFFFFFF
© 1990 PAWS, INC. All Rights Reserved.
JOHN WAYNE?
JIM DAVIS 12-6

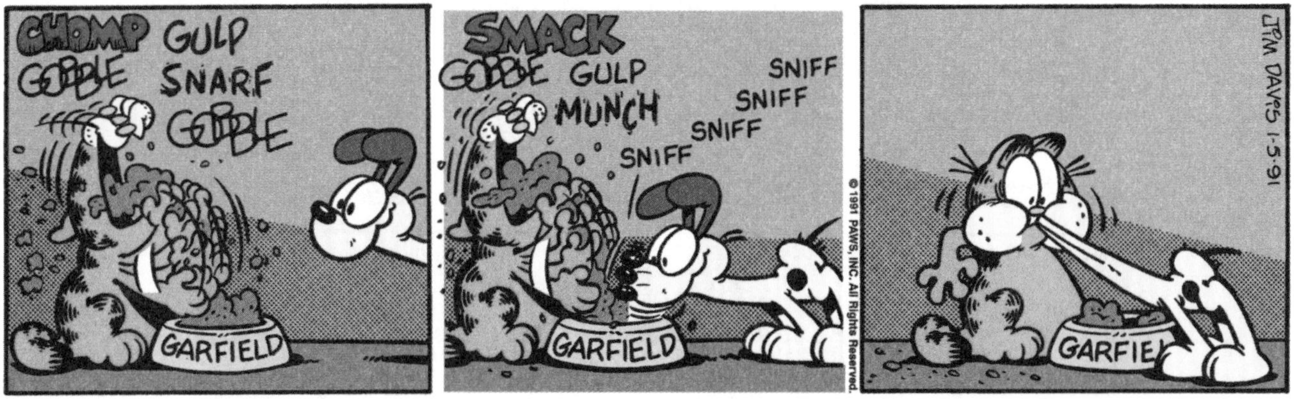
CHOMP GULP
GOBBLE SNARF
GOBBLE
SMACK
GOBBLE GULP
MUNCH
SNIFF
SNIFF
SNIFF
SNIFF
© 1991 PAWS, INC. All Rights Reserved.
JIM DAVIS 1-5-91

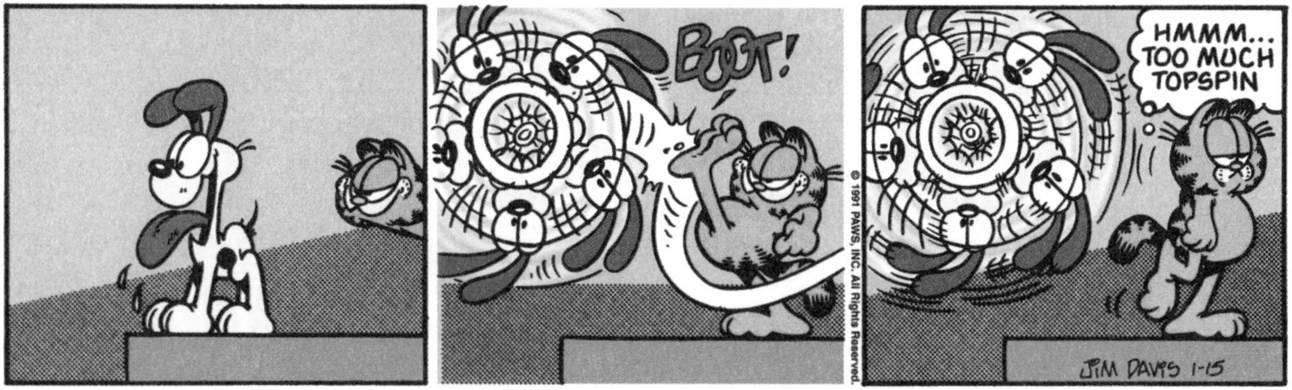
BOOT!
© 1991 PAWS, INC. All Rights Reserved.
HMMM... TOO MUCH TOPSPIN
JIM DAVIS 1-15

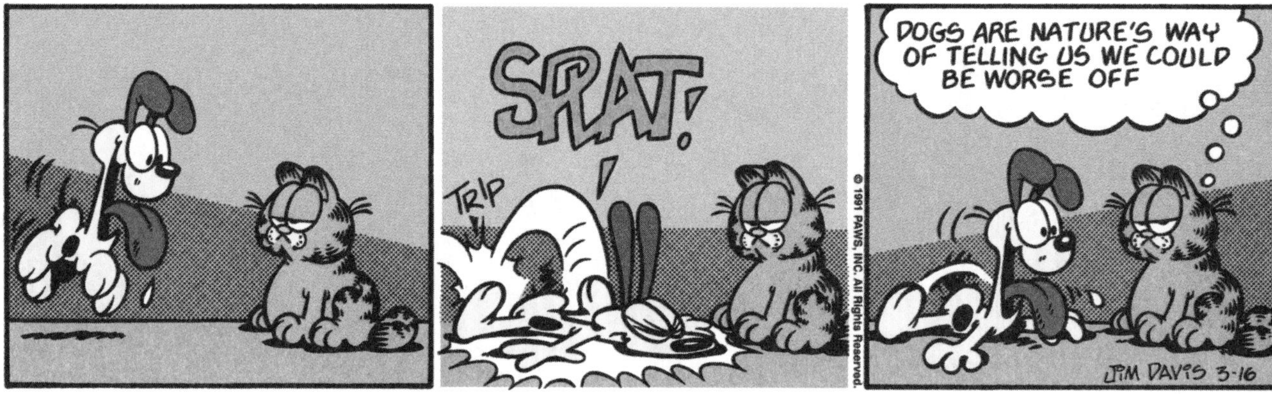
SPLAT!
TRIP
© 1991 PAWS, INC. All Rights Reserved.
DOGS ARE NATURE'S WAY OF TELLING US WE COULD BE WORSE OFF
JIM DAVIS 3-16

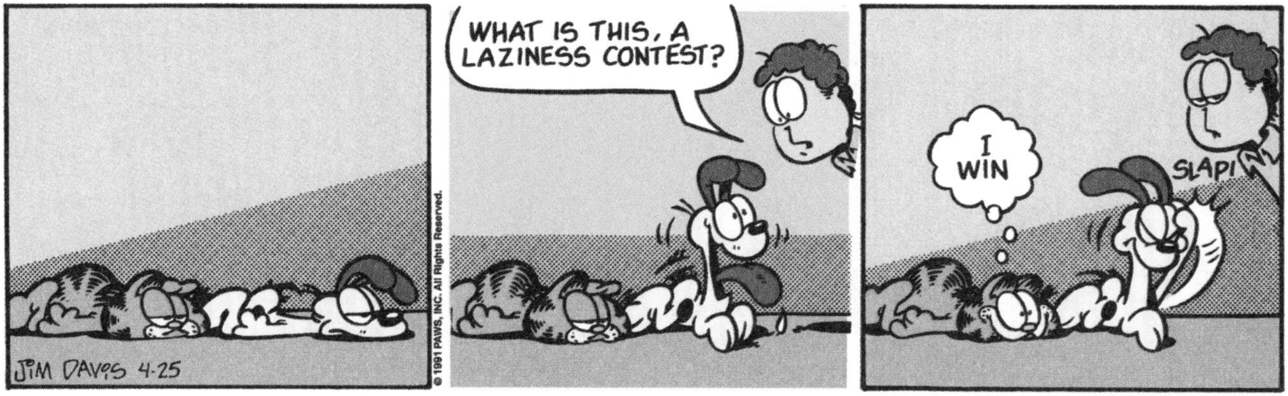
JIM DAVIS 4-25
© 1991 PAWS, INC. All Rights Reserved.
WHAT IS THIS, A LAZINESS CONTEST?
I WIN
SLAP!

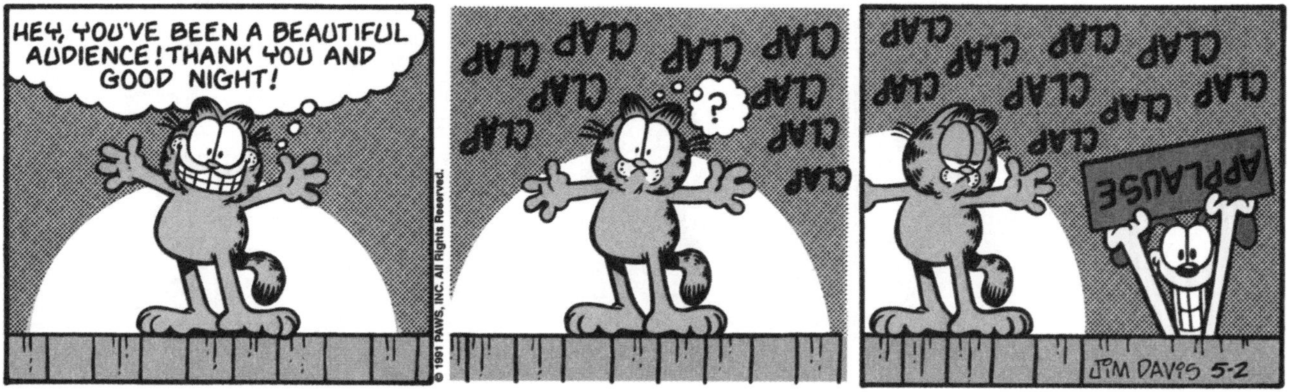
HEY, YOU'VE BEEN A BEAUTIFUL AUDIENCE! THANK YOU AND GOOD NIGHT!
© 1991 PAWS, INC. All Rights Reserved.
CLAP CLAP CLAP CLAP
CLAP CLAP CLAP
CLAP CLAP
CLAP
?
CLAP CLAP CLAP CLAP
CLAP CLAP CLAP CLAP
CLAP CLAP CLAP
APPLAUSE
JIM DAVIS 5-2

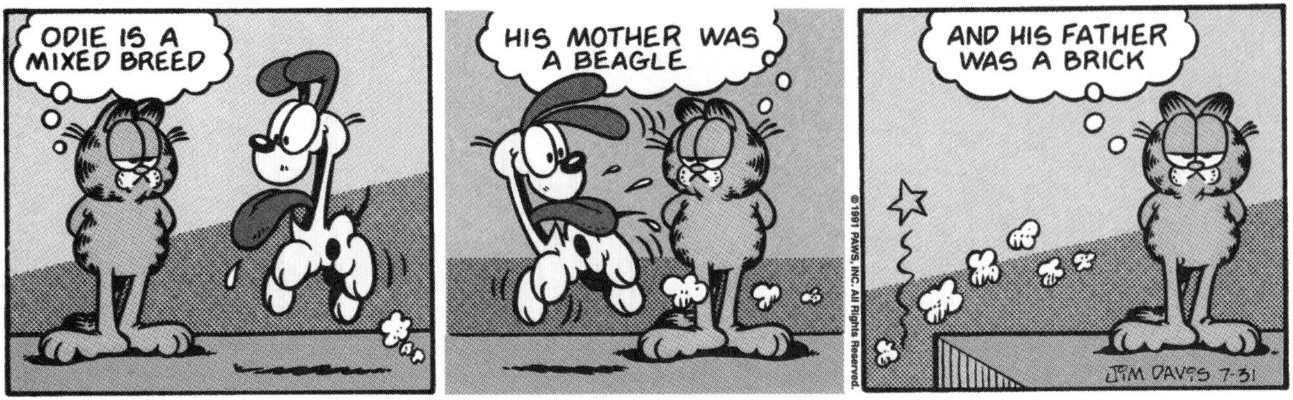
ODIE IS A MIXED BREED
HIS MOTHER WAS A BEAGLE
© 1991 PAWS, INC. All Rights Reserved.
AND HIS FATHER WAS A BRICK
JIM DAVIS 7-31

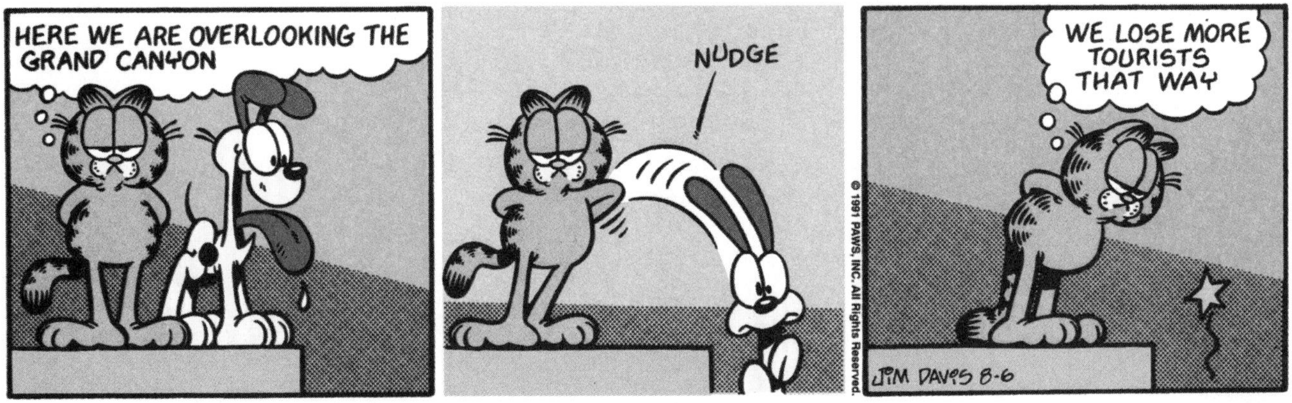
HERE WE ARE OVERLOOKING THE GRAND CANYON
NUDGE
© 1991 PAWS, INC. All Rights Reserved.
WE LOSE MORE TOURISTS THAT WAY
JIM DAVIS 8-6

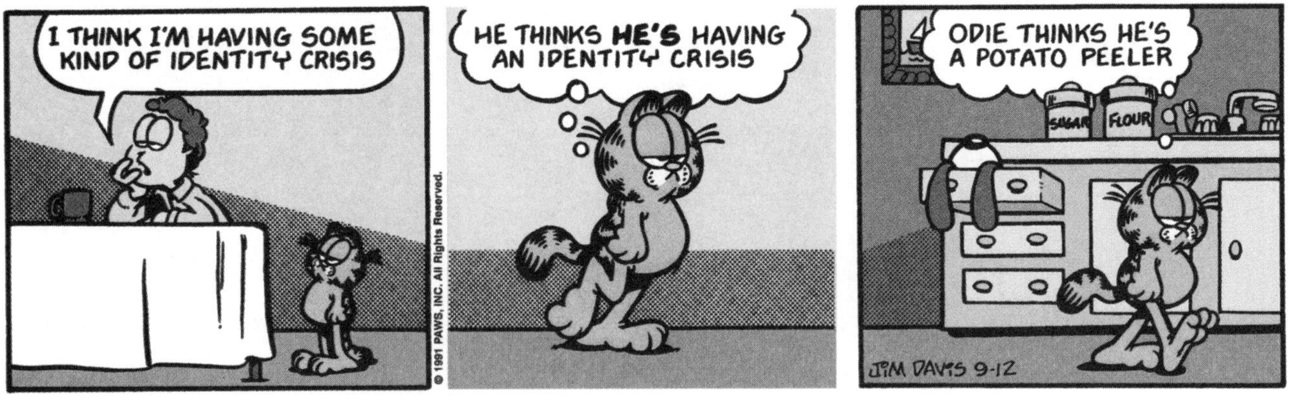
I THINK I'M HAVING SOME KIND OF IDENTITY CRISIS
© 1991 PAWS, INC. All Rights Reserved.
HE THINKS **HE'S** HAVING AN IDENTITY CRISIS
ODIE THINKS HE'S A POTATO PEELER
SUGAR
FLOUR
JIM DAVIS 9-12

NOW PLAYING
CANINE CINEMA

RAMBONE
NO CAT, NO VET,
NO DOGCATCHER
CAN STOP HIM!

The Dogfather

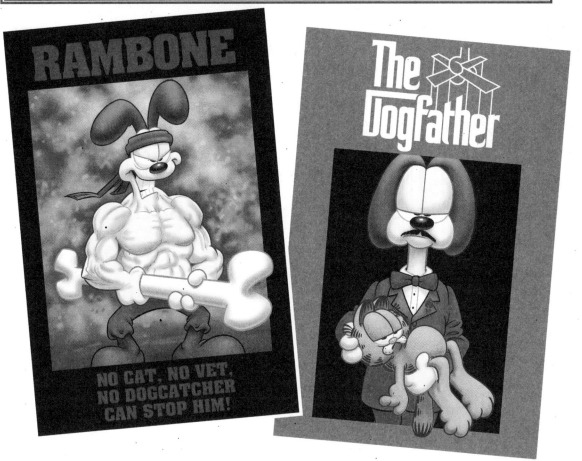

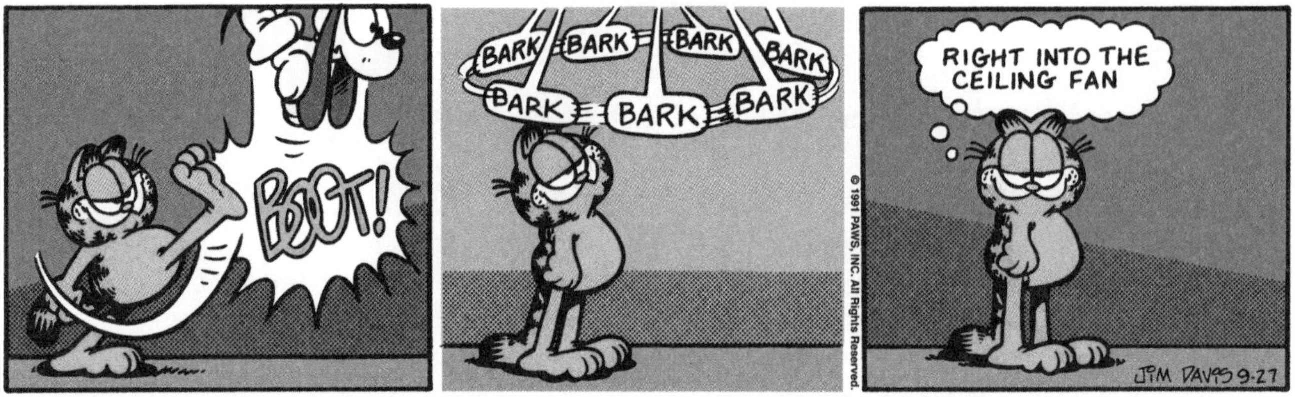
BOOT!
BARK BARK BARK BARK
BARK BARK BARK
© 1991 PAWS, INC. All Rights Reserved.
RIGHT INTO THE CEILING FAN
JIM DAVIS 9-27

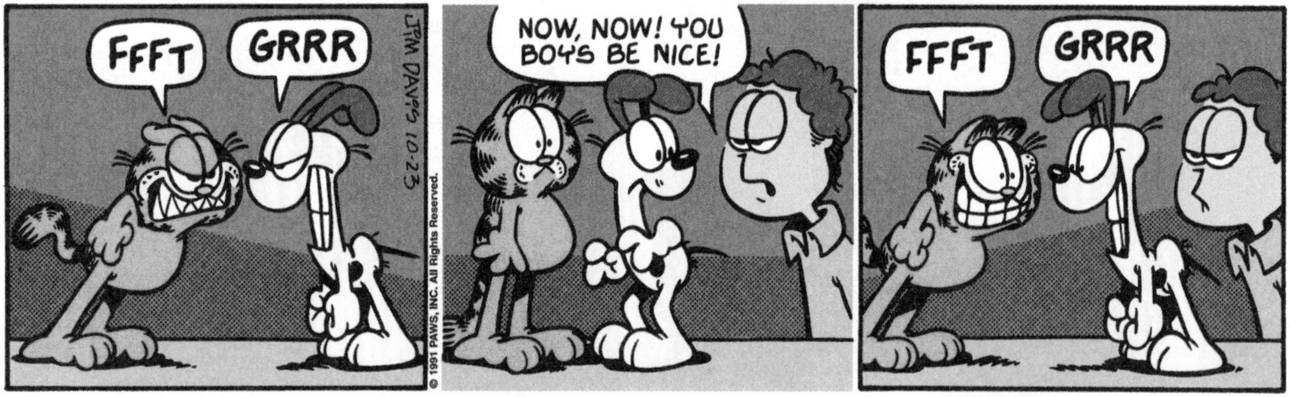
FFFT
GRRR
JIM DAVIS 10-23
© 1991 PAWS, INC. All Rights Reserved.
NOW, NOW! YOU BOYS BE NICE!
FFFT
GRRR

Very Important Pooch

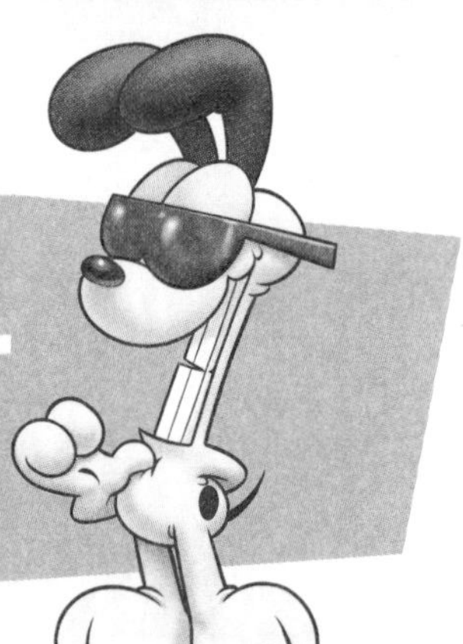

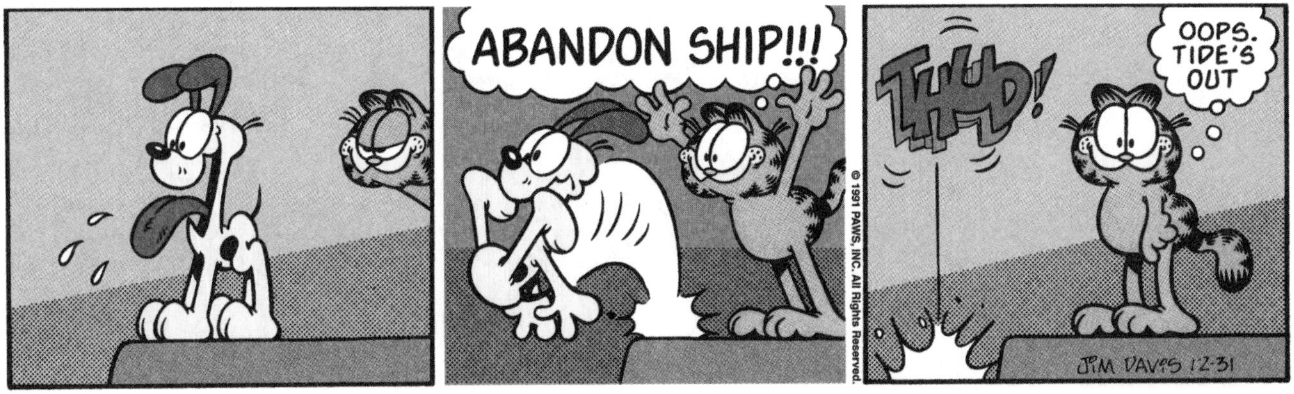
ABANDON SHIP!!!
© 1991 PAWS, INC. All Rights Reserved.
THUD!
OOPS. TIDE'S OUT
JIM DAVIS 12-31

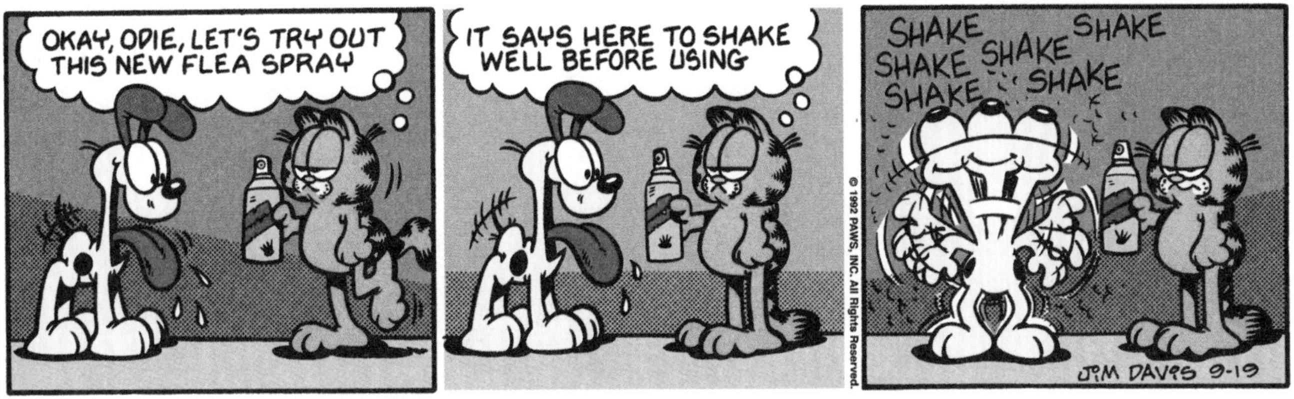
OKAY, ODIE, LET'S TRY OUT THIS NEW FLEA SPRAY
IT SAYS HERE TO SHAKE WELL BEFORE USING
© 1992 PAWS, INC. All Rights Reserved.
SHAKE SHAKE SHAKE SHAKE SHAKE SHAKE SHAKE
JIM DAVIS 9-19

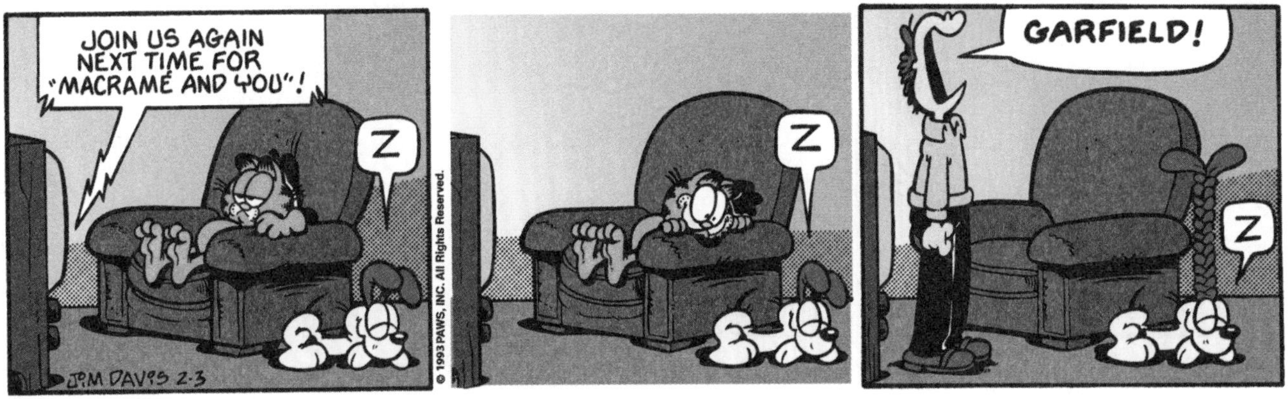
JOIN US AGAIN NEXT TIME FOR "MACRAMÉ AND YOU"!
Z
JIM DAVIS 2-3
© 1993 PAWS, INC. All Rights Reserved.
Z
GARFIELD!
Z

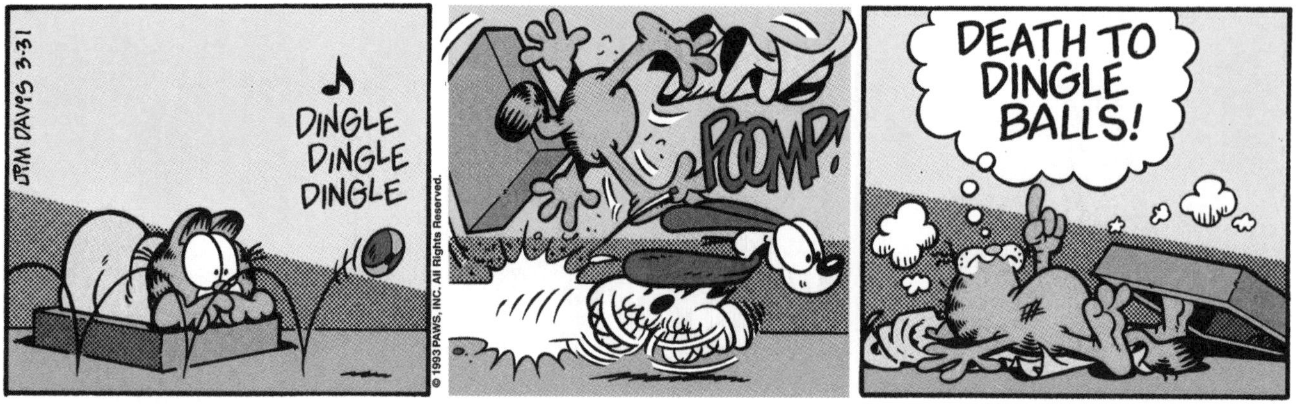
JIM DAVIS 3-31
DINGLE DINGLE DINGLE
POOMP!
© 1993 PAWS, INC. All Rights Reserved.
DEATH TO DINGLE BALLS!

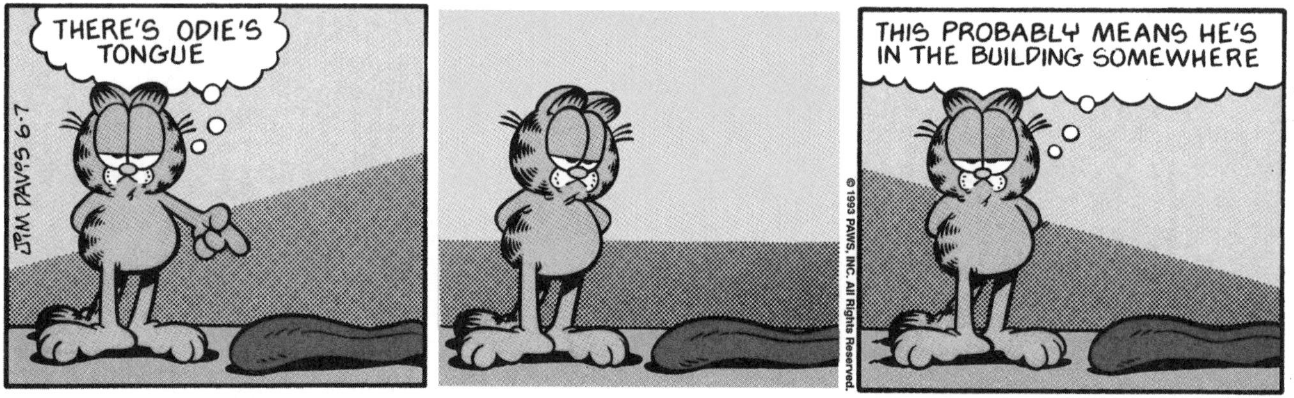
THERE'S ODIE'S TONGUE
JIM DAVIS 6-7
© 1993 PAWS, INC. All Rights Reserved.
THIS PROBABLY MEANS HE'S IN THE BUILDING SOMEWHERE

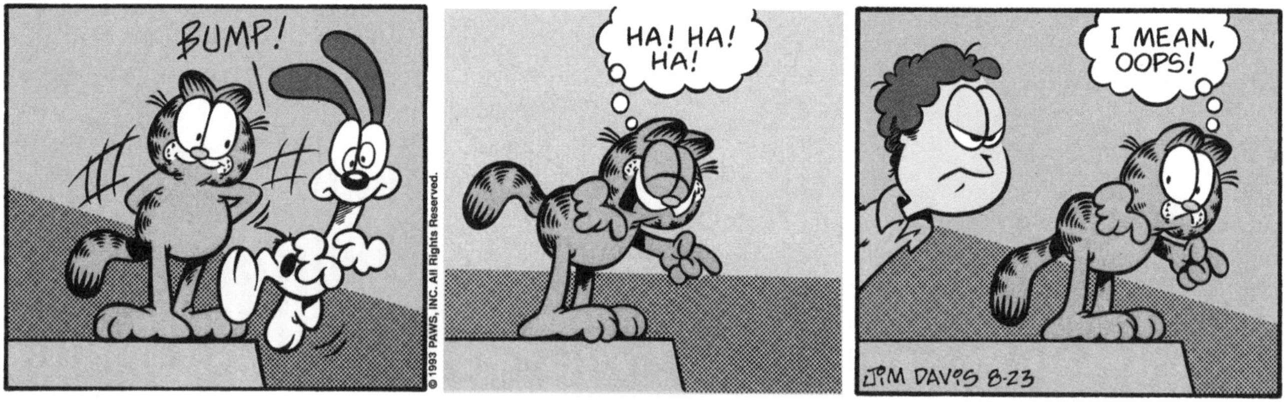
BUMP!
© 1993 PAWS, INC. All Rights Reserved.
HA! HA! HA!
I MEAN, OOPS!
JIM DAVIS 8-23

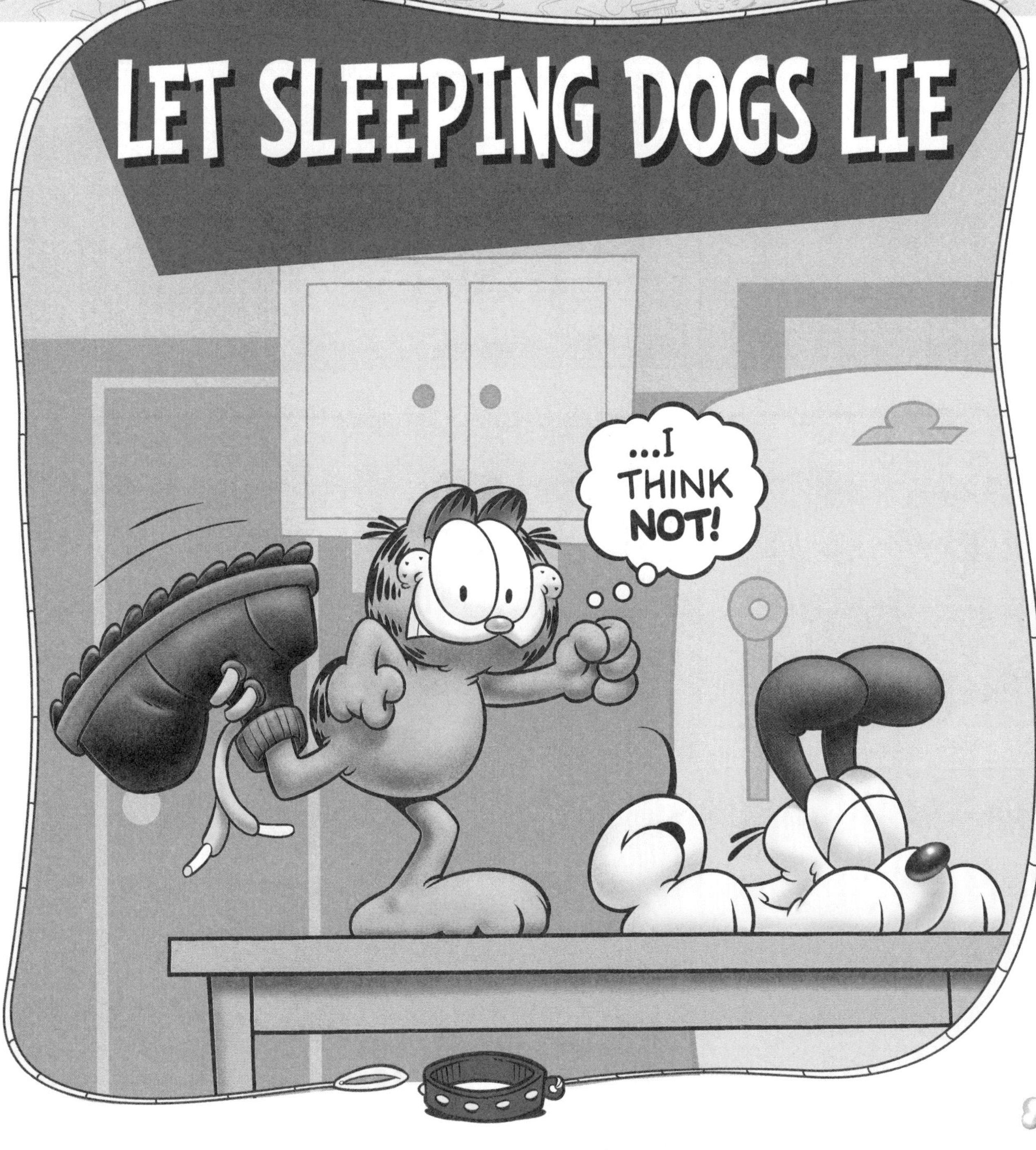
LET SLEEPING DOGS LIE
...I THINK NOT!

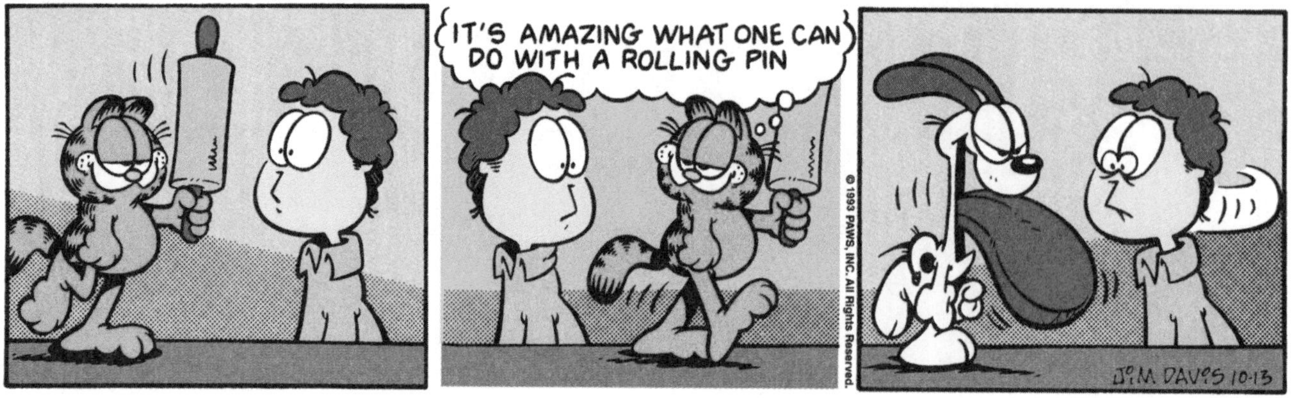
IT'S AMAZING WHAT ONE CAN DO WITH A ROLLING PIN
© 1993 PAWS, INC. All Rights Reserved.
JIM DAVIS 10-13

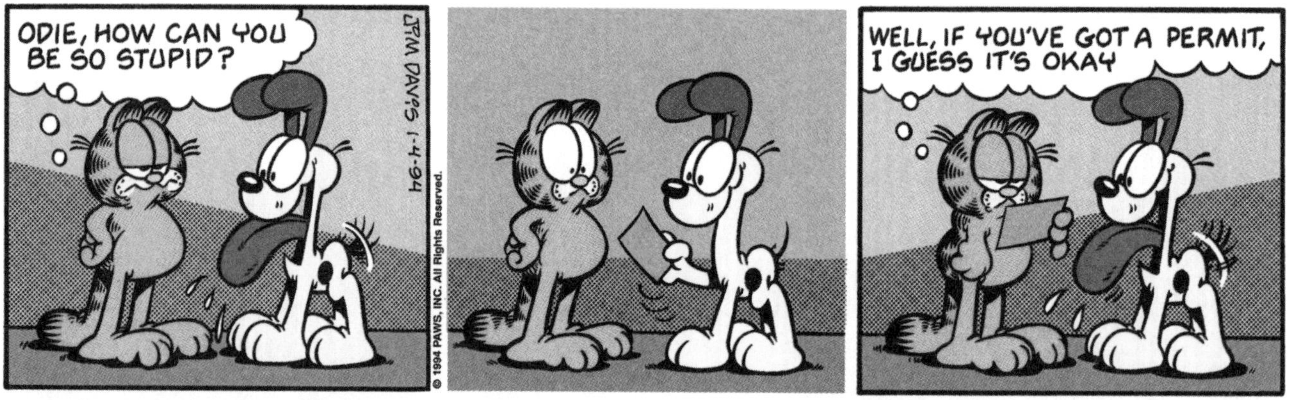
ODIE, HOW CAN YOU BE SO STUPID?
JIM DAVIS 1-4-94
© 1994 PAWS, INC. All Rights Reserved.
WELL, IF YOU'VE GOT A PERMIT, I GUESS IT'S OKAY

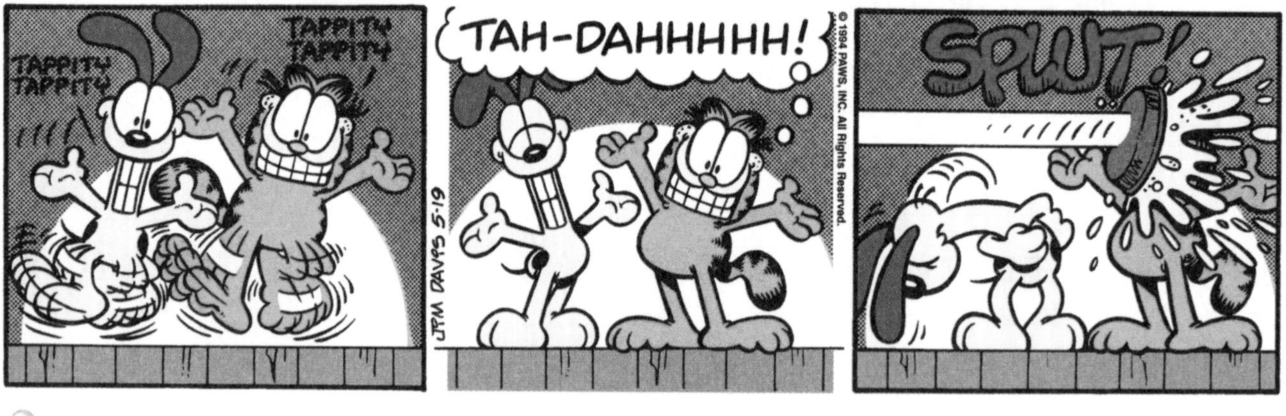
TAPPITY TAPPITY
TAPPITY TAPPITY
JIM DAVIS 5-19
TAH-DAHHHHH!
© 1994 PAWS, INC. All Rights Reserved.
SPLUT!

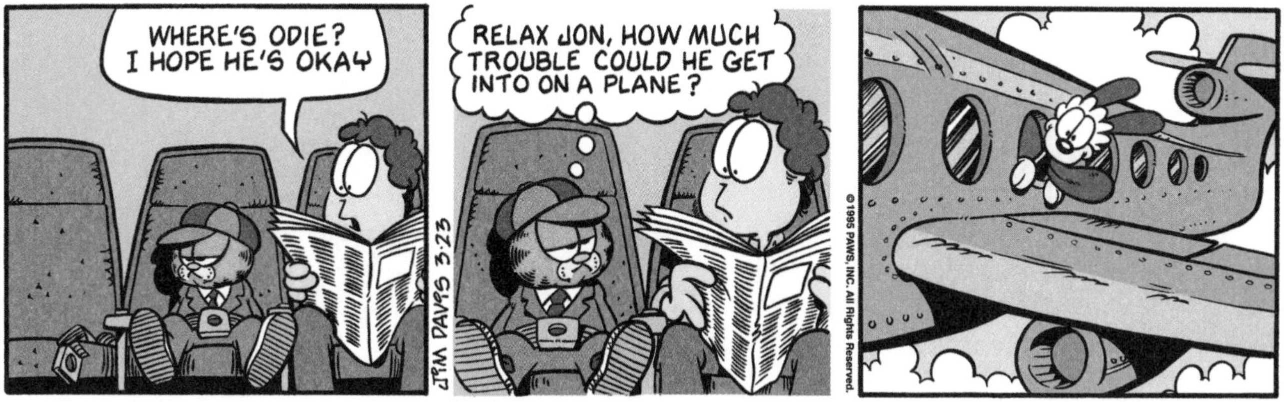
WHERE'S ODIE? I HOPE HE'S OKAY
JIM DAVIS 3-23
RELAX JON, HOW MUCH TROUBLE COULD HE GET INTO ON A PLANE?
© 1995 PAWS, INC. All Rights Reserved.

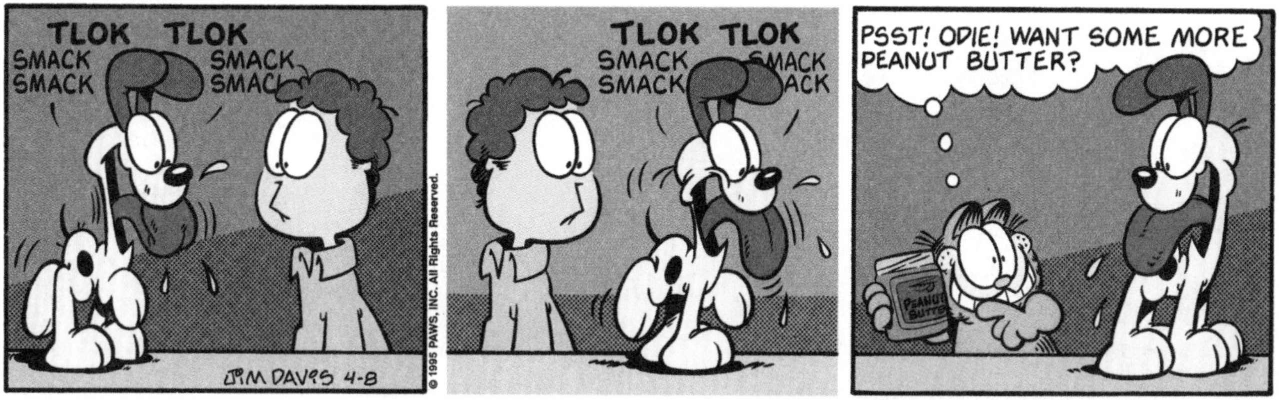
TLOK TLOK
SMACK SMACK
SMACK SMACK
JIM DAVIS 4-8
© 1995 PAWS, INC. All Rights Reserved.
TLOK TLOK
SMACK SMACK
PSST! ODIE! WANT SOME MORE PEANUT BUTTER?
PEANUT BUTTER

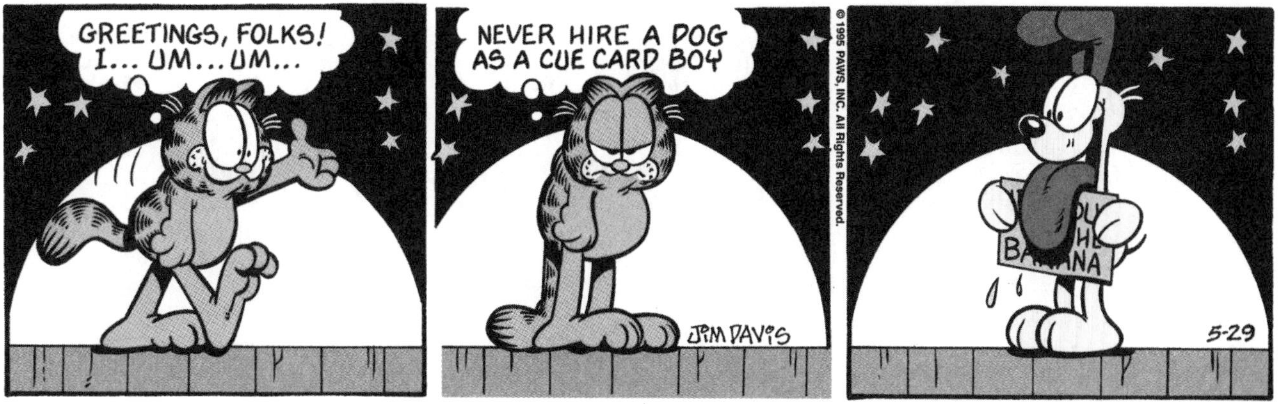
GREETINGS, FOLKS! I... UM... UM...
NEVER HIRE A DOG AS A CUE CARD BOY
JIM DAVIS
© 1995 PAWS, INC. All Rights Reserved.
5-29

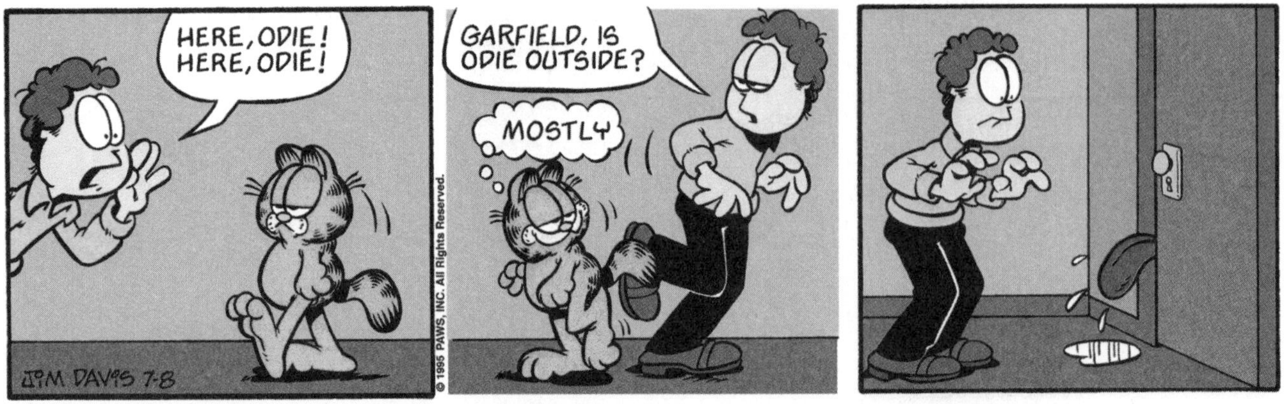
HERE, ODIE! HERE, ODIE!
JIM DAVIS 7-8
© 1995 PAWS, INC. All Rights Reserved.
GARFIELD, IS ODIE OUTSIDE?
MOSTLY

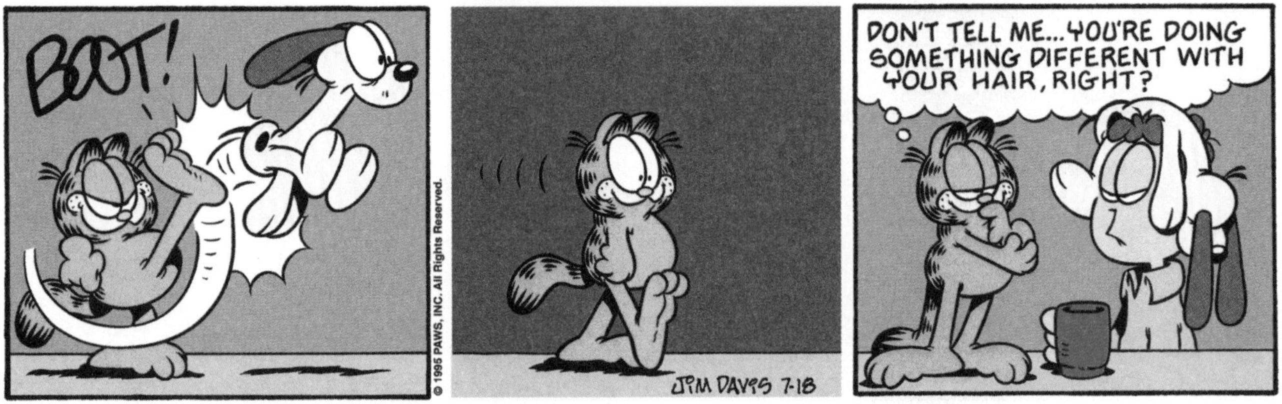
BOOT!
© 1995 PAWS, INC. All Rights Reserved.
JIM DAVIS 7-18
DON'T TELL ME...YOU'RE DOING SOMETHING DIFFERENT WITH YOUR HAIR, RIGHT?

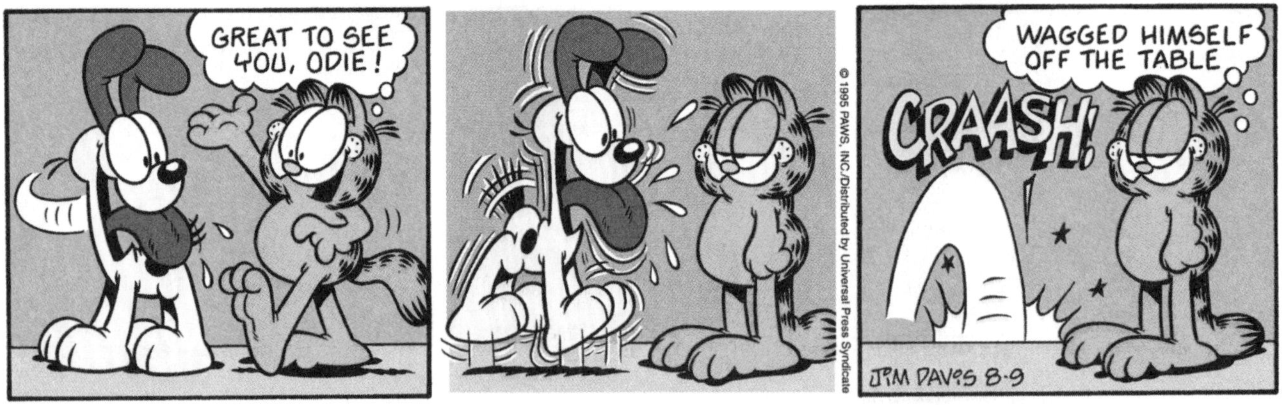
GREAT TO SEE YOU, ODIE!
© 1995 PAWS, INC./Distributed by Universal Press Syndicate
WAGGED HIMSELF OFF THE TABLE
CRAASH!
JIM DAVIS 8-9

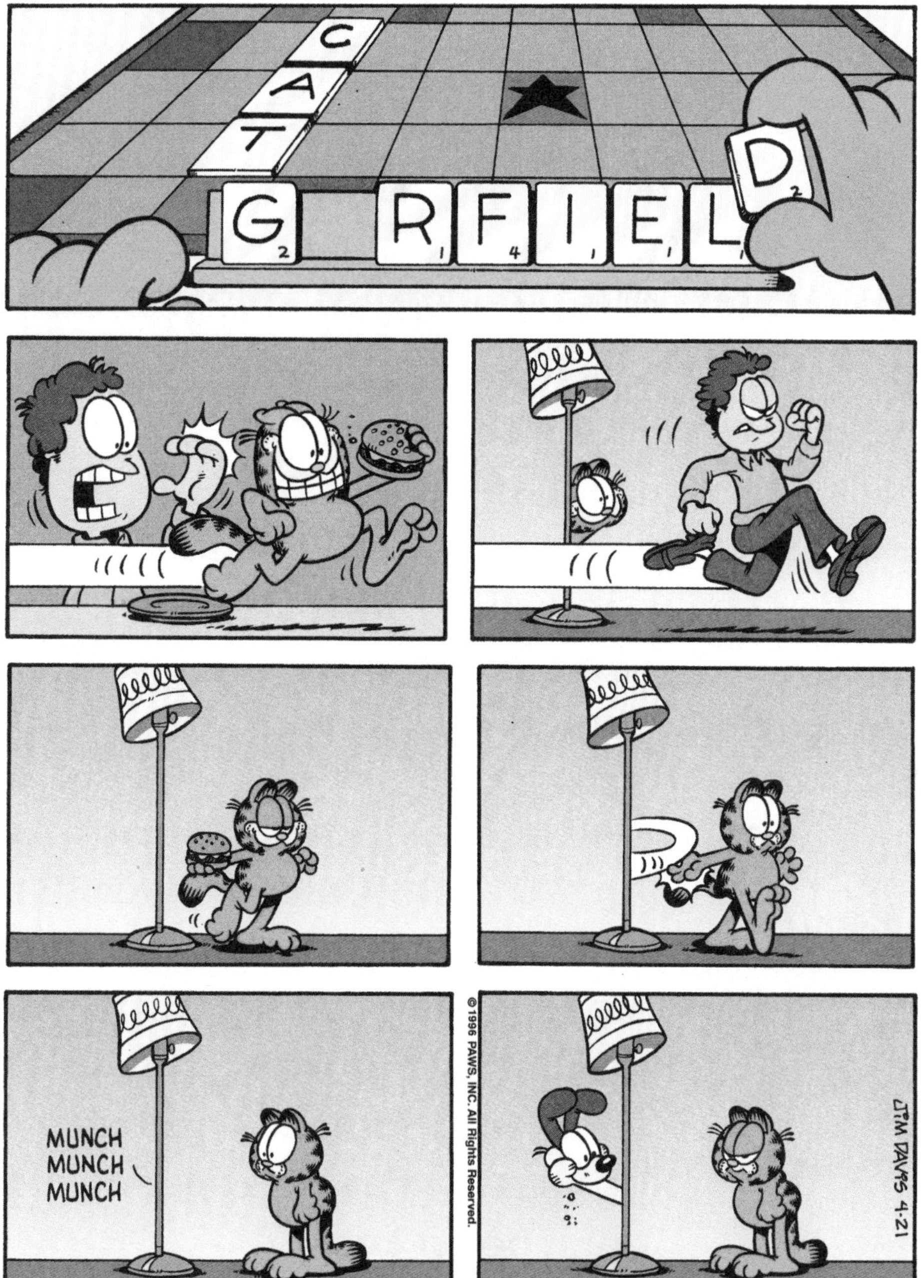
C
A
T
G
R
F
I
E
L
D
MUNCH
MUNCH
MUNCH
© 1996 PAWS, INC. All Rights Reserved.
JIM DAVIS 4-21

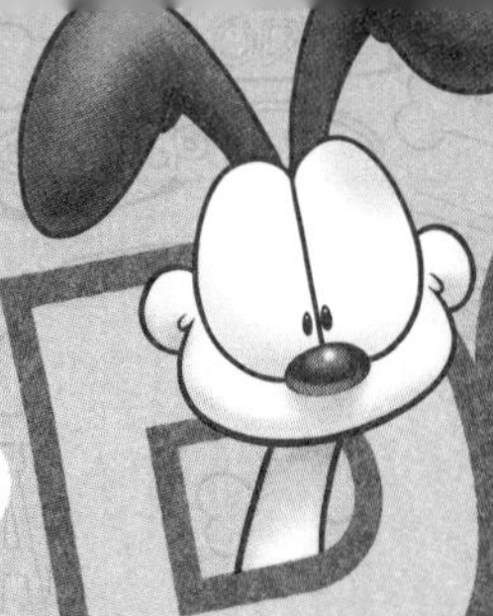

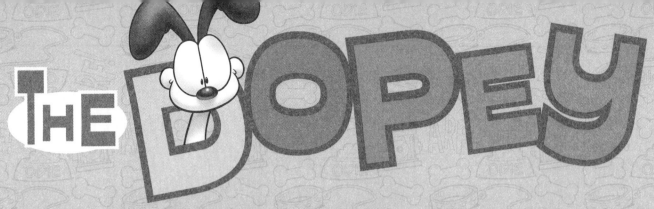

THE DOPEY

JIM DAVIS'S FAVORITE ODIE STRIPS

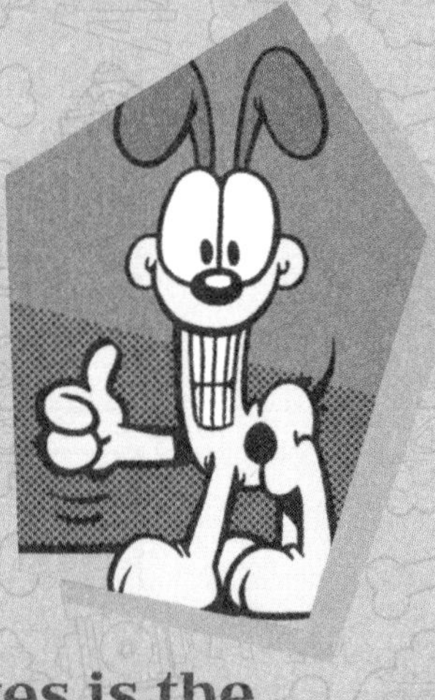

Over the years, we've done some 1,400 Odie strips—that's a lot of drool and dopiness. Picking just twelve was no easy task. I tried to pull a variety of strips and show both visual and verbal humor. Odie's a natural for physical comedy and sight gags.

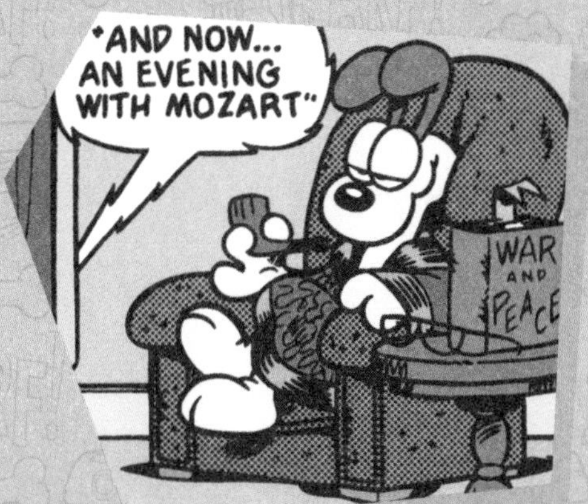
"AND NOW... AN EVENING WITH MOZART"
WAR AND PEACE

One of my all-time favorites is the April 27, 1989, strip, which depicts Odie alone at home listening to Mozart and reading *War and Peace*. I think it's what we've always suspected about him. I mean, Odie can't possibly be as stupid as he appears, right? It must be an act.

DOZEN

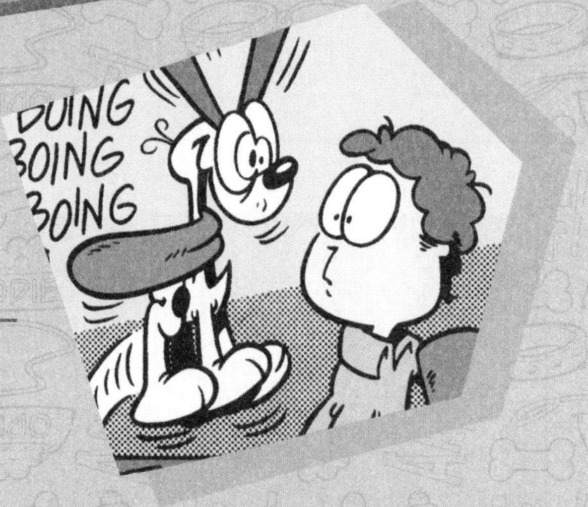

Odie's a great character to write for; he's so playful and pliable. And he's a great foil for Garfield—a punching bag with a tongue.

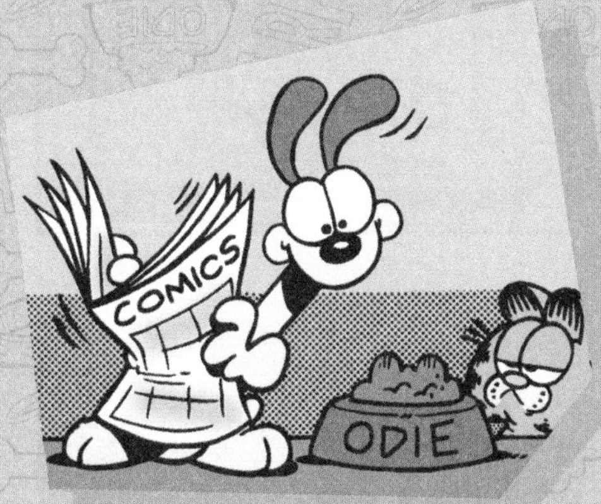
COMICS
ODIE

But writing for Odie is different from writing for Garfield. I come at it from a different place. It's not so much a thought process as it is a feeling, a mood. When I write Odie strips, I clear my mind, relax, and get silly (I might even slobber a little). I guess you could say I "Odie-ize" myself.

-JIM DAVIS

THE DOPEY DOZEN

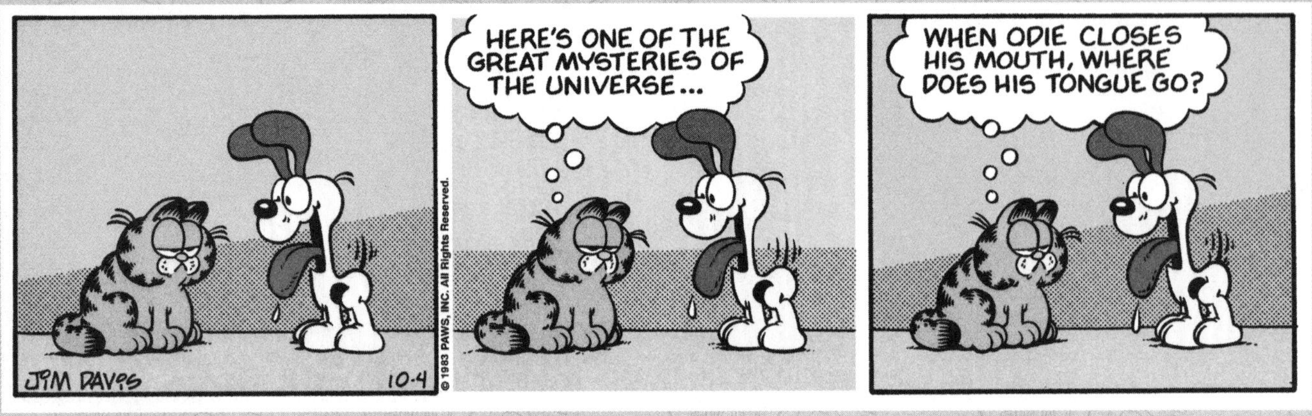

JIM DAVIS
10-4
© 1983 PAWS, INC. All Rights Reserved.
HERE'S ONE OF THE GREAT MYSTERIES OF THE UNIVERSE...
WHEN ODIE CLOSES HIS MOUTH, WHERE DOES HIS TONGUE GO?

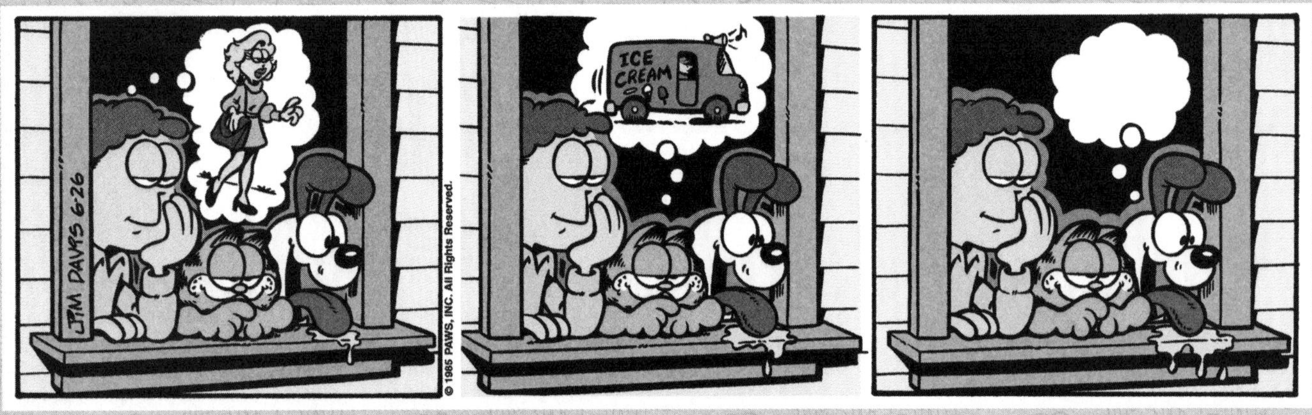

JIM DAVIS 6-26
© 1985 PAWS, INC. All Rights Reserved.
ICE CREAM

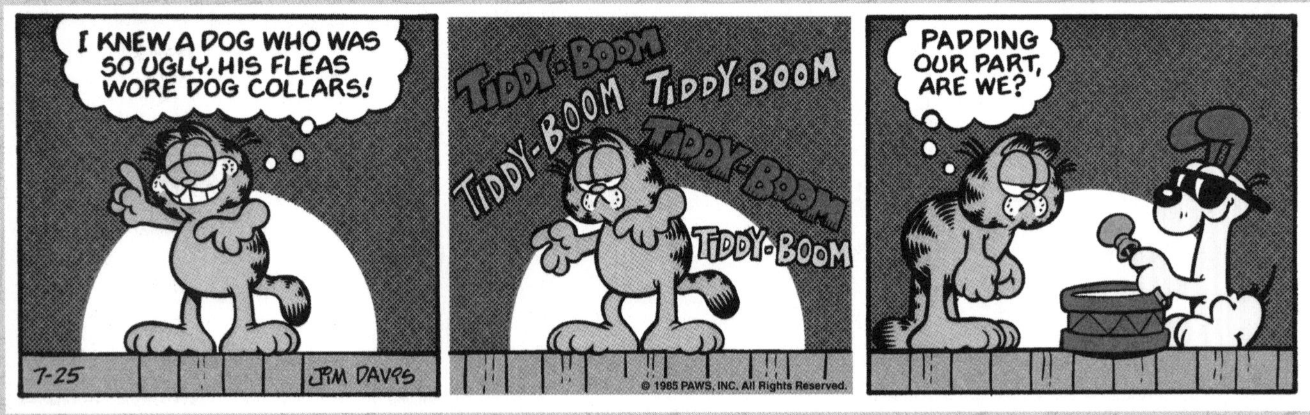

I KNEW A DOG WHO WAS SO UGLY, HIS FLEAS WORE DOG COLLARS!
7-25
JIM DAVIS
TIDDY-BOOM
TIDDY-BOOM
TIDDY-BOOM
TIDDY-BOOM
TIDDY-BOOM
© 1985 PAWS, INC. All Rights Reserved.
PADDING OUR PART, ARE WE?

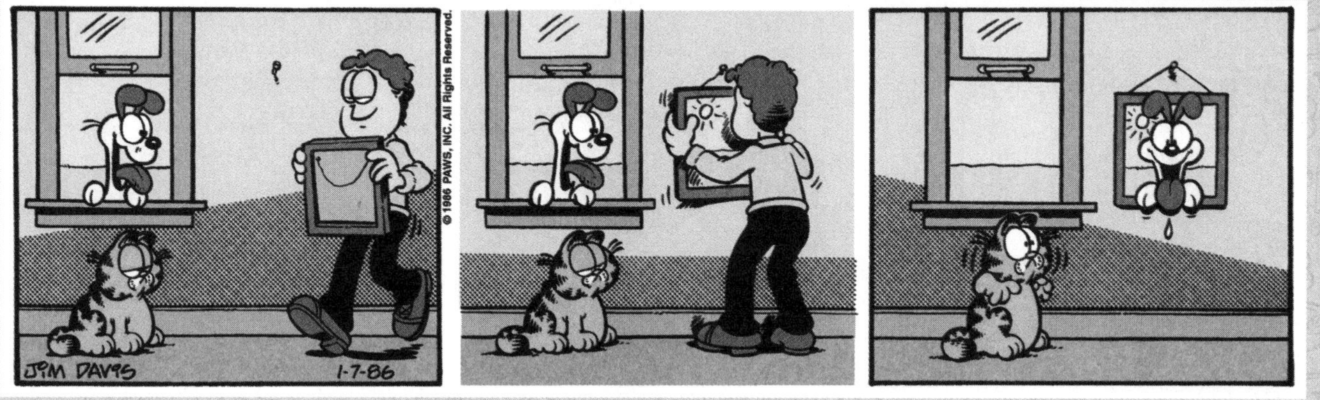
JIM DAVIS
1-7-86
© 1986 PAWS, INC. All Rights Reserved.

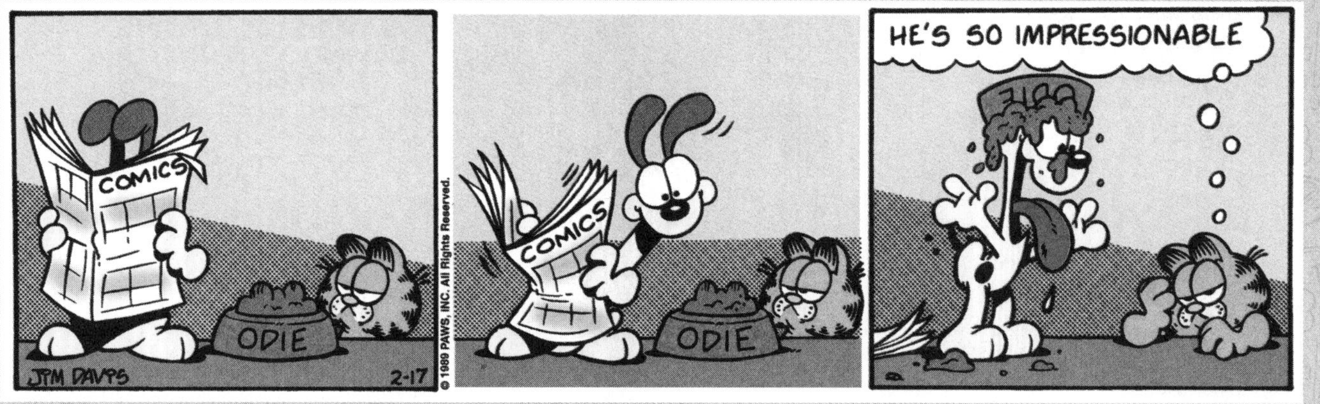
COMICS
ODIE
JIM DAVIS
2-17
© 1989 PAWS, INC. All Rights Reserved.
COMICS
ODIE
HE'S SO IMPRESSIONABLE

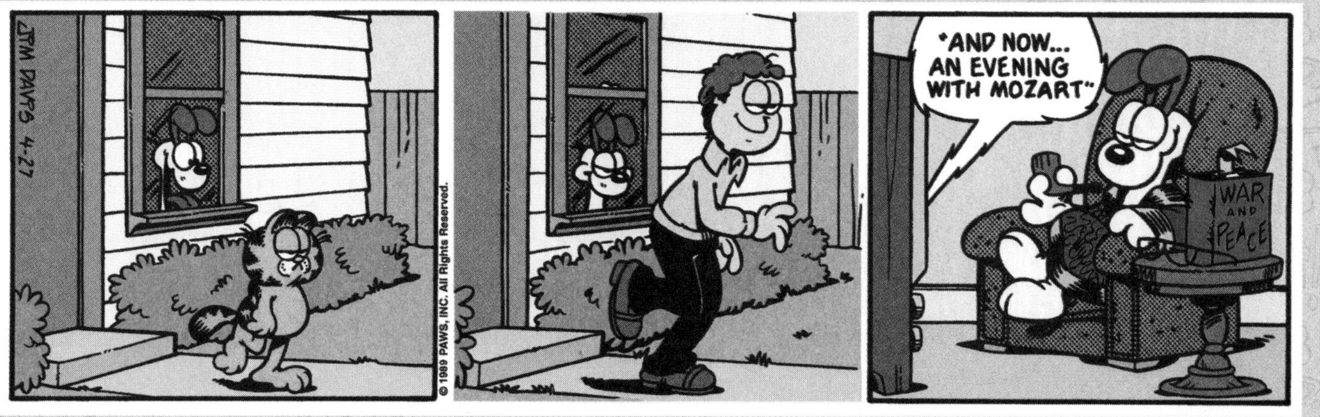
JIM DAVIS 4-27
© 1989 PAWS, INC. All Rights Reserved.
"AND NOW... AN EVENING WITH MOZART"
WAR AND PEACE

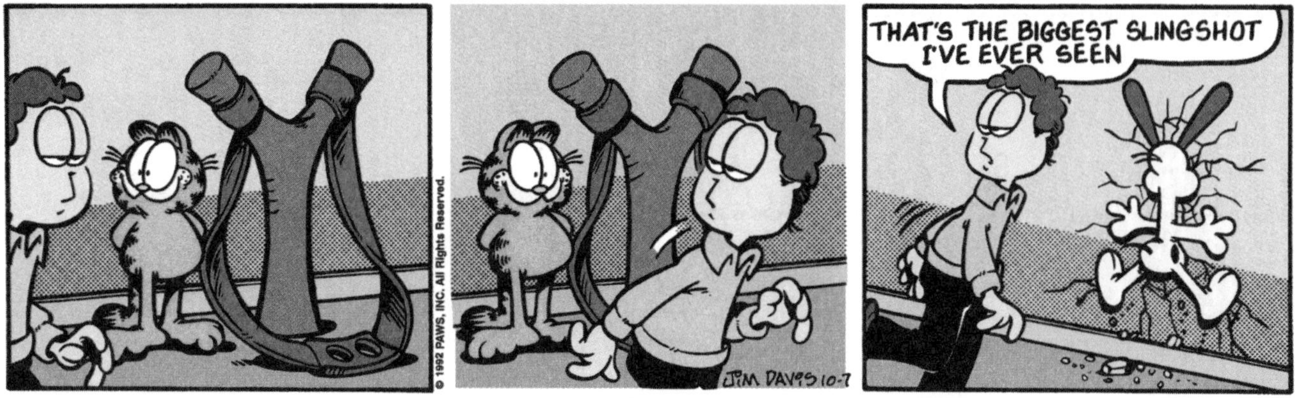
© 1992 PAWS, INC. All Rights Reserved.
JIM DAVIS 10-7
THAT'S THE BIGGEST SLINGSHOT I'VE EVER SEEN

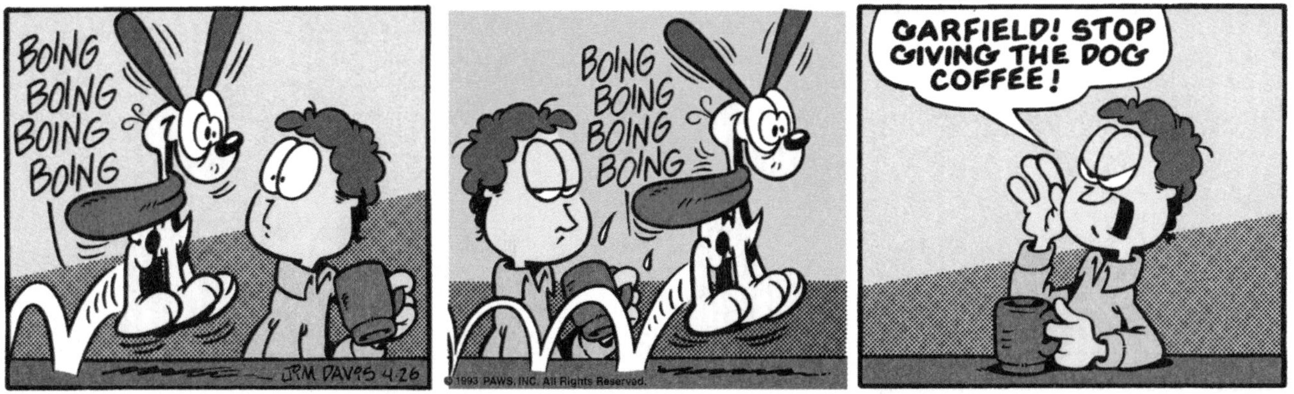
BOING BOING BOING BOING
JIM DAVIS 4-26
BOING BOING BOING BOING
© 1993 PAWS, INC. All Rights Reserved.
GARFIELD! STOP GIVING THE DOG COFFEE!

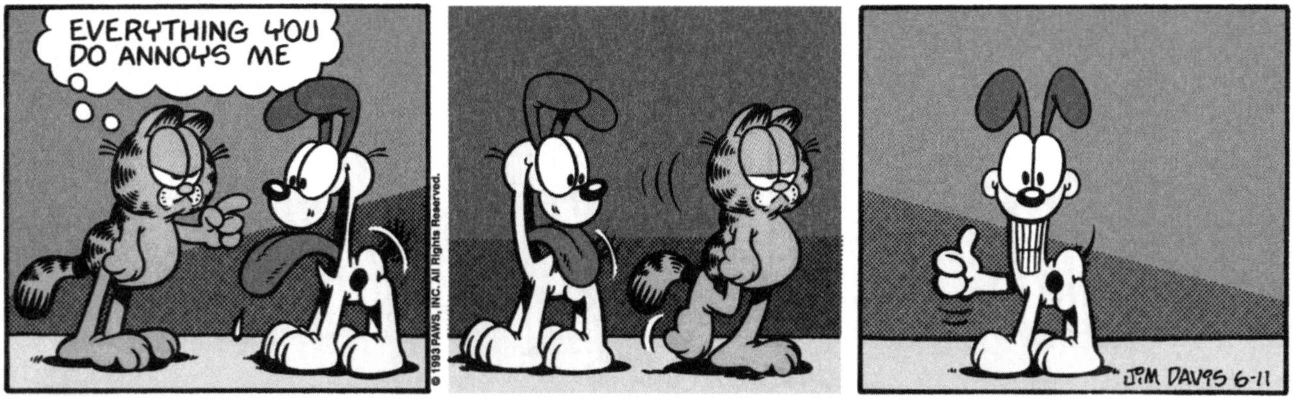
EVERYTHING YOU DO ANNOYS ME
© 1993 PAWS, INC. All Rights Reserved.
JIM DAVIS 6-11

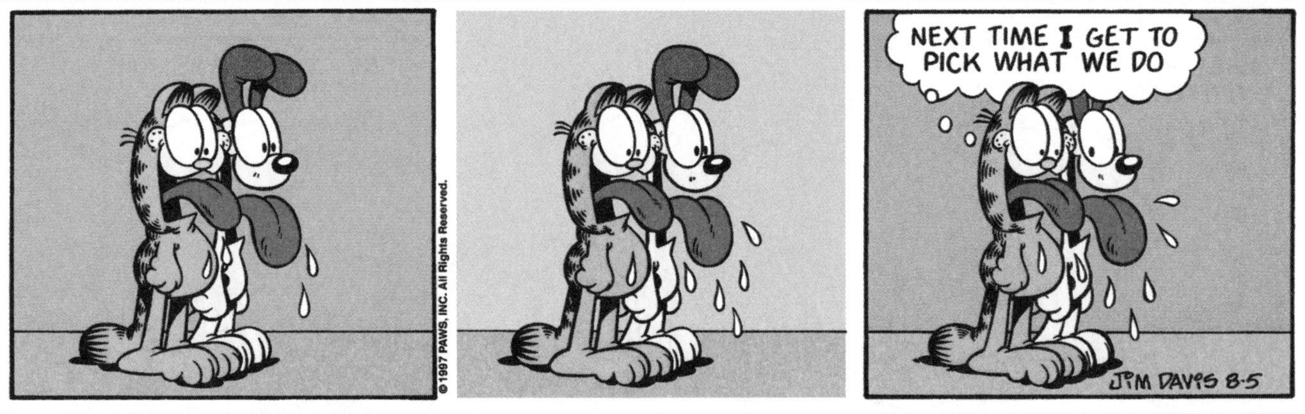
© 1997 PAWS, INC. All Rights Reserved.
NEXT TIME I GET TO PICK WHAT WE DO
JIM DAVIS 8-5

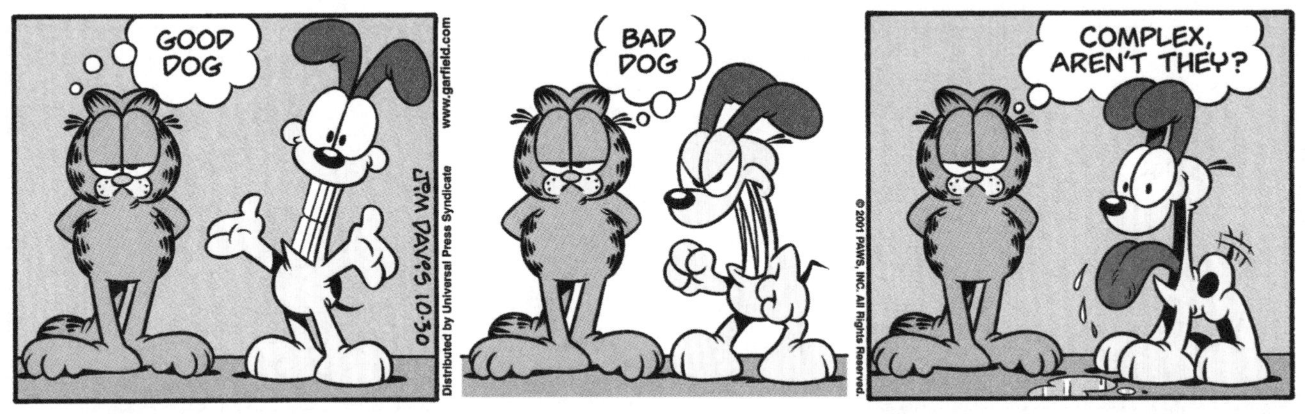
GOOD DOG
JIM DAVIS 10-30
Distributed by Universal Press Syndicate www.garfield.com
BAD DOG
© 2001 PAWS, INC. All Rights Reserved.
COMPLEX, AREN'T THEY?

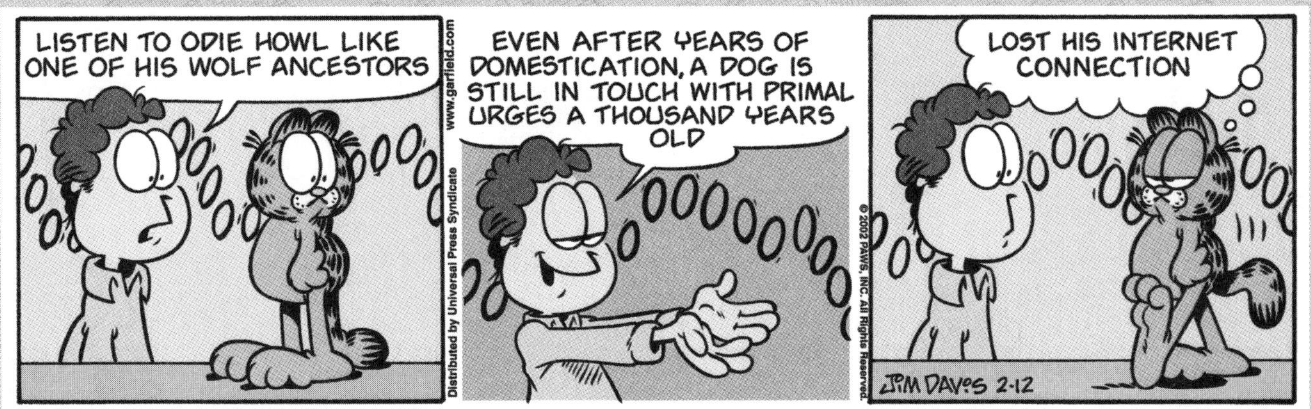
LISTEN TO ODIE HOWL LIKE ONE OF HIS WOLF ANCESTORS
Distributed by Universal Press Syndicate www.garfield.com
EVEN AFTER YEARS OF DOMESTICATION, A DOG IS STILL IN TOUCH WITH PRIMAL URGES A THOUSAND YEARS OLD
© 2002 PAWS, INC. All Rights Reserved.
LOST HIS INTERNET CONNECTION
JIM DAVIS 2-12

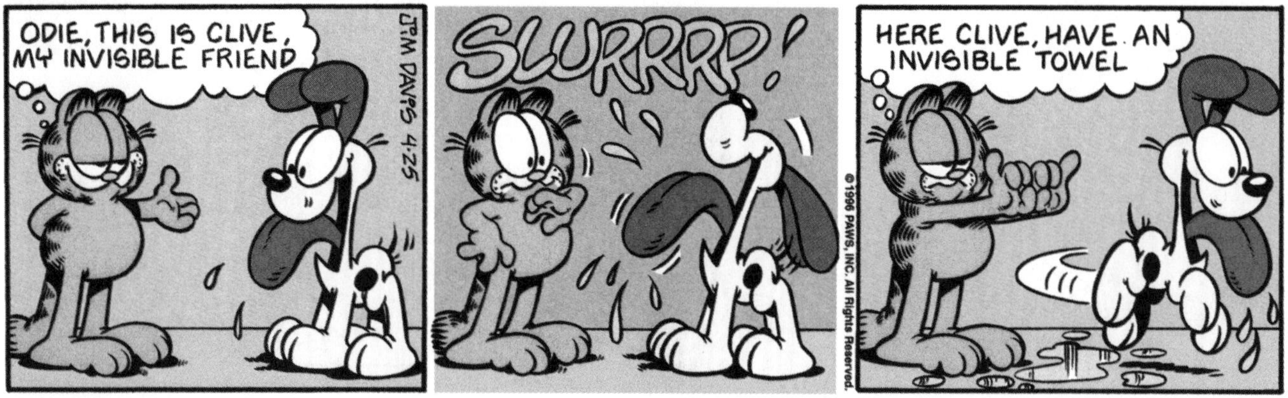
ODIE, THIS IS CLIVE, MY INVISIBLE FRIEND
JIM DAVIS 4-25
SLURRRP!
HERE CLIVE, HAVE AN INVISIBLE TOWEL
© 1996 PAWS, INC. All Rights Reserved.

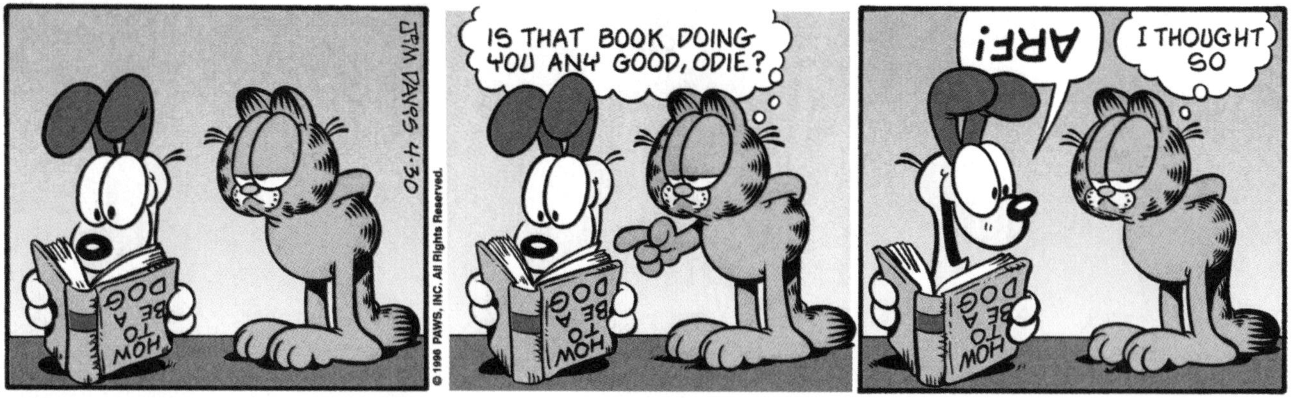
JIM DAVIS 4-30
HOW TO BE A DOG
© 1996 PAWS, INC. All Rights Reserved.
IS THAT BOOK DOING YOU ANY GOOD, ODIE?
HOW TO BE A DOG
ARF!
I THOUGHT SO
HOW TO BE A DOG

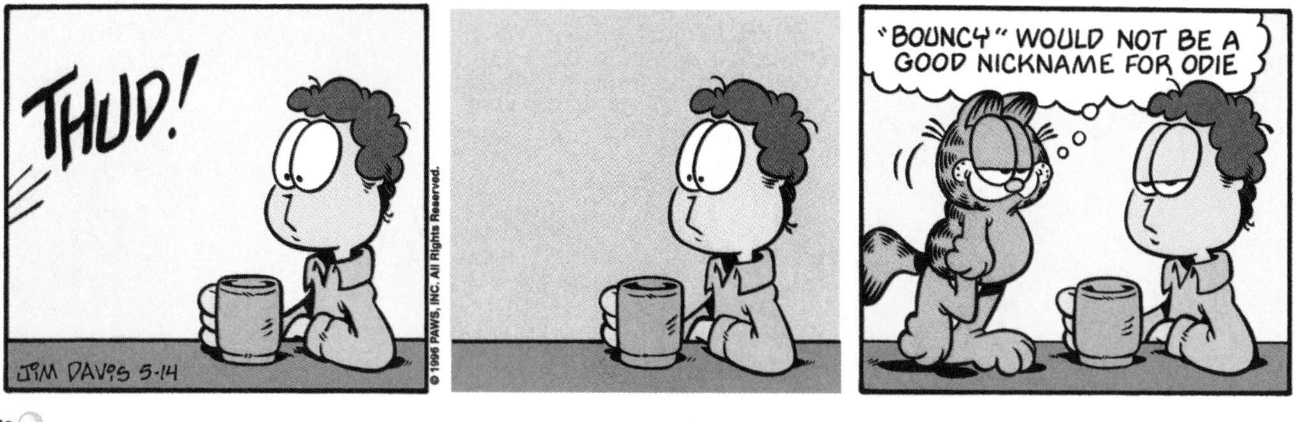
THUD!
JIM DAVIS 5-14
© 1996 PAWS, INC. All Rights Reserved.
"BOUNCY" WOULD NOT BE A GOOD NICKNAME FOR ODIE

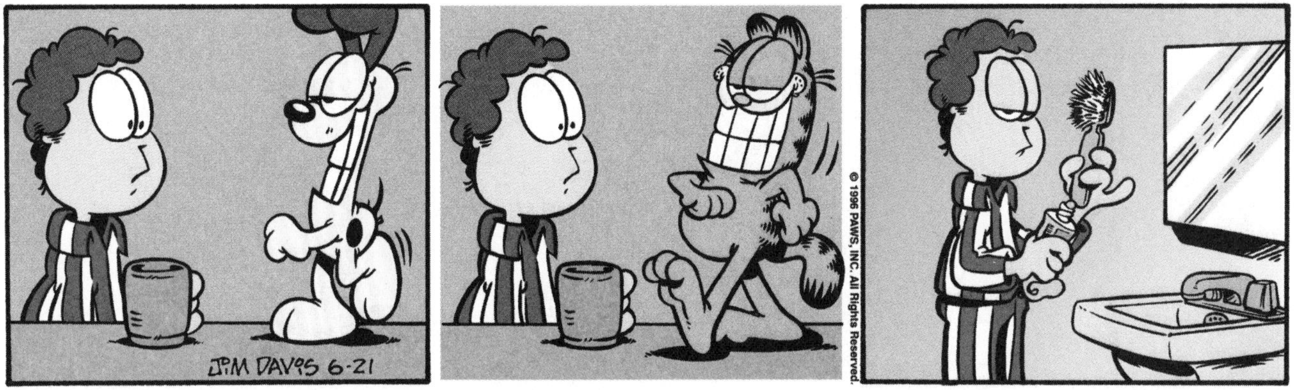
JIM DAVIS 6-21
© 1996 PAWS, INC. All Rights Reserved.

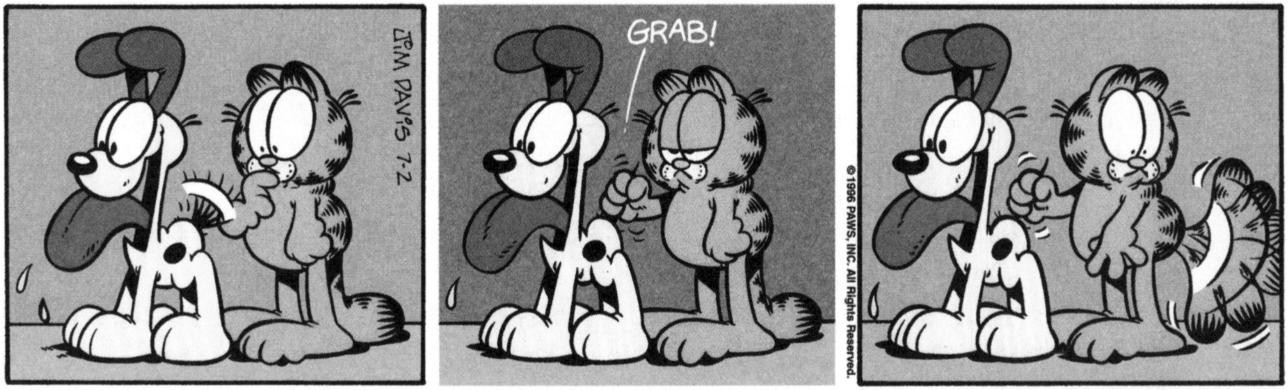
JIM DAVIS 7-2
GRAB!
© 1996 PAWS, INC. All Rights Reserved.

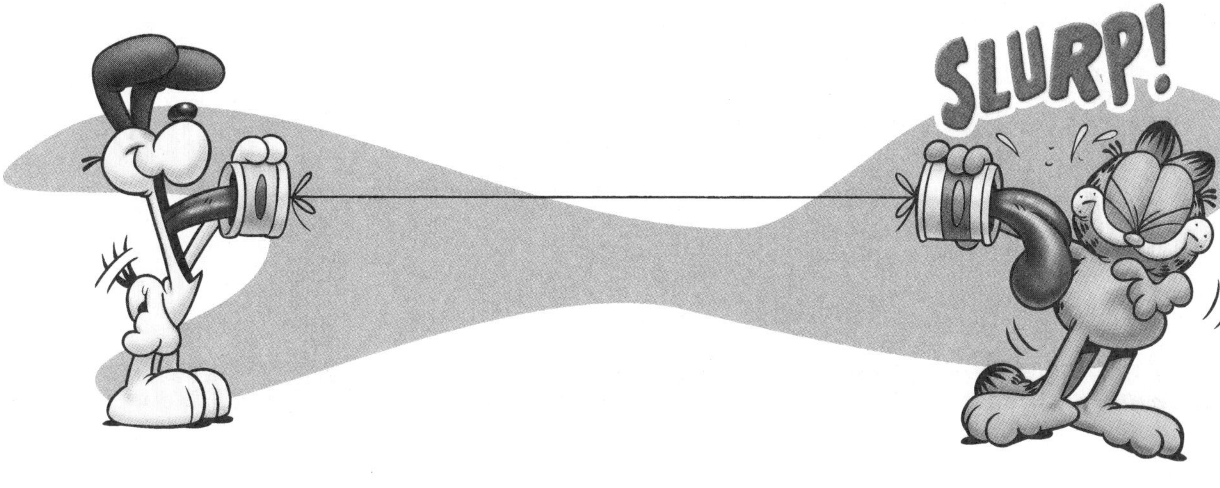
SLURP!

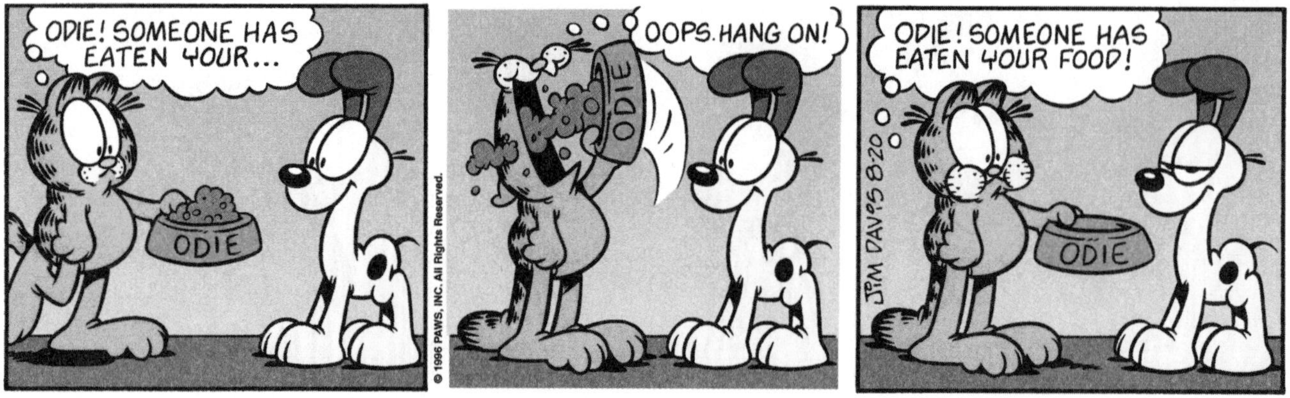
ODIE! SOMEONE HAS EATEN YOUR...
© 1996 PAWS, INC. All Rights Reserved.
OOPS. HANG ON!
ODIE
ODIE! SOMEONE HAS EATEN YOUR FOOD!
JIM DAVIS 8-20
ODIE

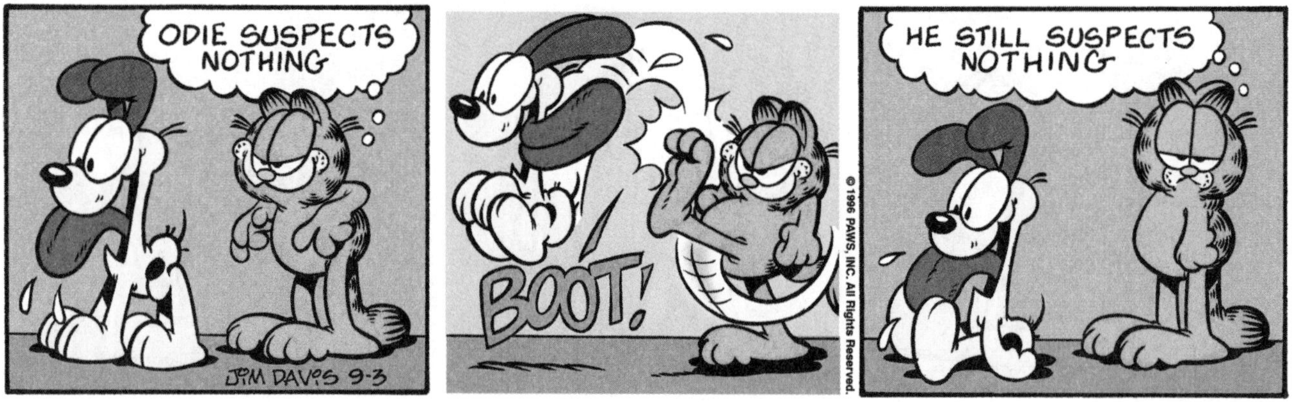
ODIE SUSPECTS NOTHING
JIM DAVIS 9-3
BOOT!
© 1996 PAWS, INC. All Rights Reserved.
HE STILL SUSPECTS NOTHING

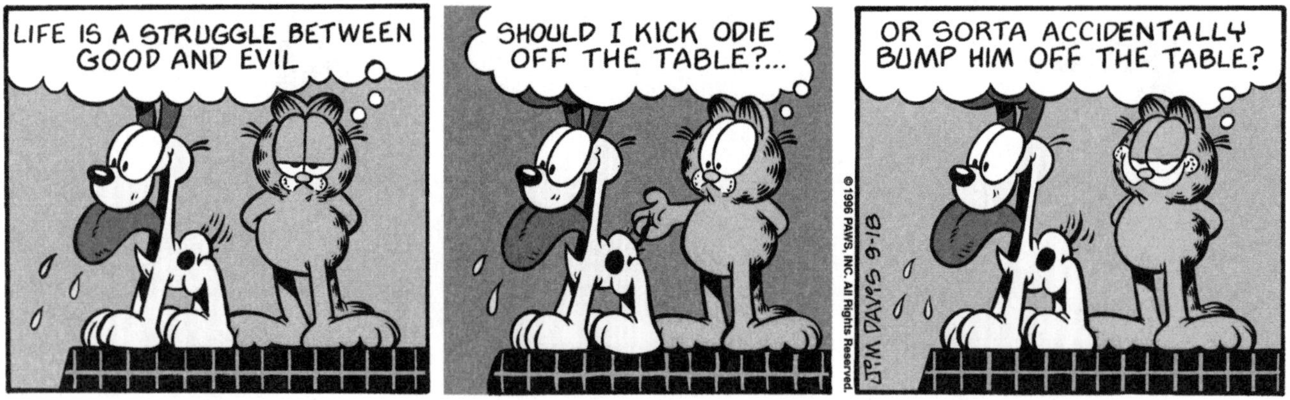
LIFE IS A STRUGGLE BETWEEN GOOD AND EVIL
SHOULD I KICK ODIE OFF THE TABLE?...
© 1996 PAWS, INC. All Rights Reserved.
JIM DAVIS 9-18
OR SORTA ACCIDENTALLY BUMP HIM OFF THE TABLE?

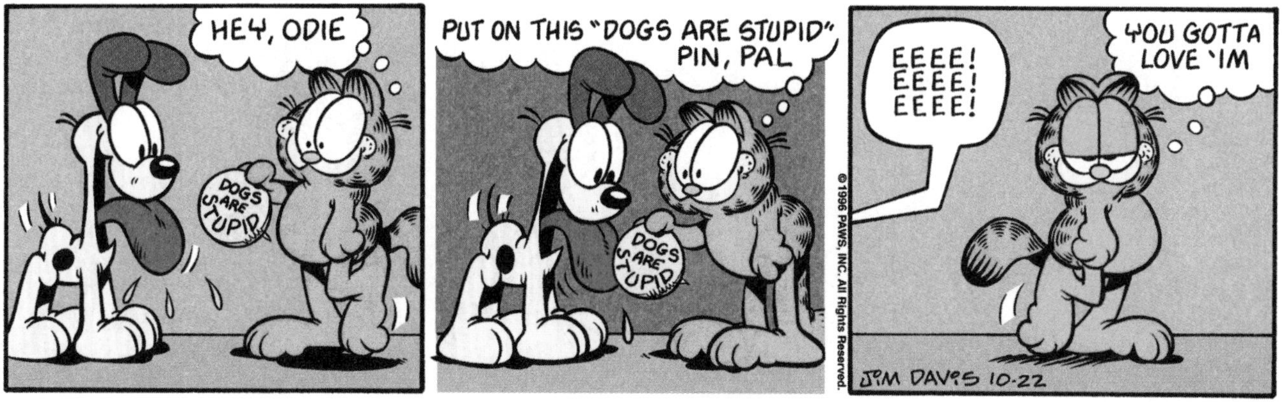
HEY, ODIE
DOGS ARE STUPID
PUT ON THIS "DOGS ARE STUPID" PIN, PAL
DOGS ARE STUPID
© 1996 PAWS, INC. All Rights Reserved.
EEEE! EEEE! EEEE!
YOU GOTTA LOVE 'IM
JIM DAVIS 10-22

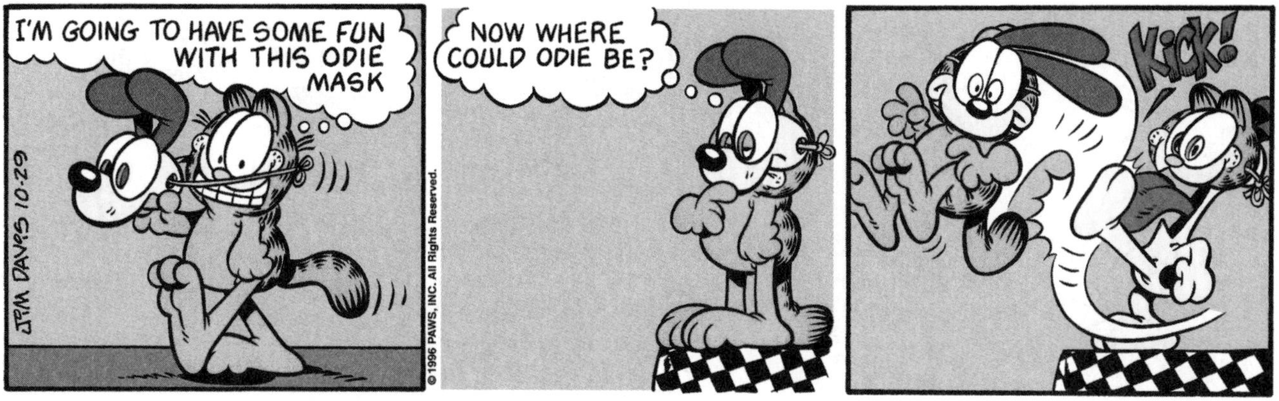
I'M GOING TO HAVE SOME FUN WITH THIS ODIE MASK
JIM DAVIS 10-29
© 1996 PAWS, INC. All Rights Reserved.
NOW WHERE COULD ODIE BE?
KICK!

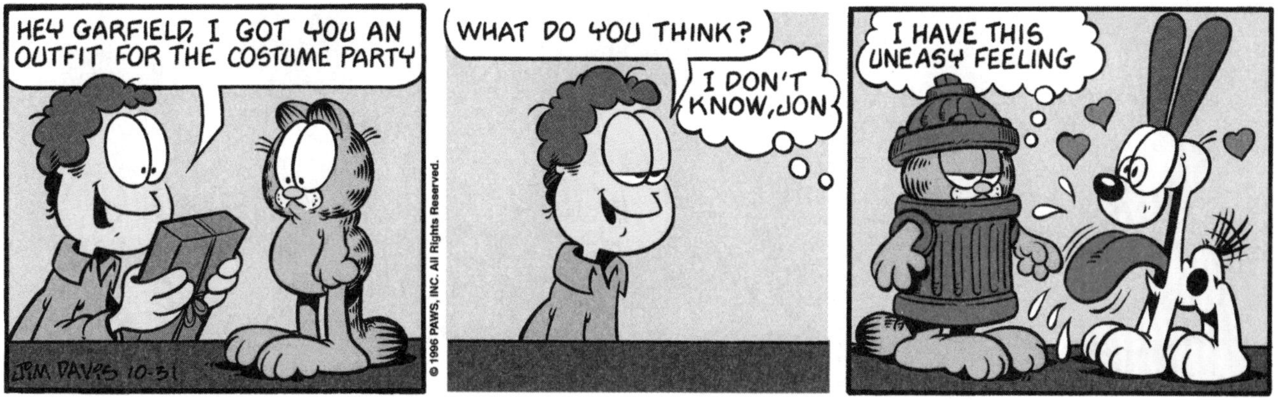
HEY GARFIELD, I GOT YOU AN OUTFIT FOR THE COSTUME PARTY
JIM DAVIS 10-31
© 1996 PAWS, INC. All Rights Reserved.
WHAT DO YOU THINK?
I DON'T KNOW, JON
I HAVE THIS UNEASY FEELING

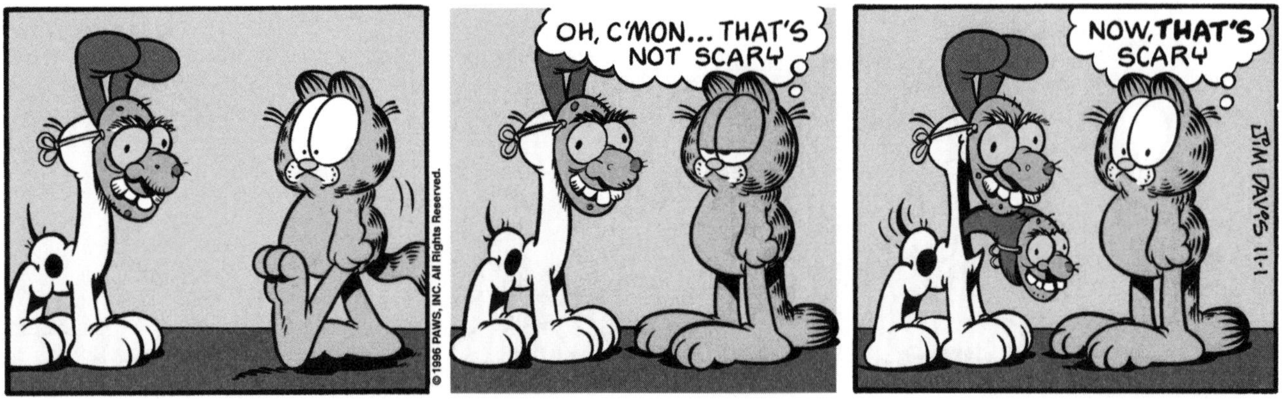
© 1996 PAWS, INC. All Rights Reserved.
OH, C'MON... THAT'S NOT SCARY
NOW, **THAT'S** SCARY
JIM DAVIS 11-1

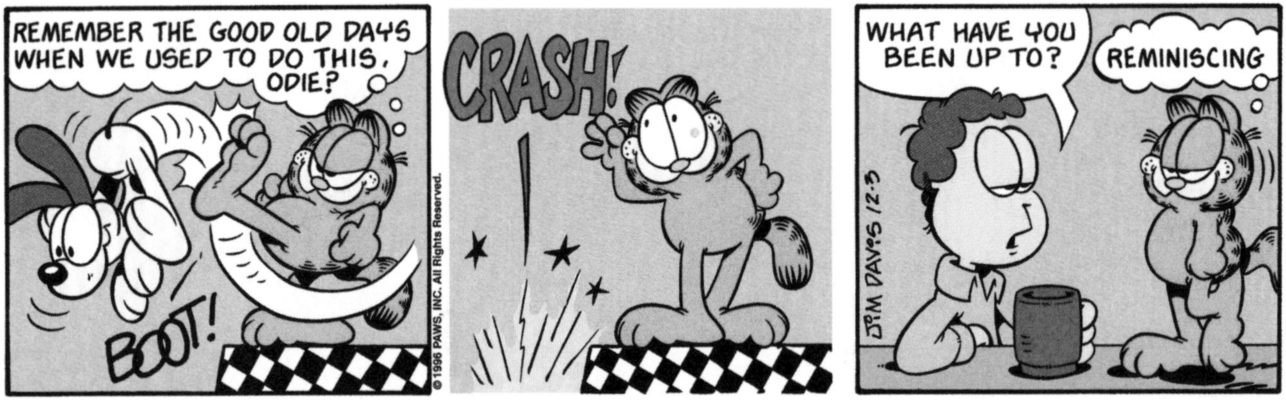
REMEMBER THE GOOD OLD DAYS WHEN WE USED TO DO THIS, ODIE?
BOOT!
© 1996 PAWS, INC. All Rights Reserved.
CRASH!
WHAT HAVE YOU BEEN UP TO?
REMINISCING
JIM DAVIS 12-3

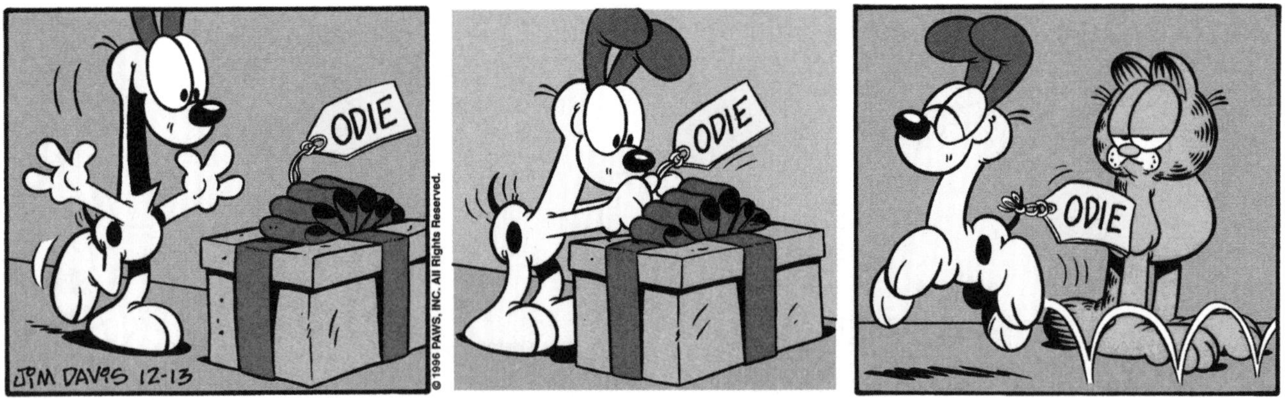
ODIE
JIM DAVIS 12-13
© 1996 PAWS, INC. All Rights Reserved.
ODIE
ODIE

Best uses for an Odie

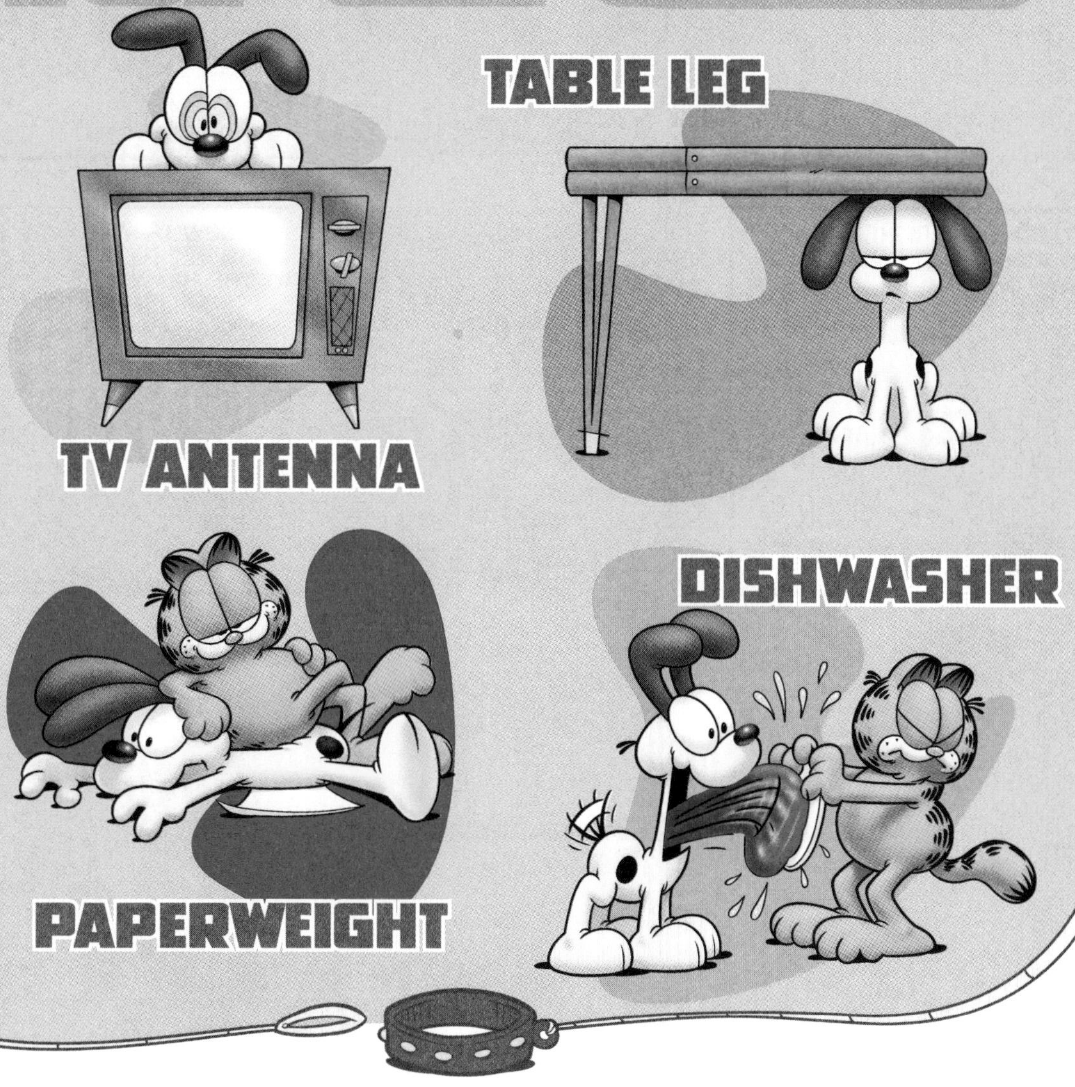
TABLE LEG
TV ANTENNA
DISHWASHER
PAPERWEIGHT

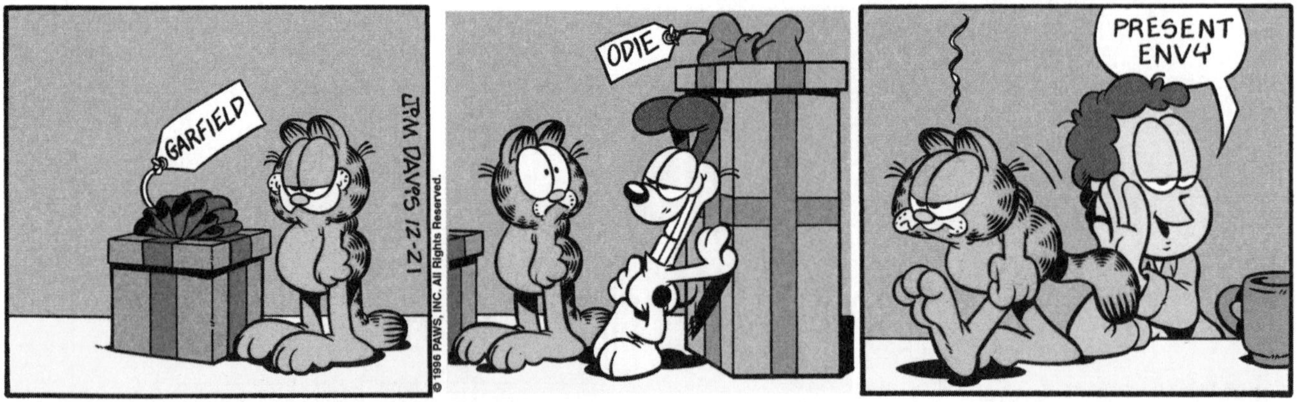
GARFIELD
JIM DAVIS 12-21
© 1996 PAWS, INC. All Rights Reserved.
ODIE
PRESENT ENVY

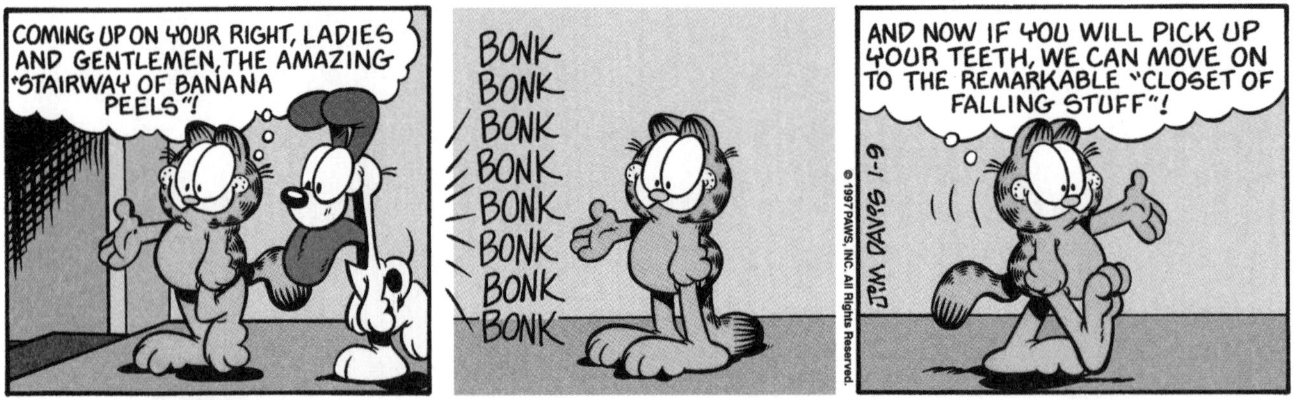
COMING UP ON YOUR RIGHT, LADIES AND GENTLEMEN, THE AMAZING "STAIRWAY OF BANANA PEELS"!
BONK BONK BONK BONK BONK BONK BONK BONK
© 1997 PAWS, INC. All Rights Reserved.
JIM DAVIS 1-9
AND NOW IF YOU WILL PICK UP YOUR TEETH, WE CAN MOVE ON TO THE REMARKABLE "CLOSET OF FALLING STUFF"!

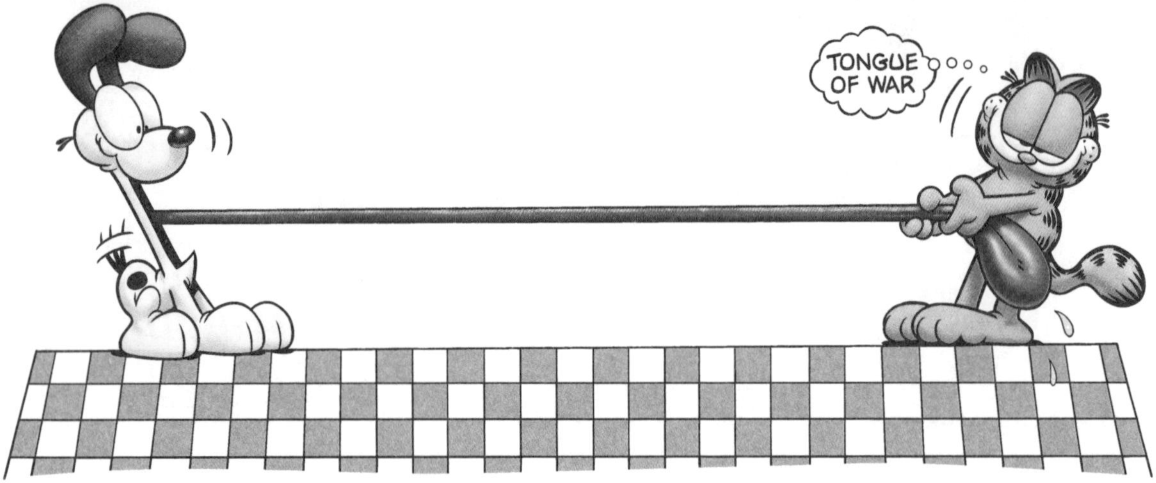
TONGUE OF WAR

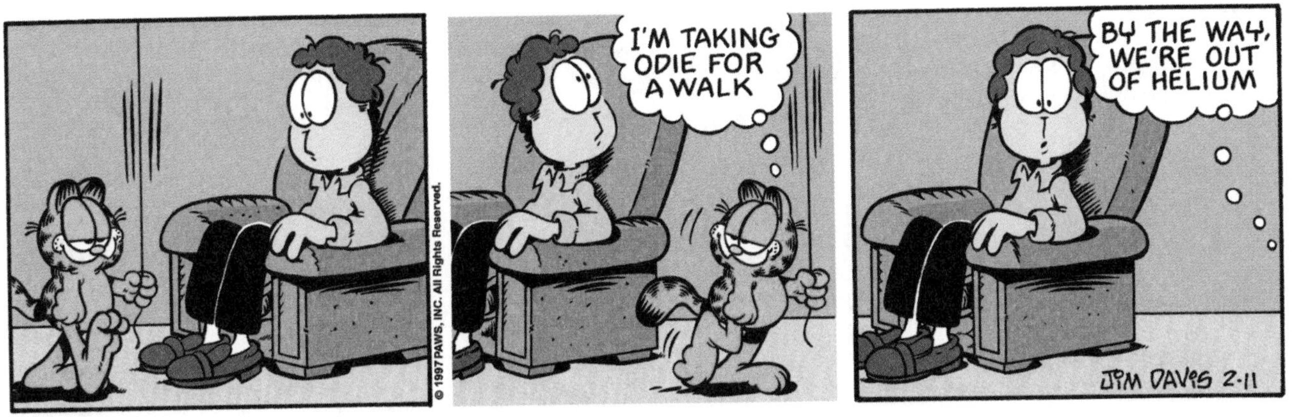
© 1997 PAWS, INC. All Rights Reserved.
I'M TAKING ODIE FOR A WALK
BY THE WAY, WE'RE OUT OF HELIUM
JIM DAVIS 2-11

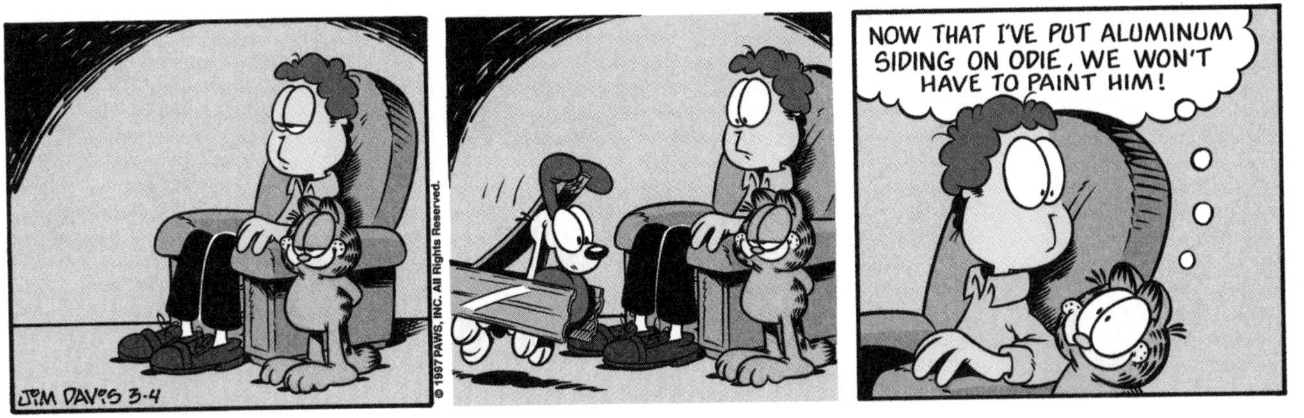
JIM DAVIS 3-4
© 1997 PAWS, INC. All Rights Reserved.
NOW THAT I'VE PUT ALUMINUM SIDING ON ODIE, WE WON'T HAVE TO PAINT HIM!

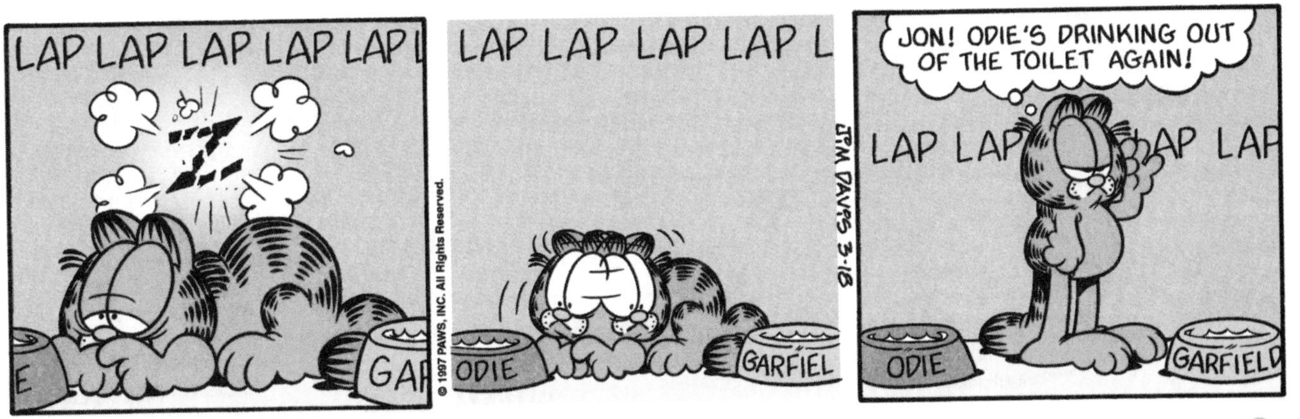
LAP LAP LAP LAP LAP L
GAF
© 1997 PAWS, INC. All Rights Reserved.
LAP LAP LAP LAP L
ODIE
GARFIEL
JIM DAVIS 3-18
JON! ODIE'S DRINKING OUT OF THE TOILET AGAIN!
LAP LAP LAP LAP
ODIE
GARFIELD

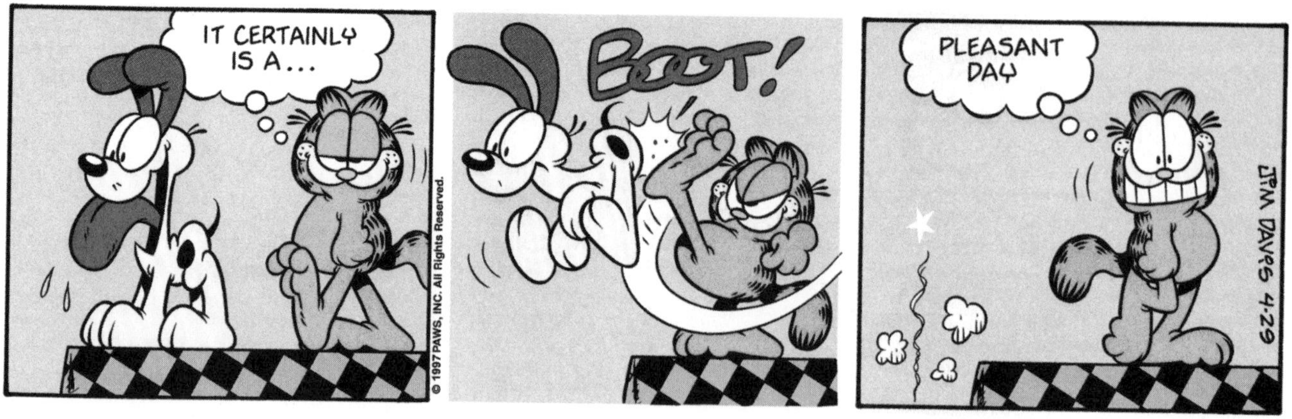
IT CERTAINLY IS A...
© 1997 PAWS, INC. All Rights Reserved.
BOOT!
PLEASANT DAY
JIM DAVIS 4-29

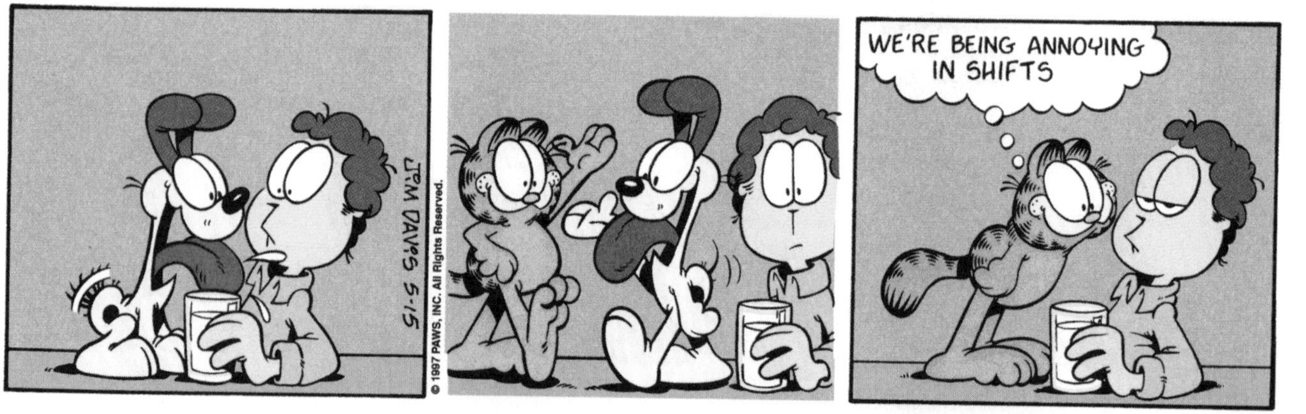
JIM DAVIS 5-15
© 1997 PAWS, INC. All Rights Reserved.
WE'RE BEING ANNOYING IN SHIFTS

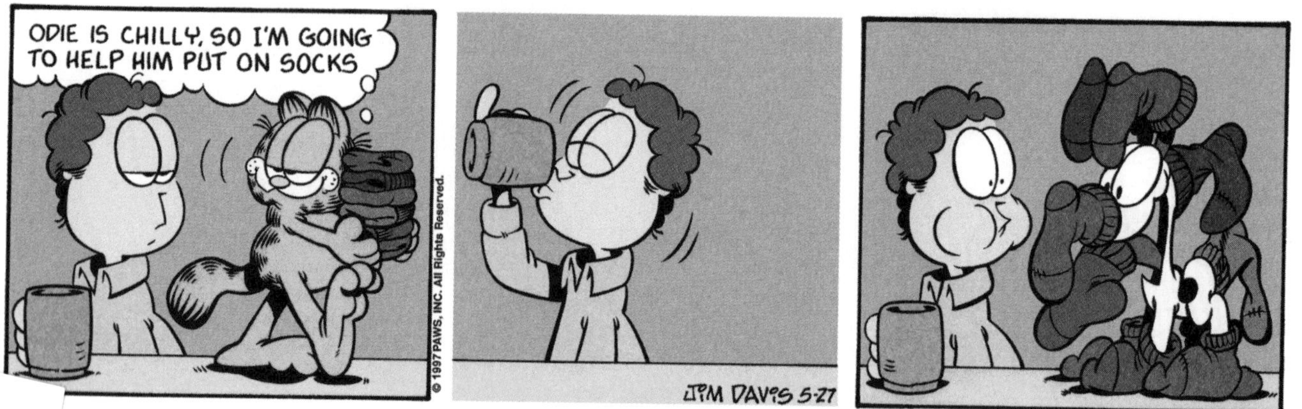
ODIE IS CHILLY, SO I'M GOING TO HELP HIM PUT ON SOCKS
© 1997 PAWS, INC. All Rights Reserved.
JIM DAVIS 5-27

Dogs are a great natural resource

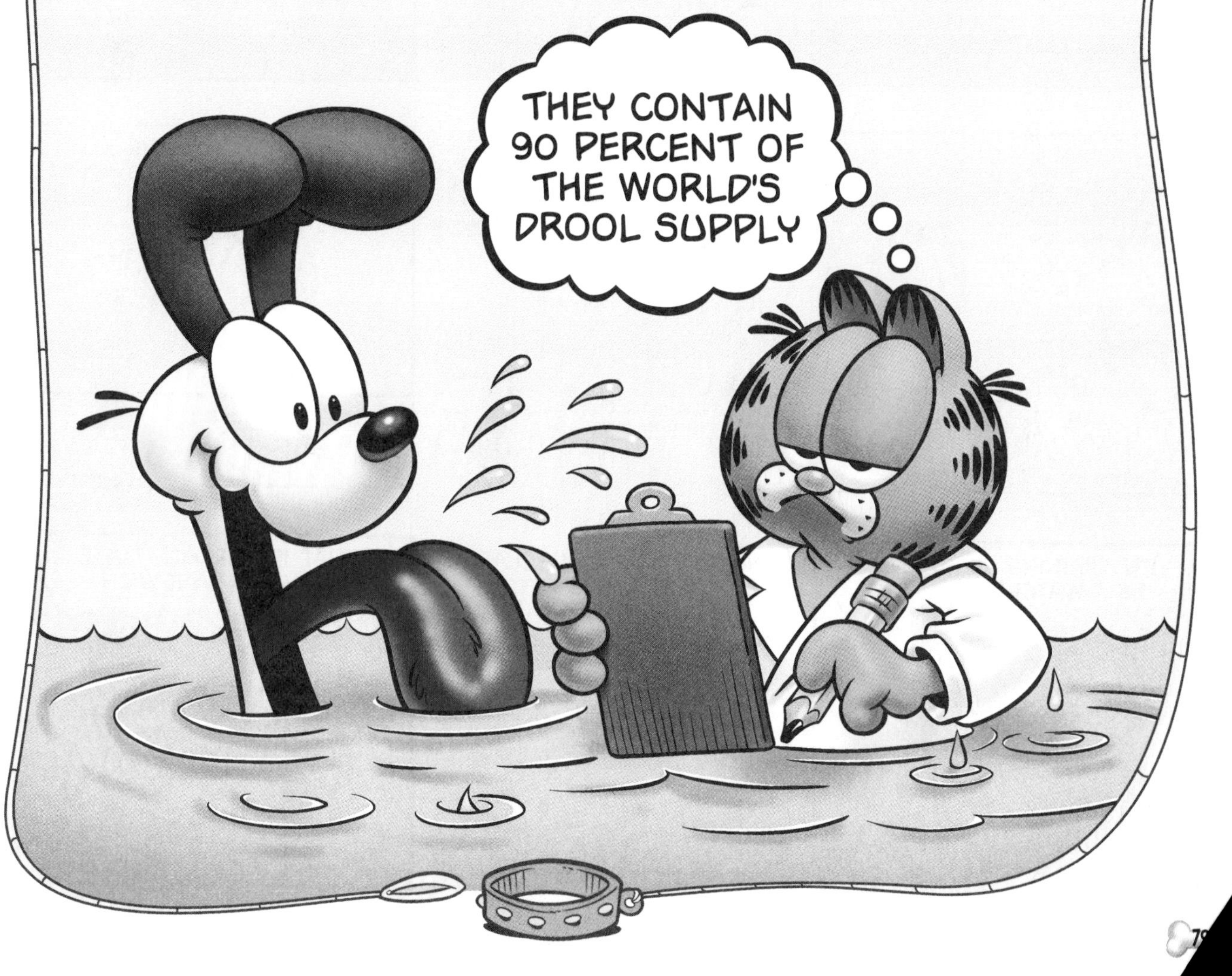
THEY CONTAIN 90 PERCENT OF THE WORLD'S DROOL SUPPLY

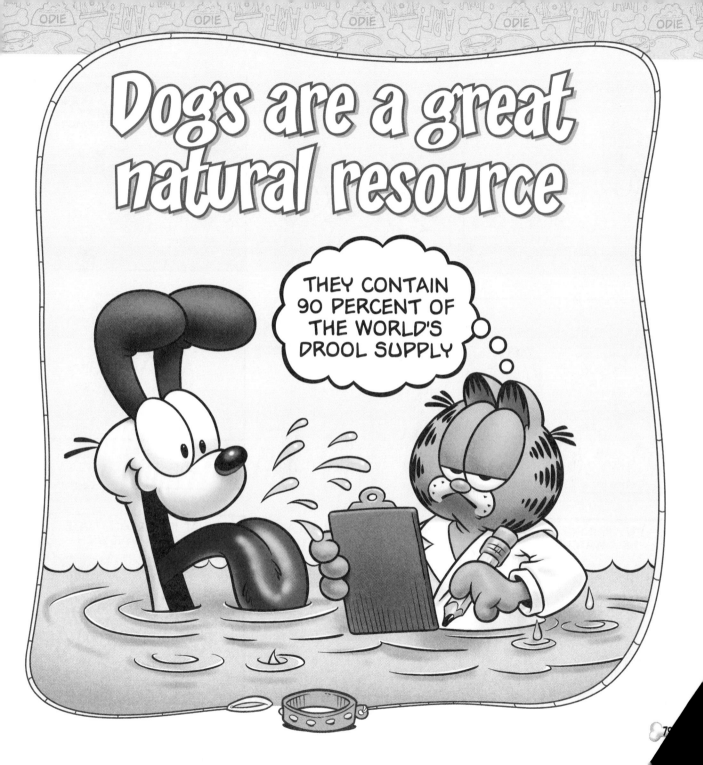

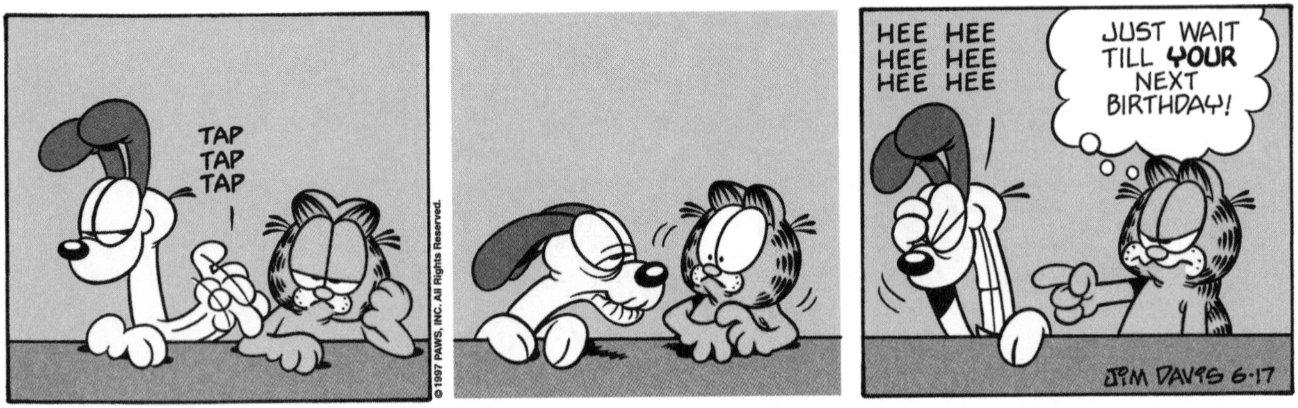
TAP
TAP
TAP
© 1997 PAWS, INC. All Rights Reserved.
HEE HEE
HEE HEE
HEE HEE
JUST WAIT TILL **YOUR** NEXT BIRTHDAY!
JIM DAVIS 6-17

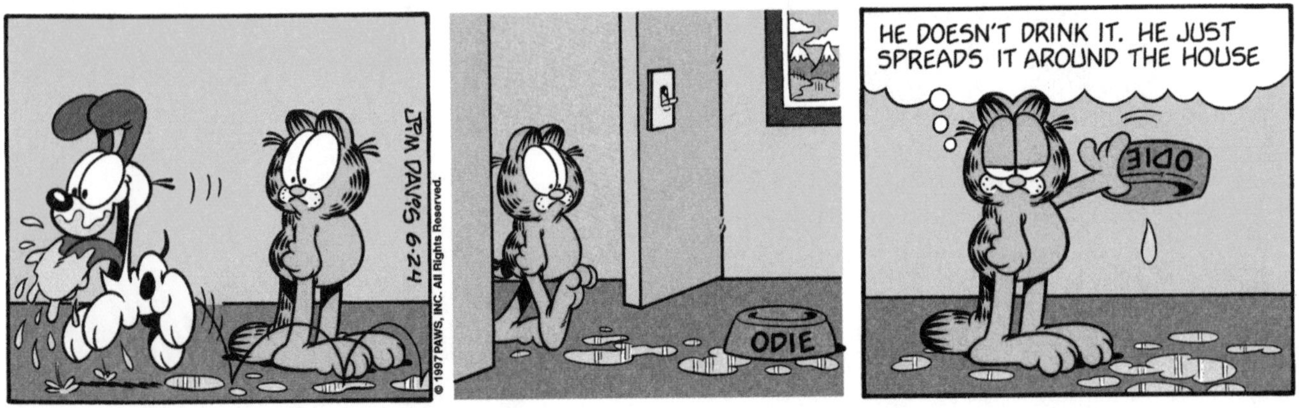
JIM DAVIS 6-24
© 1997 PAWS, INC. All Rights Reserved.
ODIE
HE DOESN'T DRINK IT. HE JUST SPREADS IT AROUND THE HOUSE
ODIE

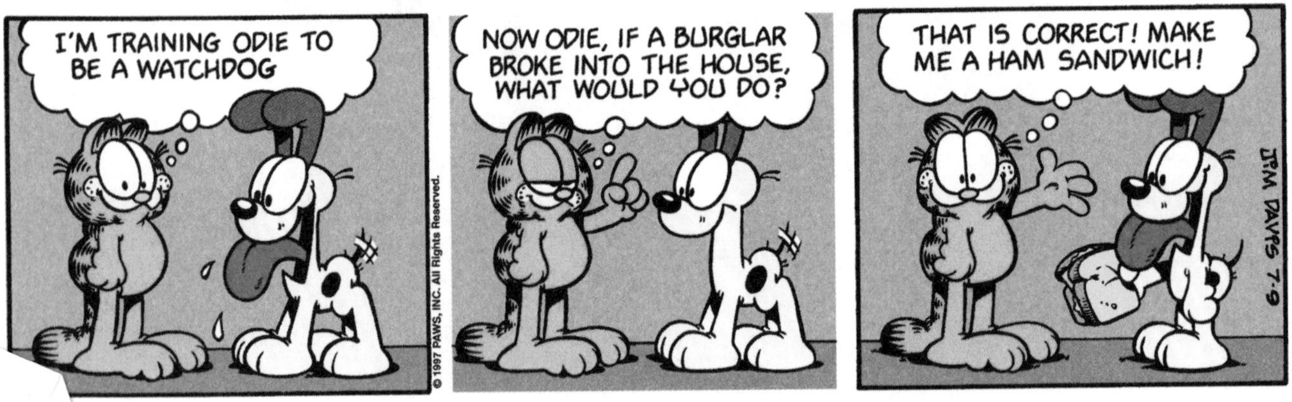
I'M TRAINING ODIE TO BE A WATCHDOG
© 1997 PAWS, INC. All Rights Reserved.
NOW ODIE, IF A BURGLAR BROKE INTO THE HOUSE, WHAT WOULD YOU DO?
THAT IS CORRECT! MAKE ME A HAM SANDWICH!
JIM DAVIS 7-9

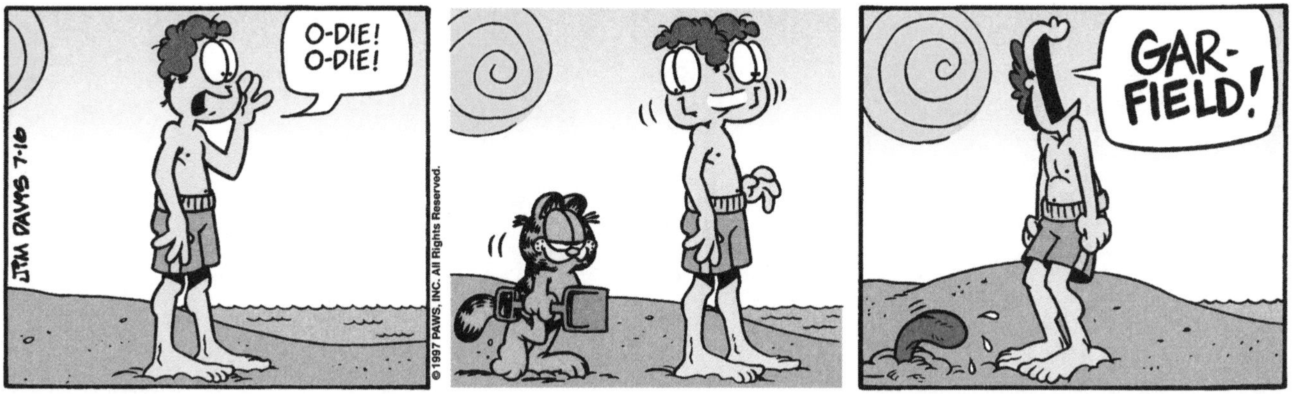
JPM DAVPS 7-10
O-DIE! O-DIE!
© 1997 PAWS, INC. All Rights Reserved.
GAR-FIELD!

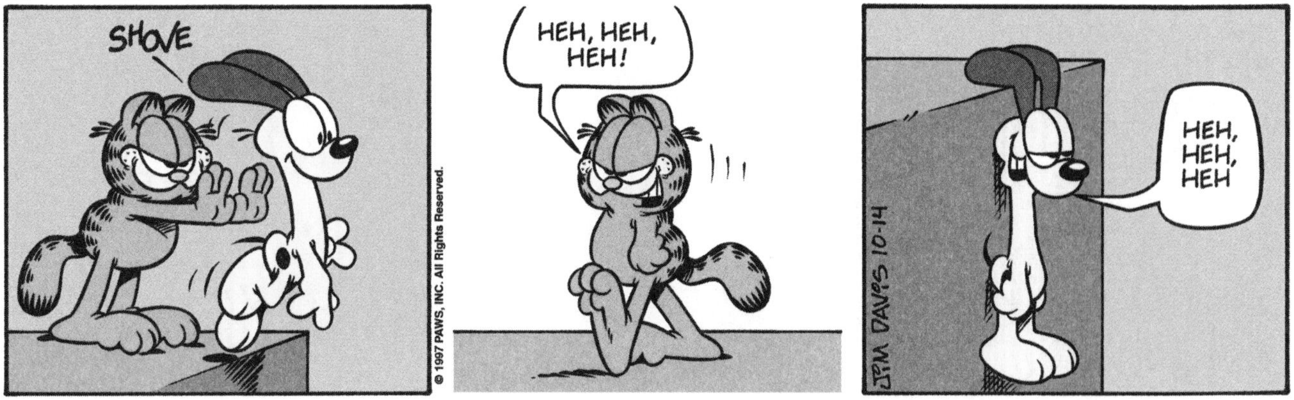
SHOVE
© 1997 PAWS, INC. All Rights Reserved.
HEH, HEH, HEH!
JPM DAVPS 10-14
HEH, HEH, HEH

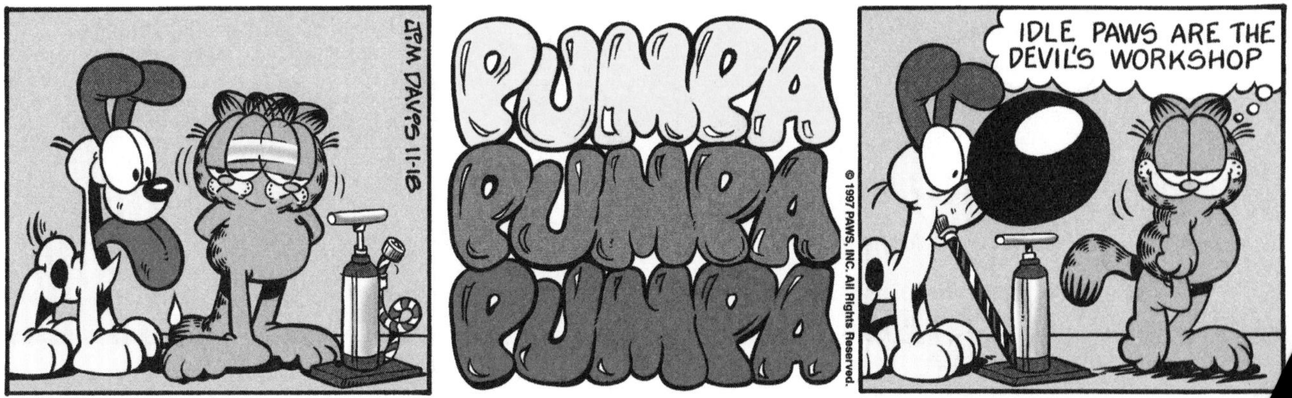
JPM DAVPS 11-18
PUMPA
PUMPA
PUMPA
© 1997 PAWS, INC. All Rights Reserved.
IDLE PAWS ARE THE DEVIL'S WORKSHOP

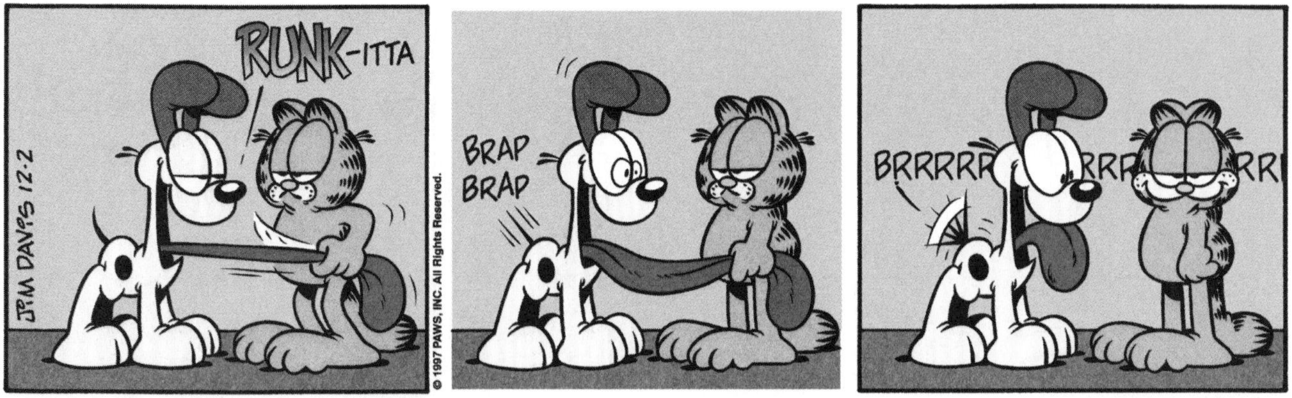
JIM DAVIS 12-2
RUNK-ITTA
© 1997 PAWS, INC. All Rights Reserved.
BRAP
BRAP
BRRRRR

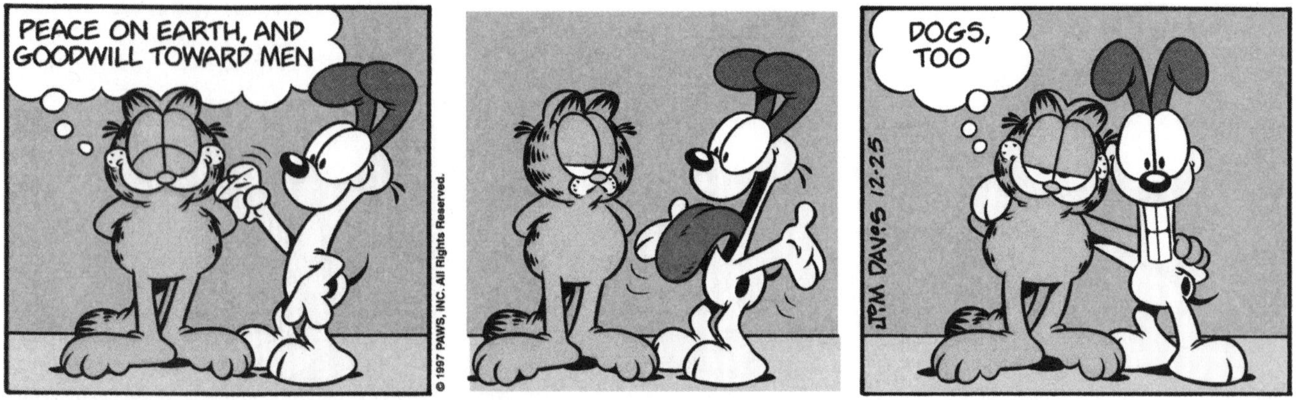
PEACE ON EARTH, AND GOODWILL TOWARD MEN
© 1997 PAWS, INC. All Rights Reserved.
JIM DAVIS 12-25
DOGS, TOO

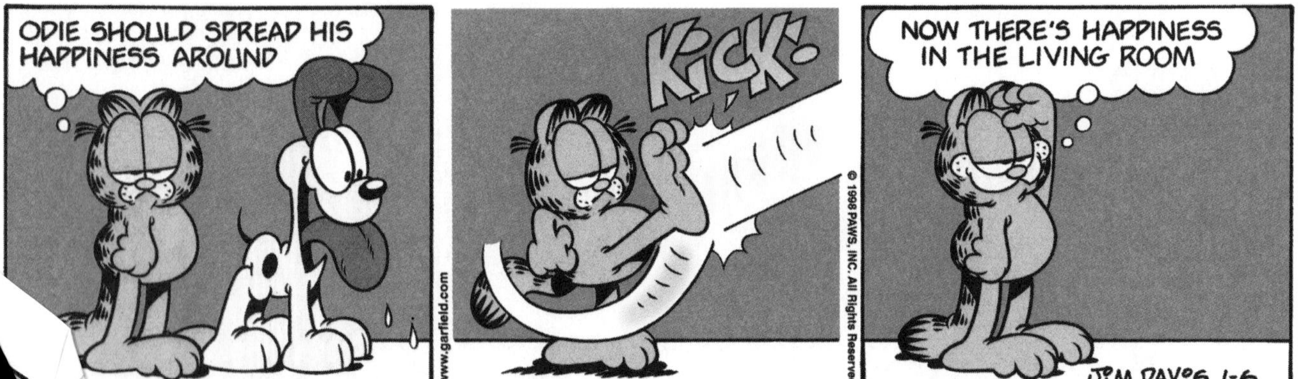
ODIE SHOULD SPREAD HIS HAPPINESS AROUND
www.garfield.com
KICK!
© 1998 PAWS, INC. All Rights Reserved.
NOW THERE'S HAPPINESS IN THE LIVING ROOM
JIM DAVIS 1-6

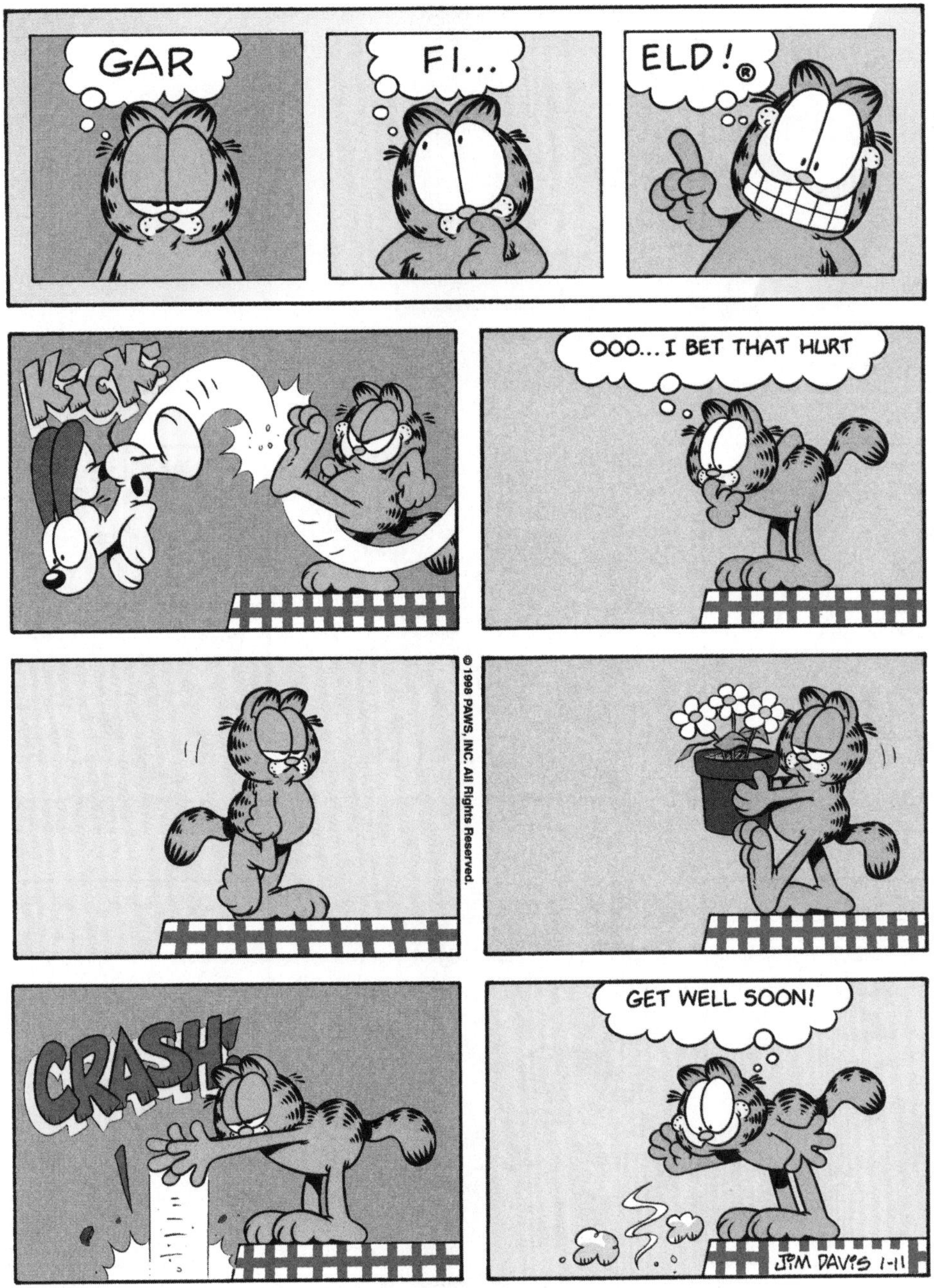
GAR
FI...
ELD!®
KICK!
OOO... I BET THAT HURT
© 1998 PAWS, INC. All Rights Reserved.
CRASH!
GET WELL SOON!
JIM DAVIS 1-11

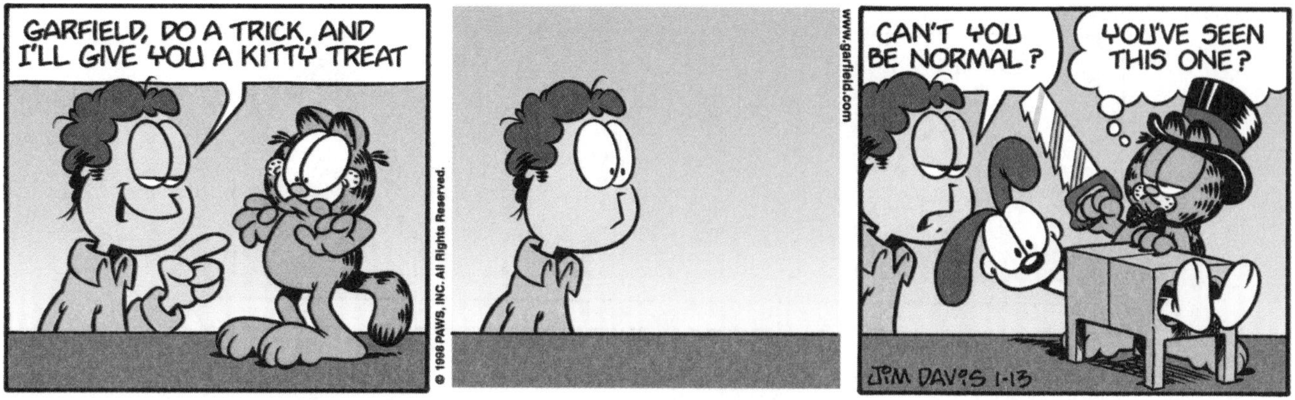
GARFIELD, DO A TRICK, AND I'LL GIVE YOU A KITTY TREAT
© 1998 PAWS, INC. All Rights Reserved.
www.garfield.com
CAN'T YOU BE NORMAL?
YOU'VE SEEN THIS ONE?
JIM DAVIS 1-13

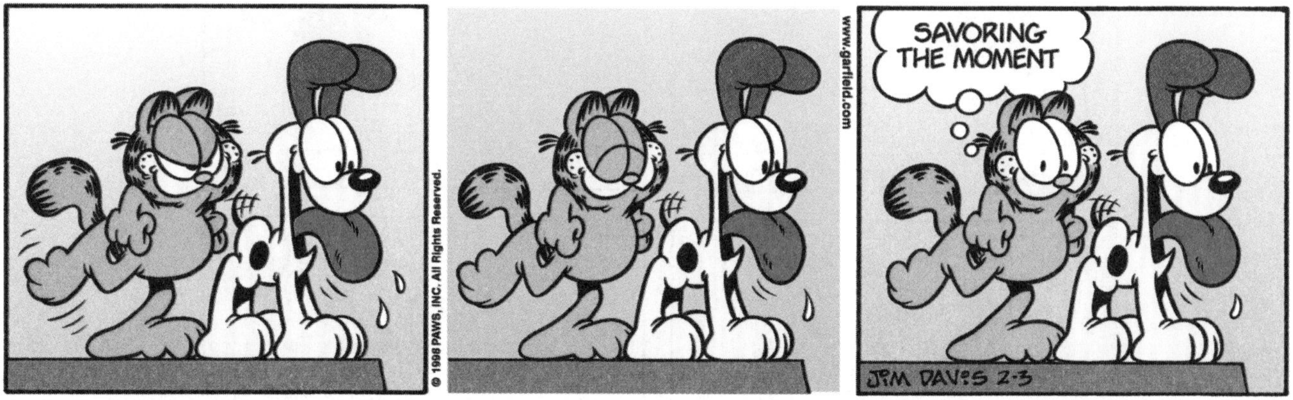
© 1998 PAWS, INC. All Rights Reserved.
www.garfield.com
SAVORING THE MOMENT
JIM DAVIS 2-3

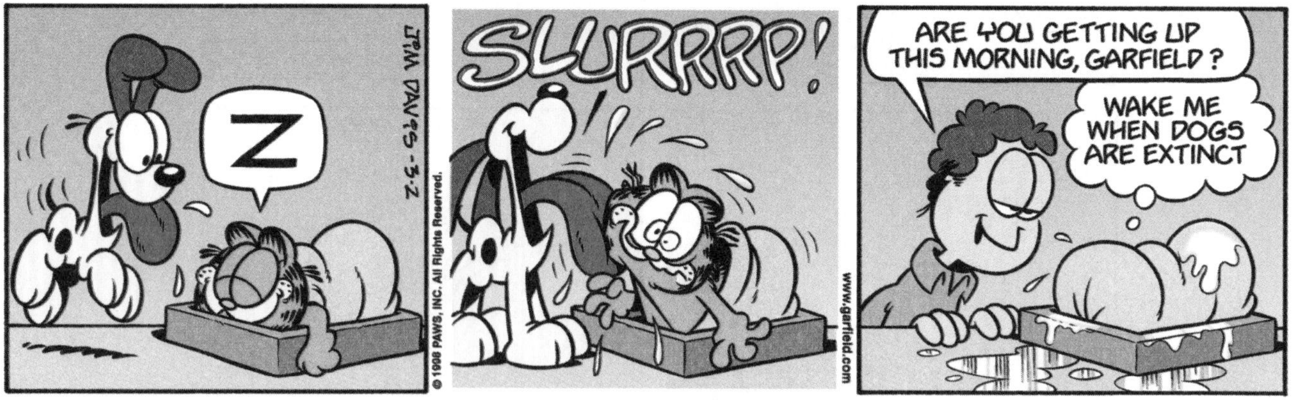
Z
JIM DAVIS 3-2
© 1998 PAWS, INC. All Rights Reserved.
SLURRRP!
www.garfield.com
ARE YOU GETTING UP THIS MORNING, GARFIELD?
WAKE ME WHEN DOGS ARE EXTINCT

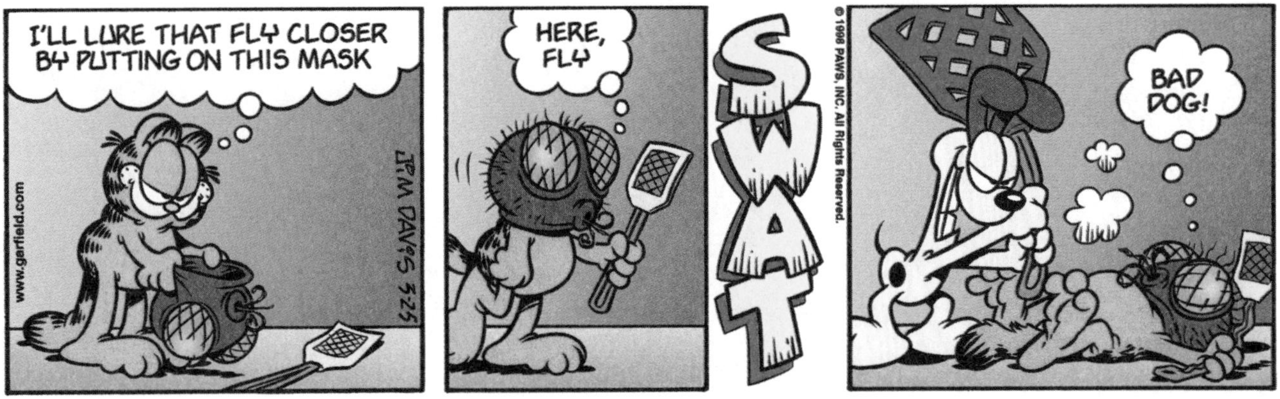
I'LL LURE THAT FLY CLOSER BY PUTTING ON THIS MASK
JIM DAVIS 3-25
www.garfield.com
HERE, FLY
SWAT
© 1998 PAWS, INC. All Rights Reserved.
BAD DOG!

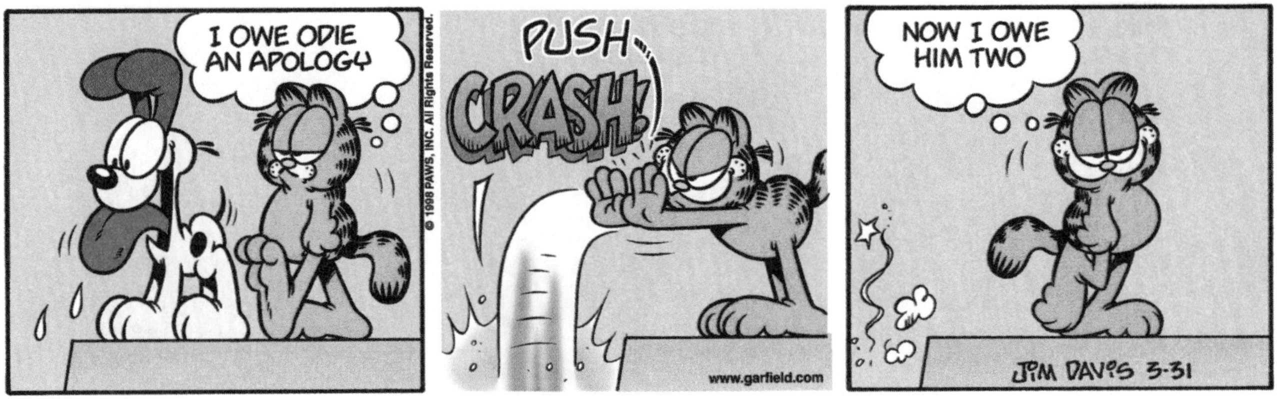
I OWE ODIE AN APOLOGY
© 1998 PAWS, INC. All Rights Reserved.
PUSH
CRASH!
www.garfield.com
NOW I OWE HIM TWO
JIM DAVIS 3-31

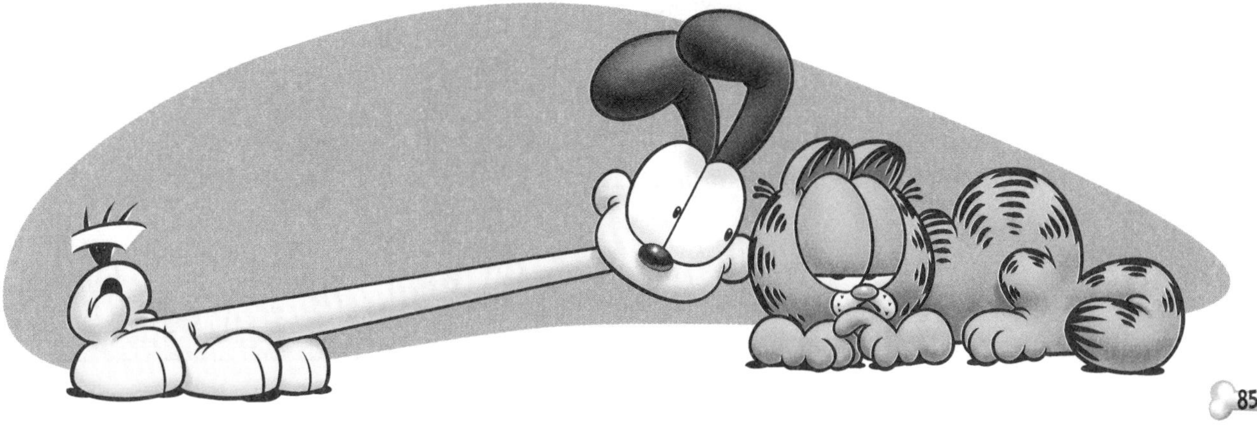

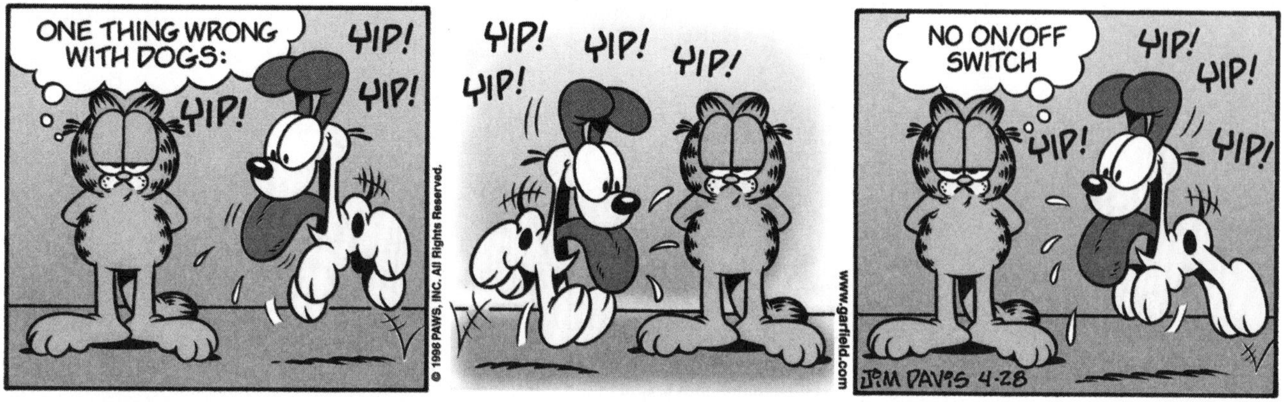
ONE THING WRONG WITH DOGS:
YIP!
YIP!
YIP!
YIP!
YIP!
YIP!
YIP!
© 1998 PAWS, INC. All Rights Reserved.
NO ON/OFF SWITCH
YIP!
YIP!
YIP!
YIP!
www.garfield.com
JIM DAVIS 4-28

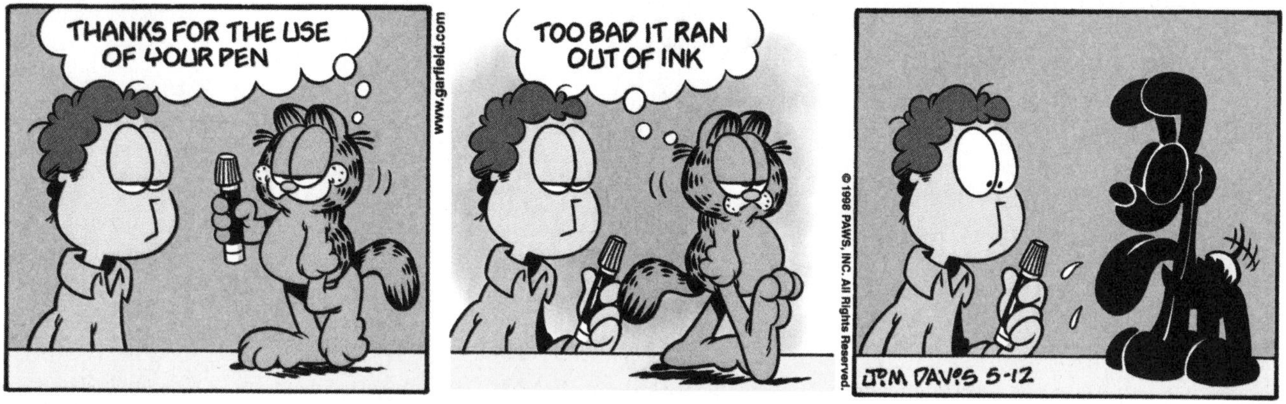
THANKS FOR THE USE OF YOUR PEN
www.garfield.com
TOO BAD IT RAN OUT OF INK
© 1998 PAWS, INC. All Rights Reserved.
JIM DAVIS 5-12

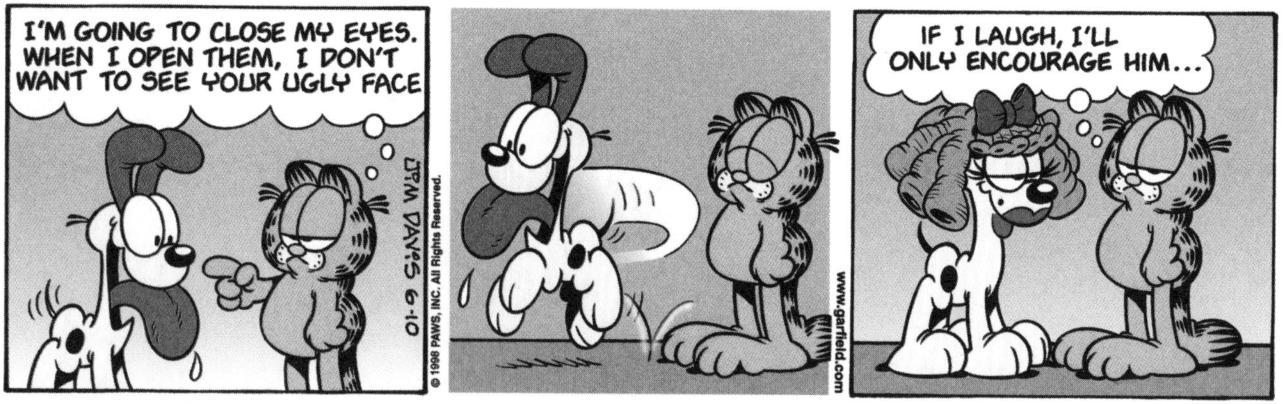
I'M GOING TO CLOSE MY EYES. WHEN I OPEN THEM, I DON'T WANT TO SEE YOUR UGLY FACE
JIM DAVIS 6-10
© 1998 PAWS, INC. All Rights Reserved.
www.garfield.com
IF I LAUGH, I'LL ONLY ENCOURAGE HIM...

OBEDIENCE SCHOOL DROPOUT

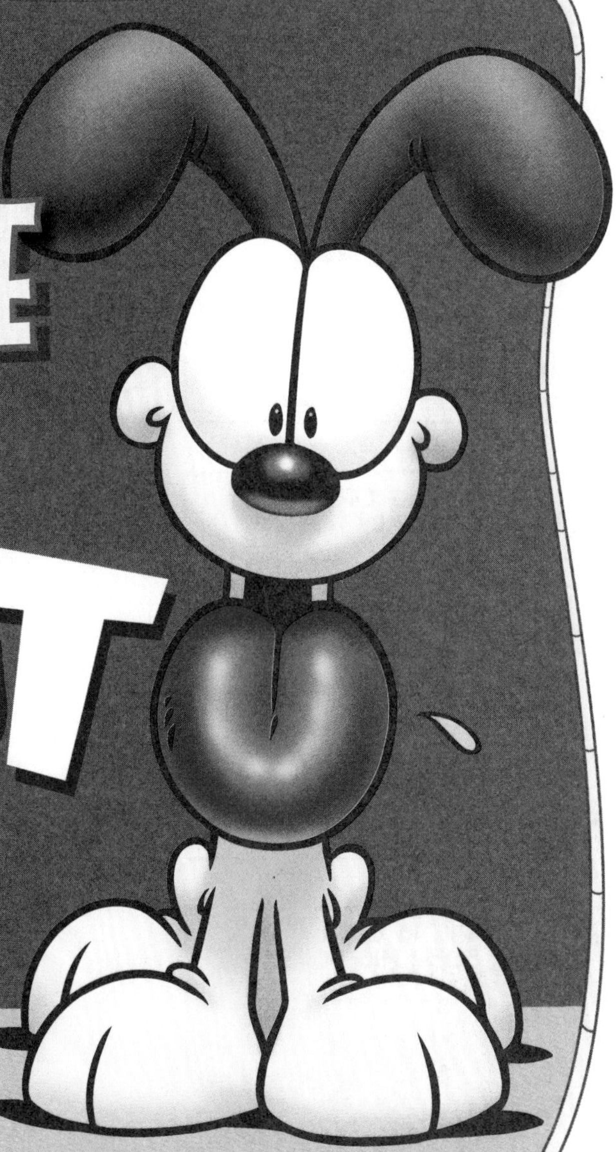

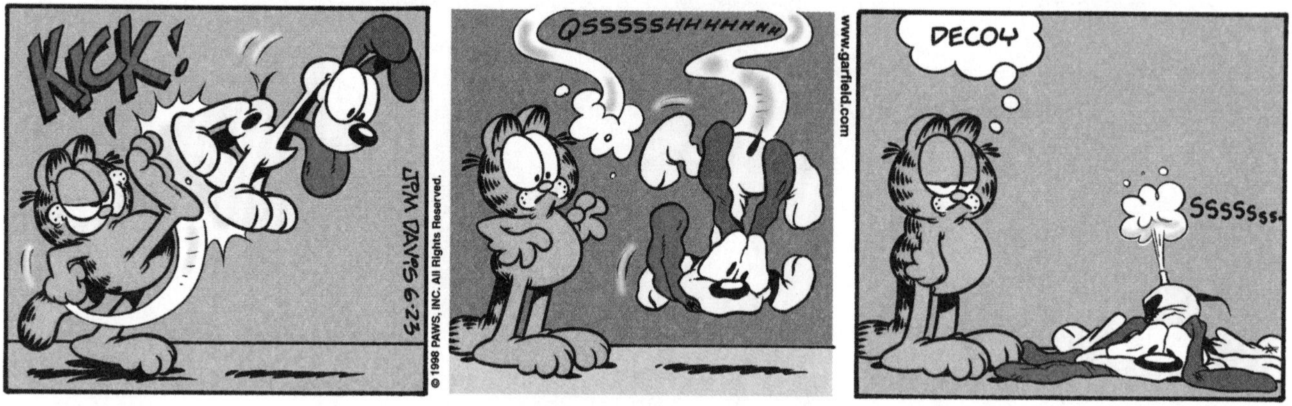
KICK!
JIM DAVIS 6-23
© 1998 PAWS, INC. All Rights Reserved.
QSSSSSHHHHHHH
www.garfield.com
DECOY
SSSSSss.

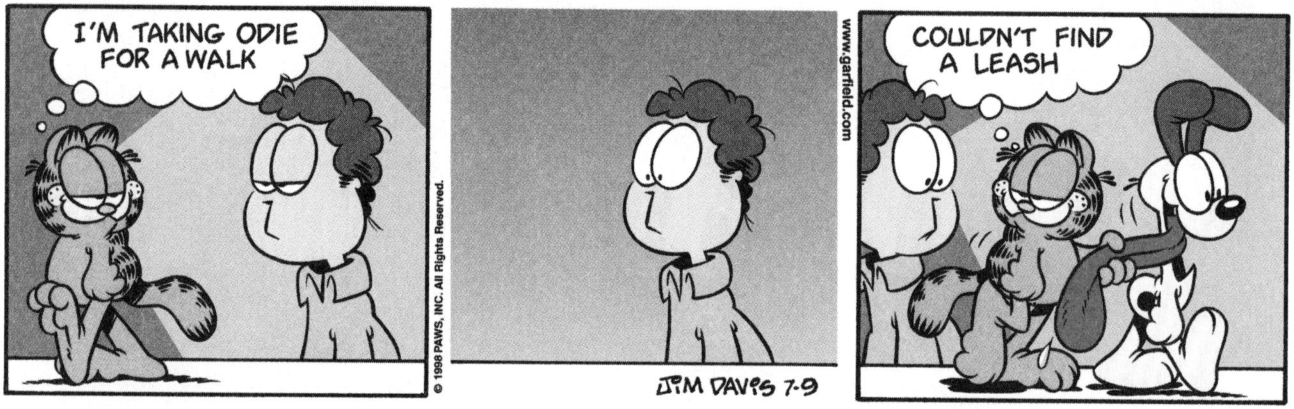
I'M TAKING ODIE FOR A WALK
© 1998 PAWS, INC. All Rights Reserved.
JIM DAVIS 7-9
www.garfield.com
COULDN'T FIND A LEASH

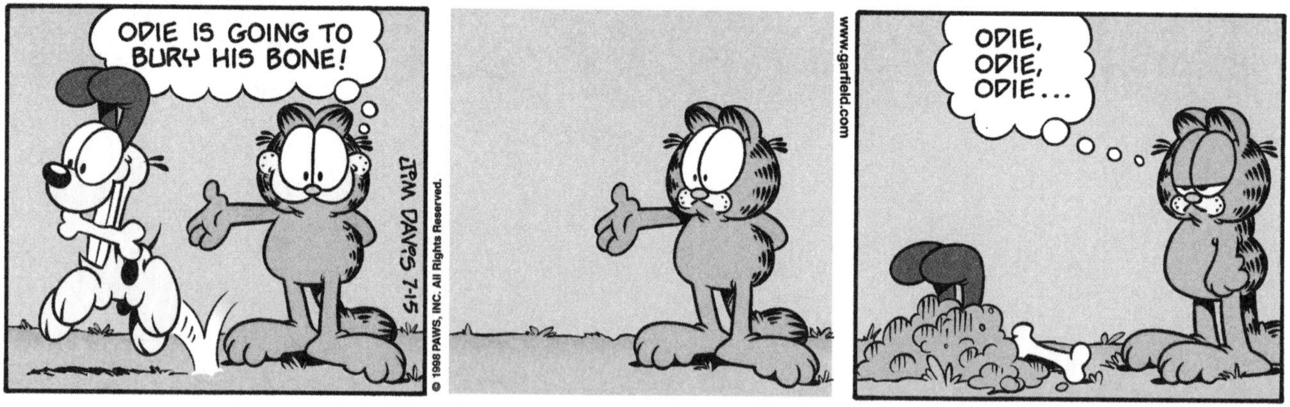
ODIE IS GOING TO BURY HIS BONE!
JIM DAVIS 7-15
© 1998 PAWS, INC. All Rights Reserved.
www.garfield.com
ODIE, ODIE, ODIE...

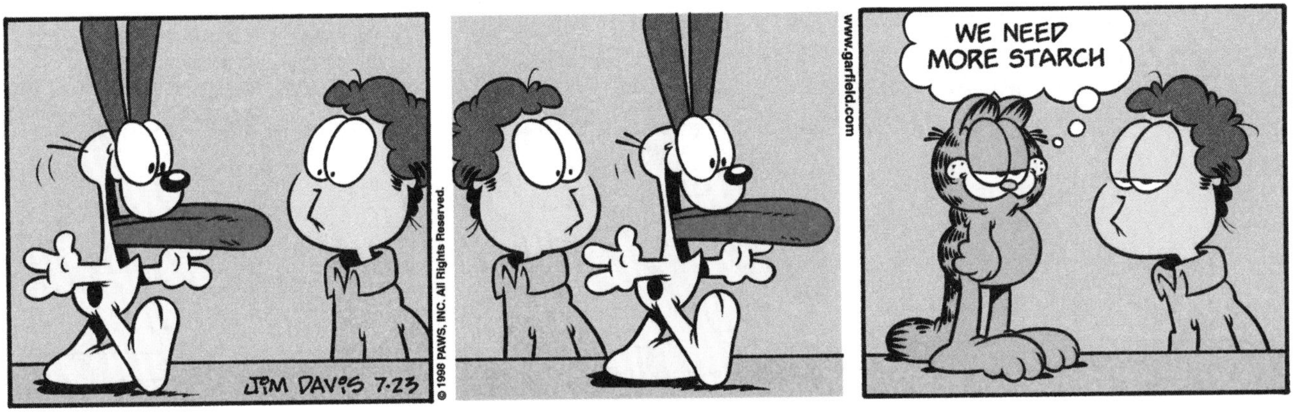
JIM DAVIS 7-23
© 1998 PAWS, INC. All Rights Reserved.
www.garfield.com
WE NEED MORE STARCH

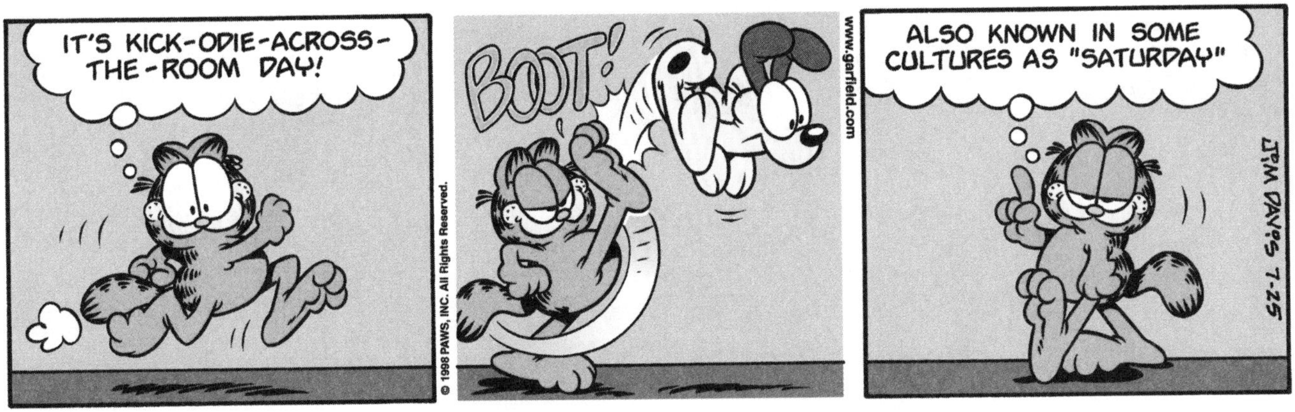
IT'S KICK-ODIE-ACROSS-THE-ROOM DAY!
© 1998 PAWS, INC. All Rights Reserved.
BOOT!
www.garfield.com
ALSO KNOWN IN SOME CULTURES AS "SATURDAY"
JIM DAVIS 7-25

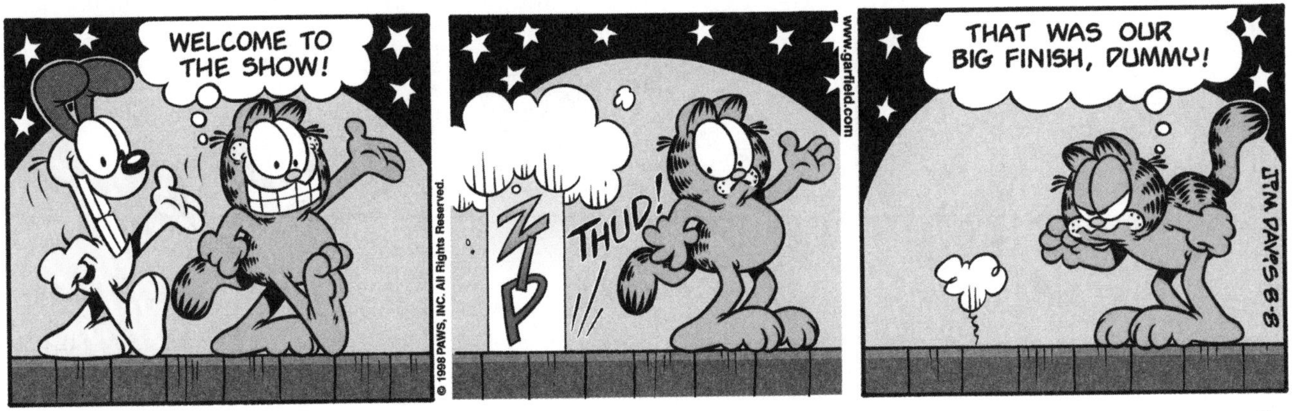
WELCOME TO THE SHOW!
© 1998 PAWS, INC. All Rights Reserved.
ZIP
THUD!
www.garfield.com
THAT WAS OUR BIG FINISH, DUMMY!
JIM DAVIS 8-8

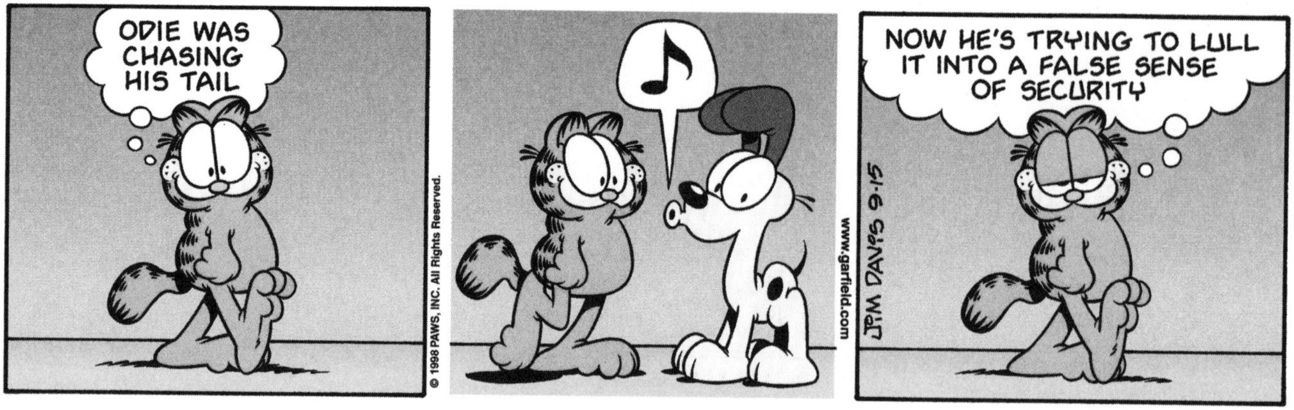
ODIE WAS CHASING HIS TAIL
© 1998 PAWS, INC. All Rights Reserved.
♪
www.garfield.com
JIM DAVIS 9-15
NOW HE'S TRYING TO LULL IT INTO A FALSE SENSE OF SECURITY

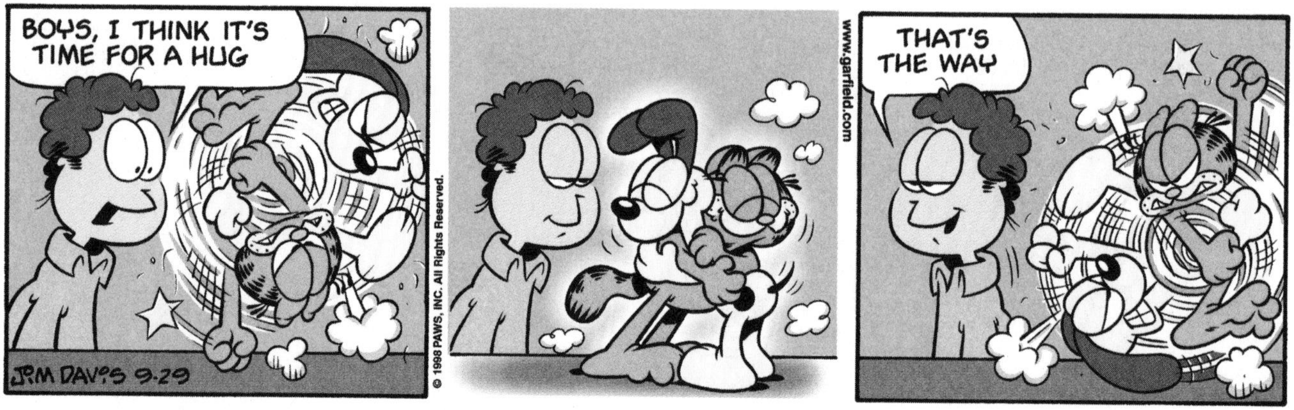
BOYS, I THINK IT'S TIME FOR A HUG
JIM DAVIS 9-29
© 1998 PAWS, INC. All Rights Reserved.
www.garfield.com
THAT'S THE WAY

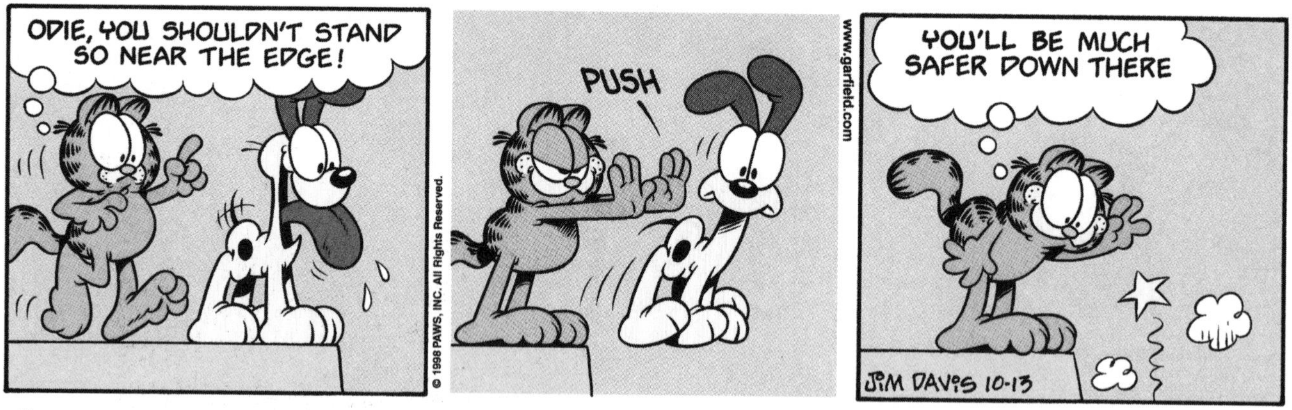
ODIE, YOU SHOULDN'T STAND SO NEAR THE EDGE!
© 1998 PAWS, INC. All Rights Reserved.
PUSH
www.garfield.com
YOU'LL BE MUCH SAFER DOWN THERE
JIM DAVIS 10-13

NOW PLAYING
CANINE CINEMA

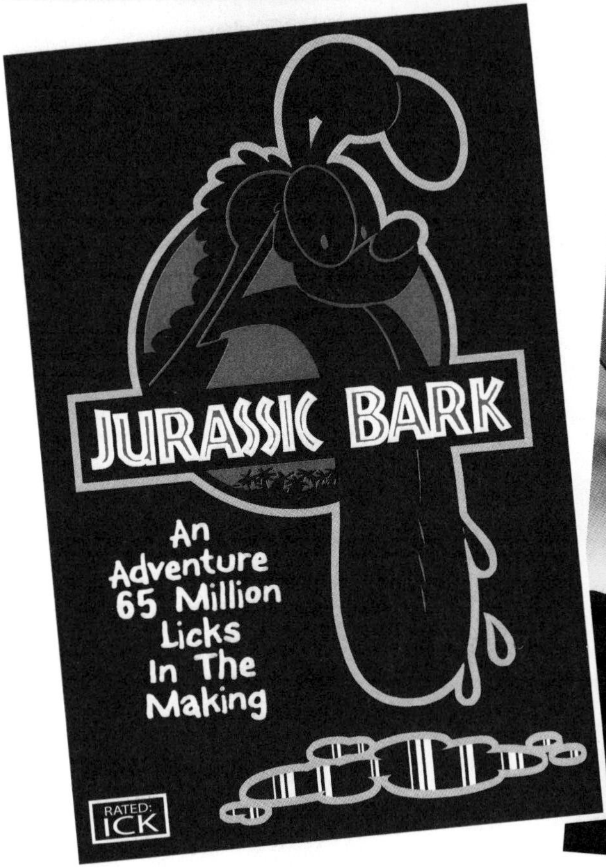
JURASSIC BARK
An Adventure 65 Million Licks In The Making
RATED: ICK

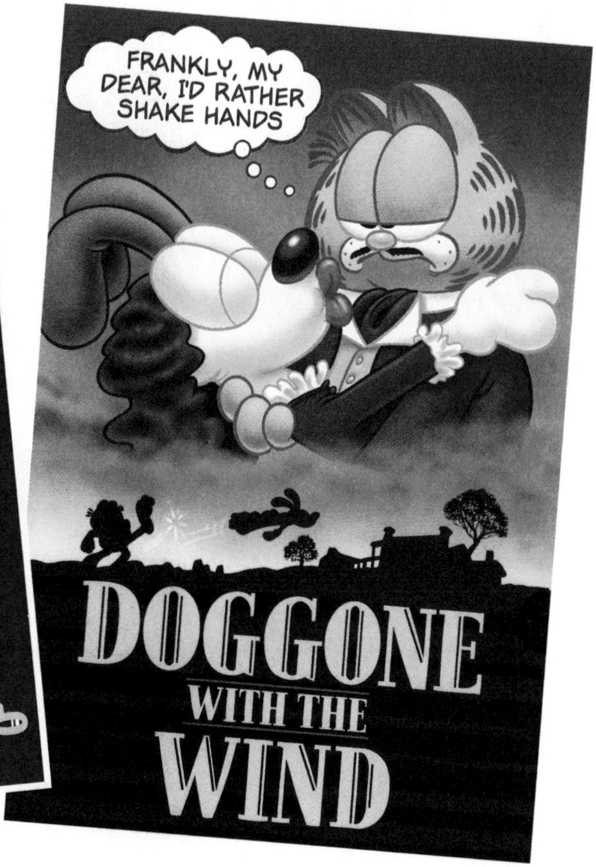
FRANKLY, MY DEAR, I'D RATHER SHAKE HANDS
DOGGONE
WITH THE
WIND

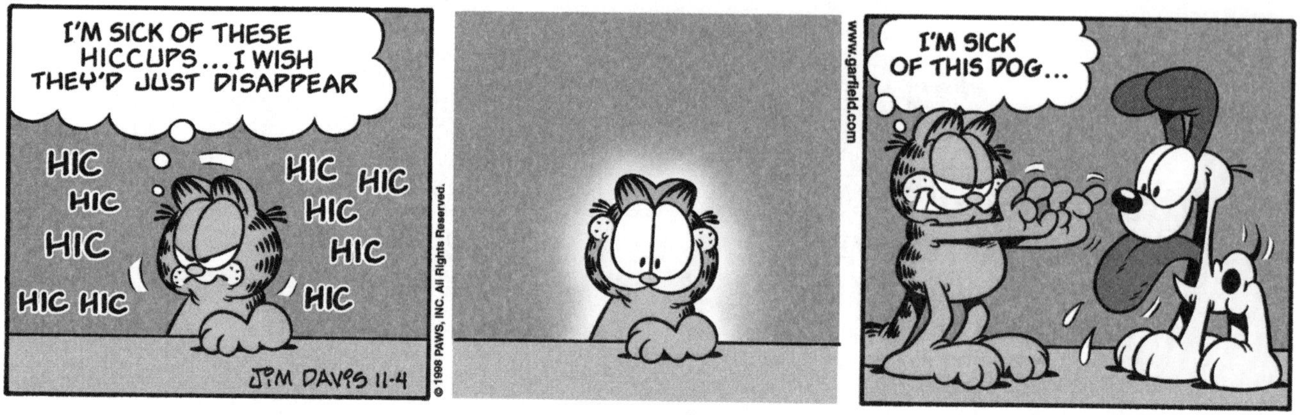
I'M SICK OF THESE HICCUPS... I WISH THEY'D JUST DISAPPEAR
HIC HIC HIC HIC HIC HIC HIC HIC HIC HIC
JIM DAVIS 11-4
© 1998 PAWS, INC. All Rights Reserved.
www.garfield.com
I'M SICK OF THIS DOG...

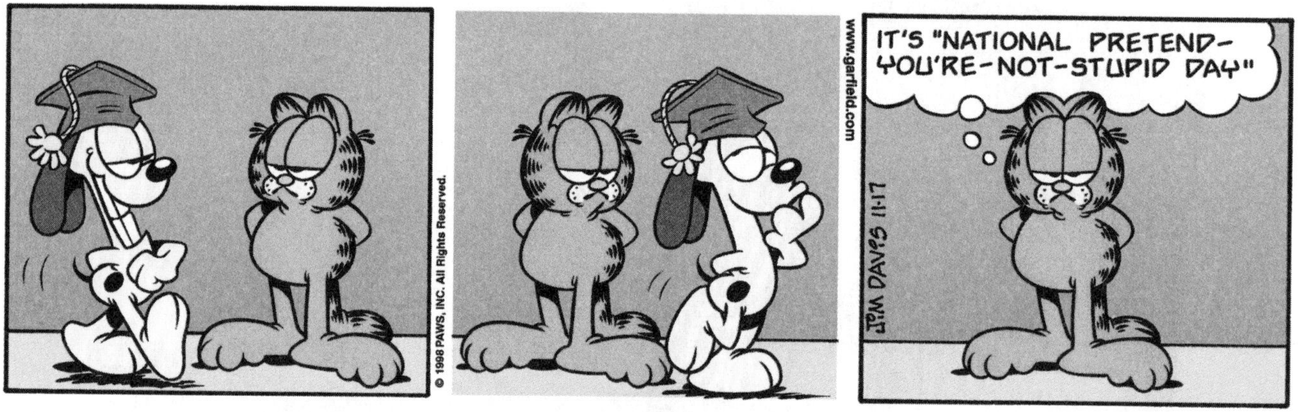
© 1998 PAWS, INC. All Rights Reserved.
www.garfield.com
IT'S "NATIONAL PRETEND-YOU'RE-NOT-STUPID DAY"
JIM DAVIS 11-17

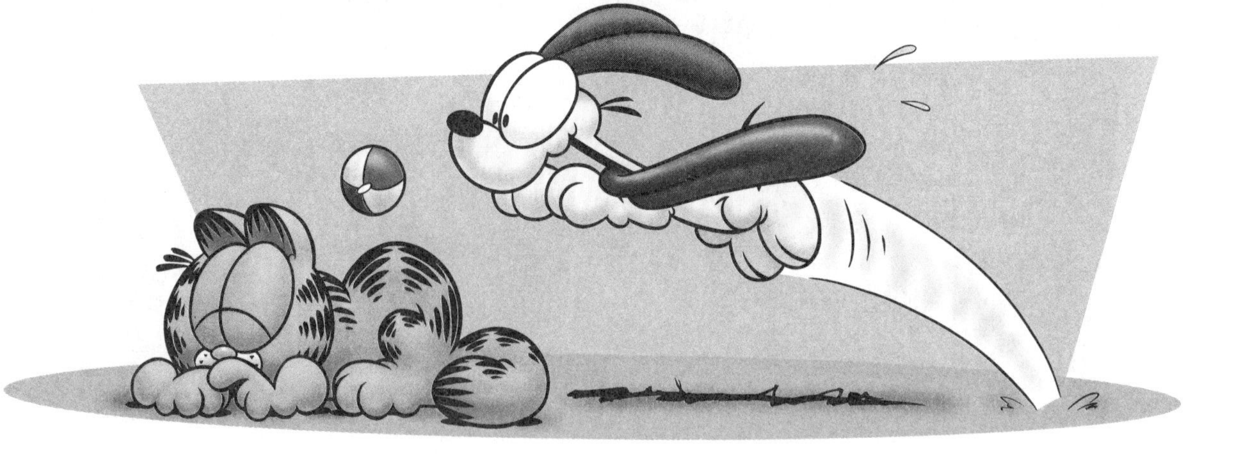

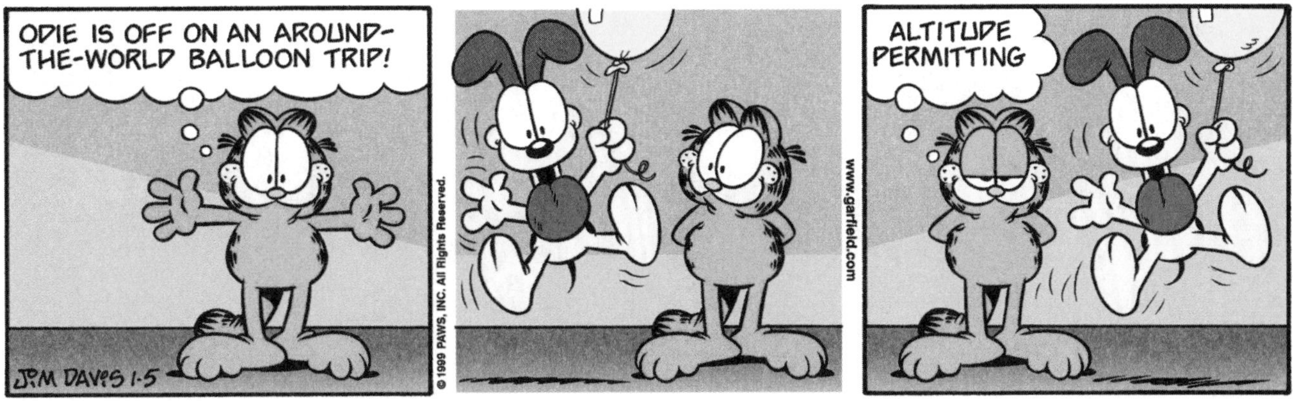
ODIE IS OFF ON AN AROUND-THE-WORLD BALLOON TRIP!
JIM DAVIS 1-5
© 1999 PAWS, INC. All Rights Reserved.
www.garfield.com
ALTITUDE PERMITTING

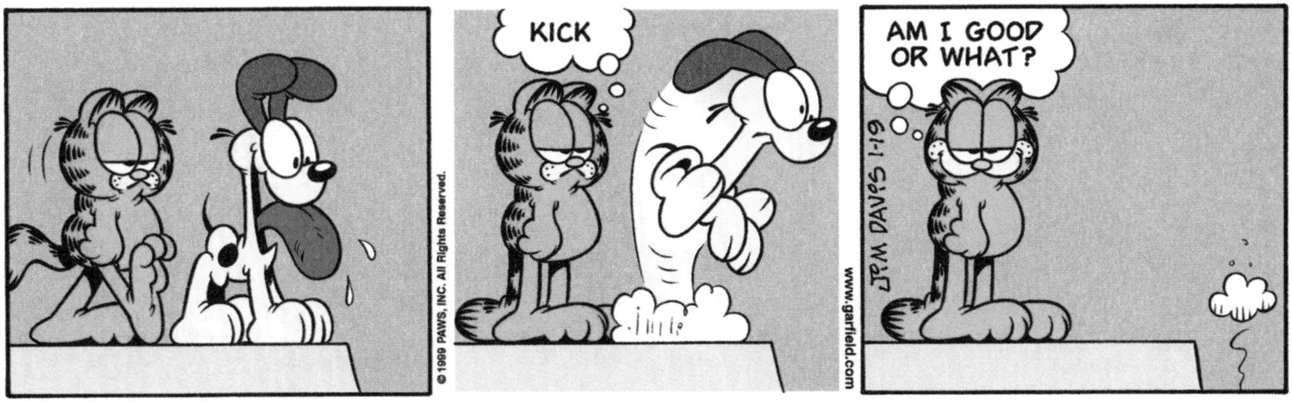
© 1999 PAWS, INC. All Rights Reserved.
KICK
www.garfield.com
AM I GOOD OR WHAT?
JIM DAVIS 1-19

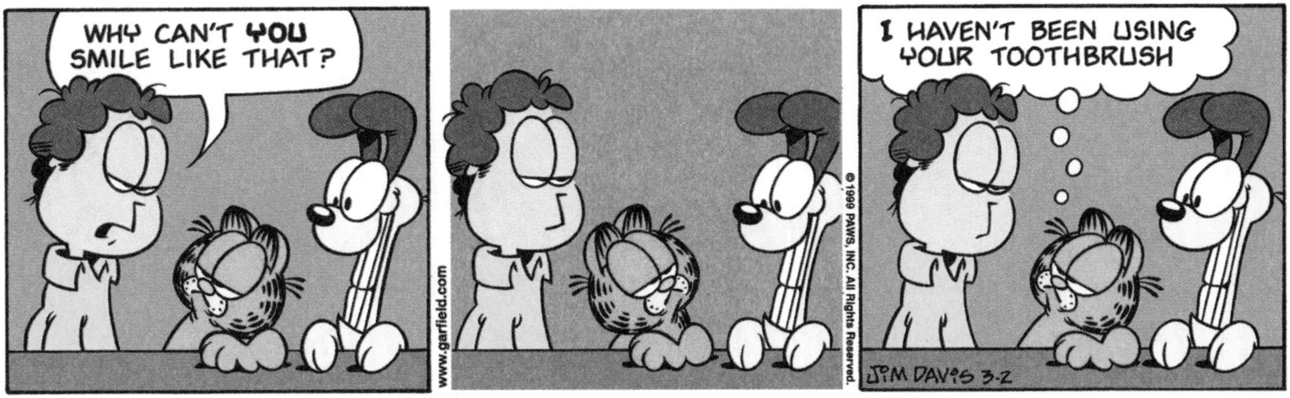
WHY CAN'T YOU SMILE LIKE THAT?
www.garfield.com
© 1999 PAWS, INC. All Rights Reserved.
I HAVEN'T BEEN USING YOUR TOOTHBRUSH
JIM DAVIS 3-2

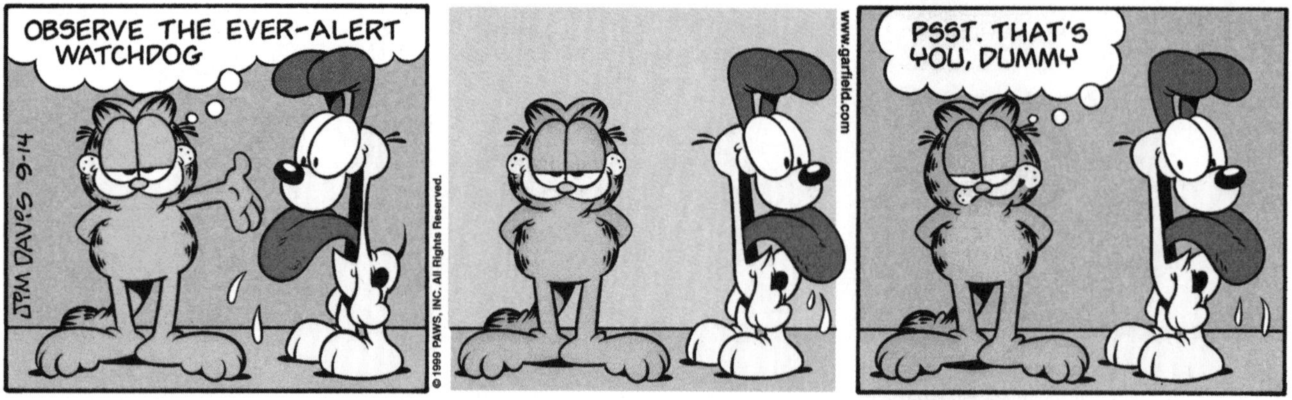
OBSERVE THE EVER-ALERT WATCHDOG
JIM DAVIS 9-14
© 1999 PAWS, INC. All Rights Reserved.
www.garfield.com
PSST. THAT'S YOU, DUMMY

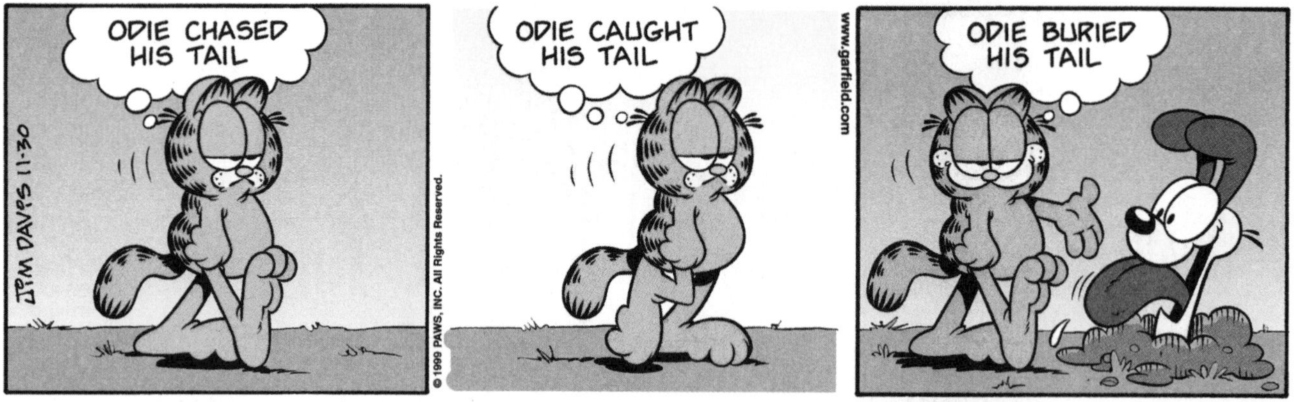
ODIE CHASED HIS TAIL
JIM DAVIS 11-30
© 1999 PAWS, INC. All Rights Reserved.
ODIE CAUGHT HIS TAIL
www.garfield.com
ODIE BURIED HIS TAIL

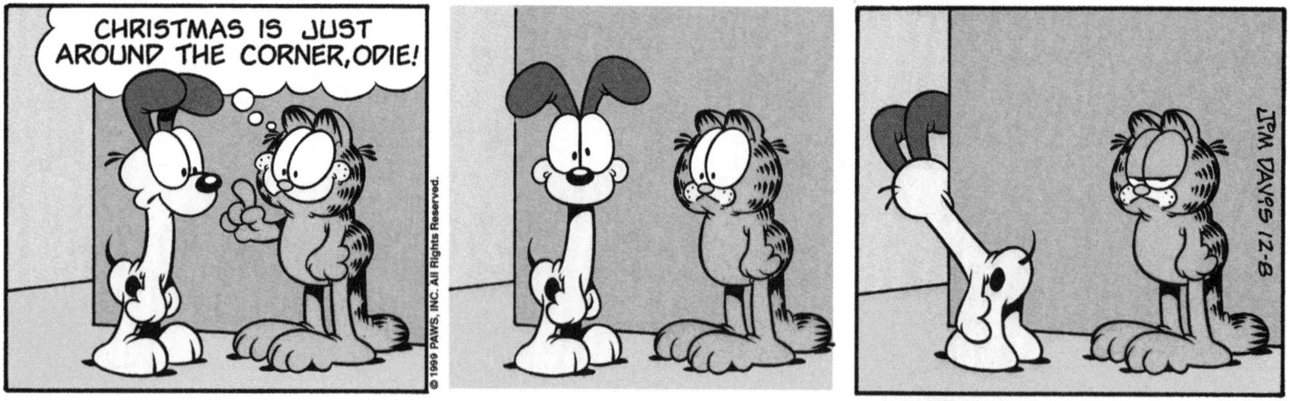
CHRISTMAS IS JUST AROUND THE CORNER, ODIE!
© 1999 PAWS, INC. All Rights Reserved.
JIM DAVIS 12-8

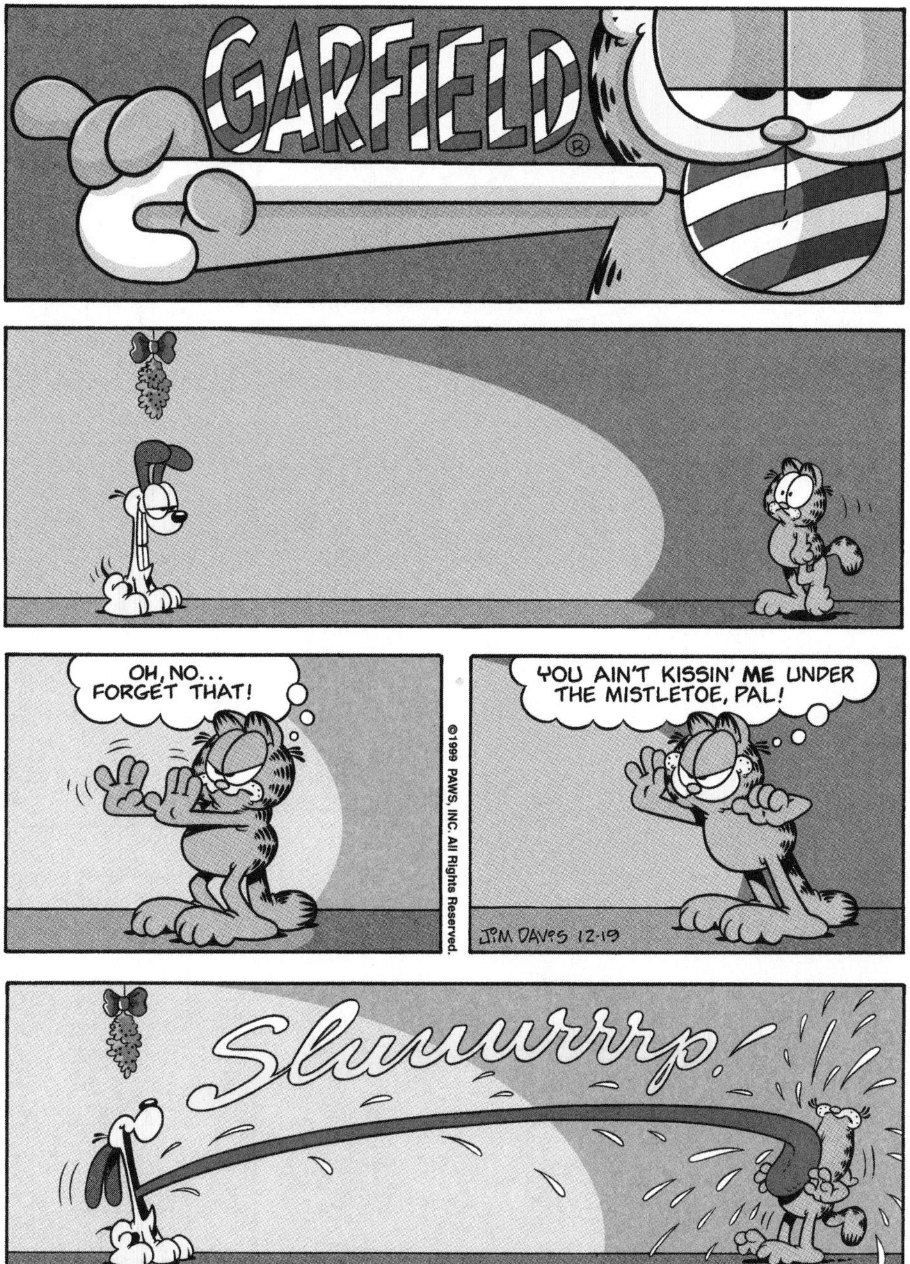
GARFIELD®
OH, NO... FORGET THAT!
©1999 PAWS, INC. All Rights Reserved.
YOU AIN'T KISSIN' ME UNDER THE MISTLETOE, PAL!
JIM DAVIS 12-19
Sluuurrrp!

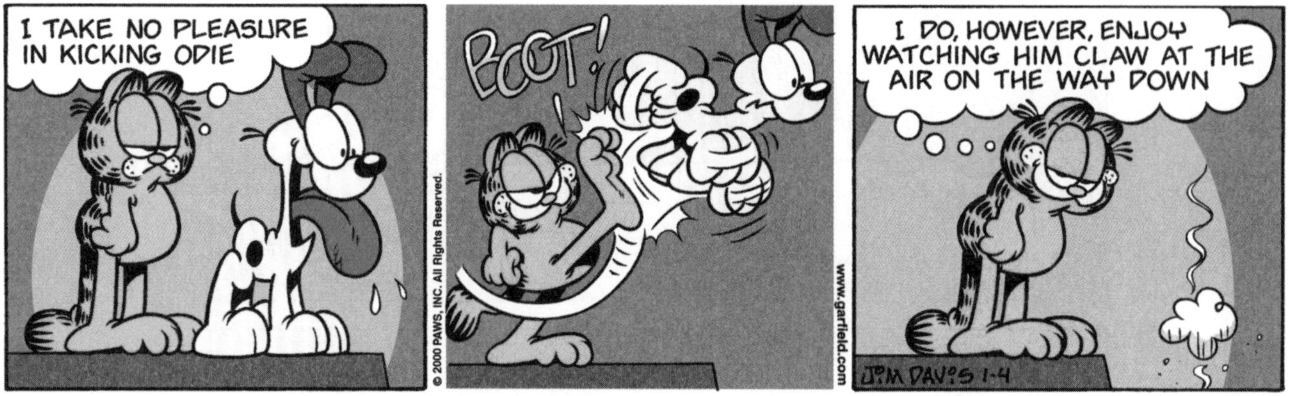
I TAKE NO PLEASURE IN KICKING ODIE
BOOT!
© 2000 PAWS, INC. All Rights Reserved.
www.garfield.com
I DO, HOWEVER, ENJOY WATCHING HIM CLAW AT THE AIR ON THE WAY DOWN
JIM DAVIS 1-4

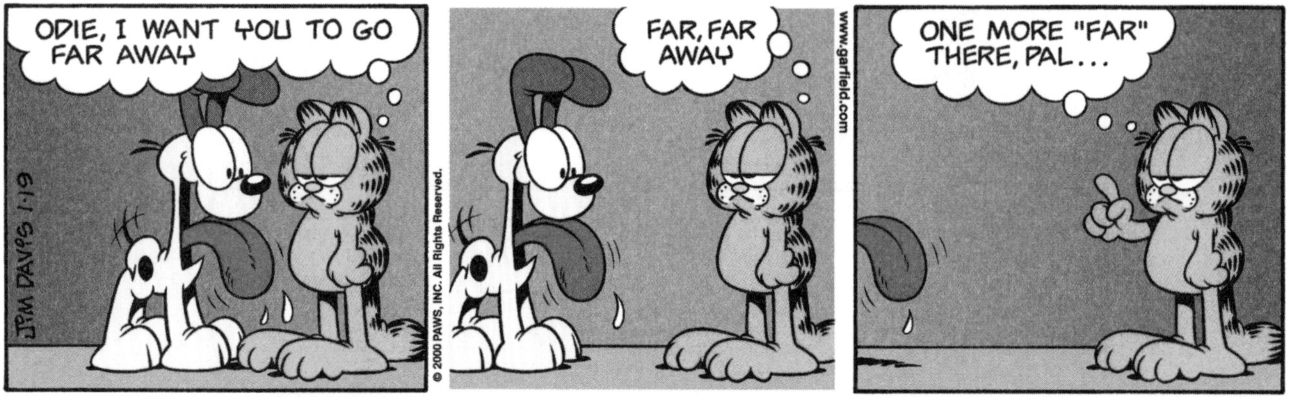
ODIE, I WANT YOU TO GO FAR AWAY
JIM DAVIS 1-19
© 2000 PAWS, INC. All Rights Reserved.
FAR, FAR AWAY
www.garfield.com
ONE MORE "FAR" THERE, PAL...

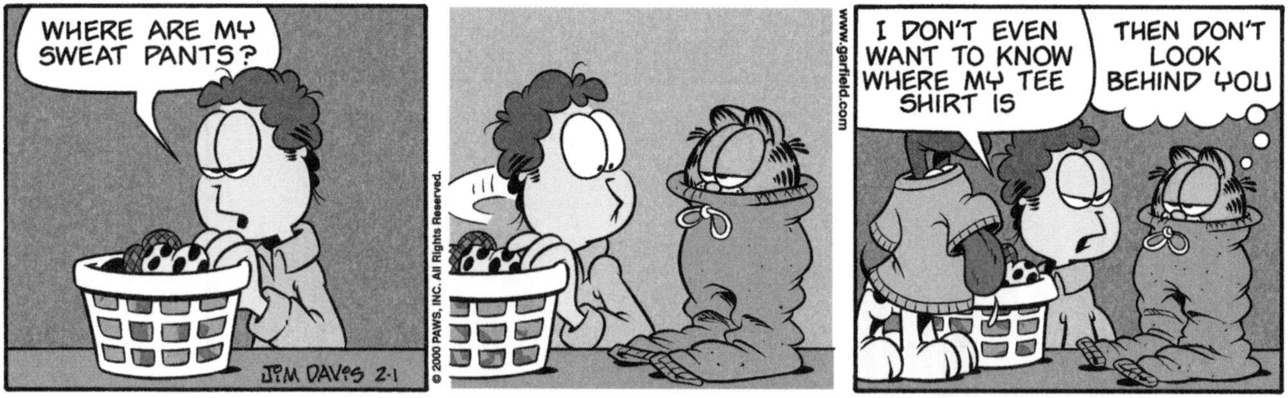
WHERE ARE MY SWEAT PANTS?
JIM DAVIS 2-1
© 2000 PAWS, INC. All Rights Reserved.
www.garfield.com
I DON'T EVEN WANT TO KNOW WHERE MY TEE SHIRT IS
THEN DON'T LOOK BEHIND YOU

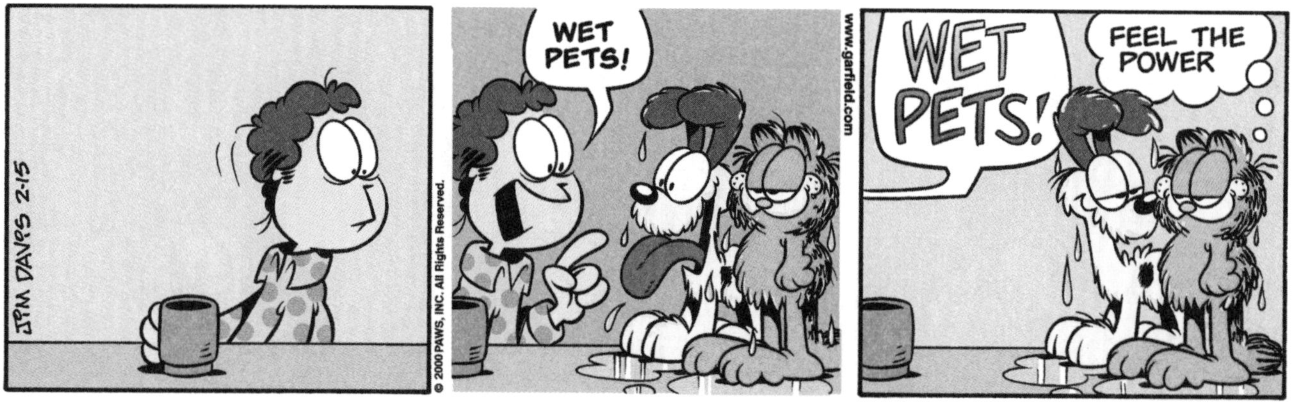
JIM DAVIS 2-15
© 2000 PAWS, INC. All Rights Reserved.
WET PETS!
www.garfield.com
WET PETS!
FEEL THE POWER

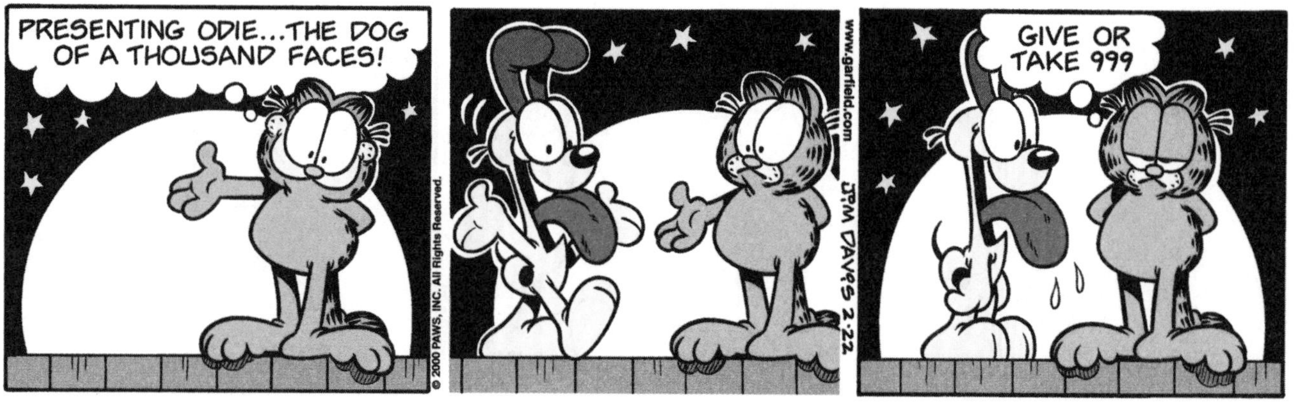
PRESENTING ODIE...THE DOG OF A THOUSAND FACES!
© 2000 PAWS, INC. All Rights Reserved.
www.garfield.com
JIM DAVIS 2-22
GIVE OR TAKE 999

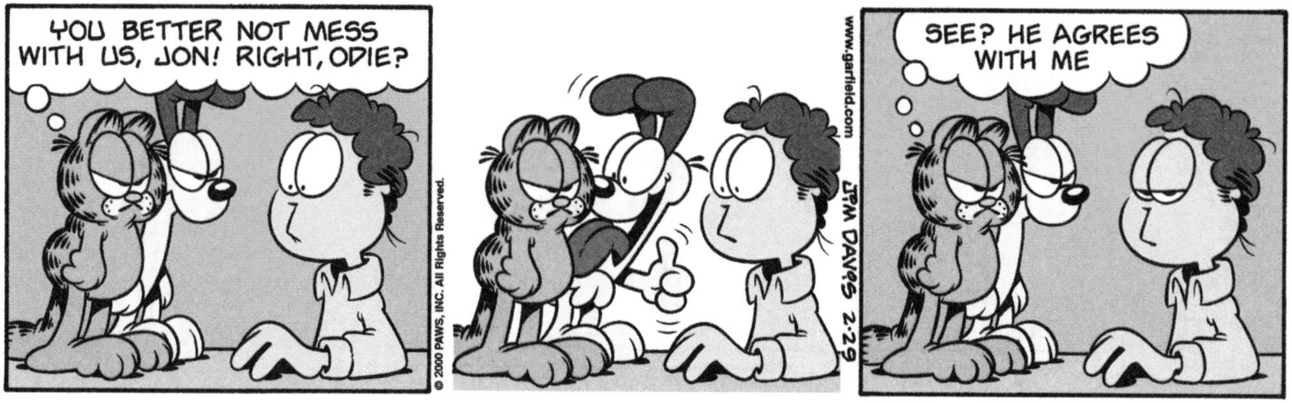
YOU BETTER NOT MESS WITH US, JON! RIGHT, ODIE?
© 2000 PAWS, INC. All Rights Reserved.
www.garfield.com
JIM DAVIS 2-29
SEE? HE AGREES WITH ME

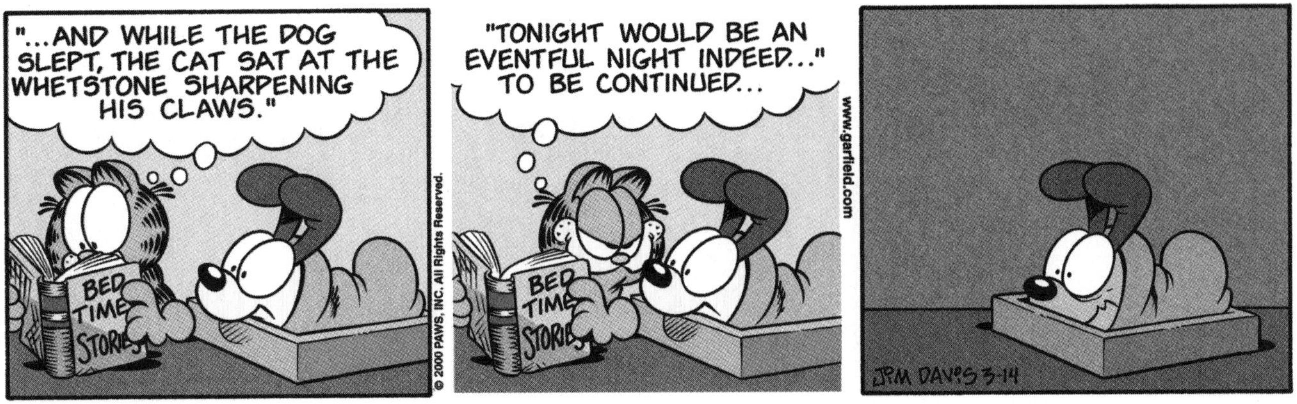
"...AND WHILE THE DOG SLEPT, THE CAT SAT AT THE WHETSTONE SHARPENING HIS CLAWS."
BED TIME STORIES
© 2000 PAWS, INC. All Rights Reserved.
"TONIGHT WOULD BE AN EVENTFUL NIGHT INDEED..." TO BE CONTINUED...
BED TIME STORIES
www.garfield.com
JIM DAVIS 3-14

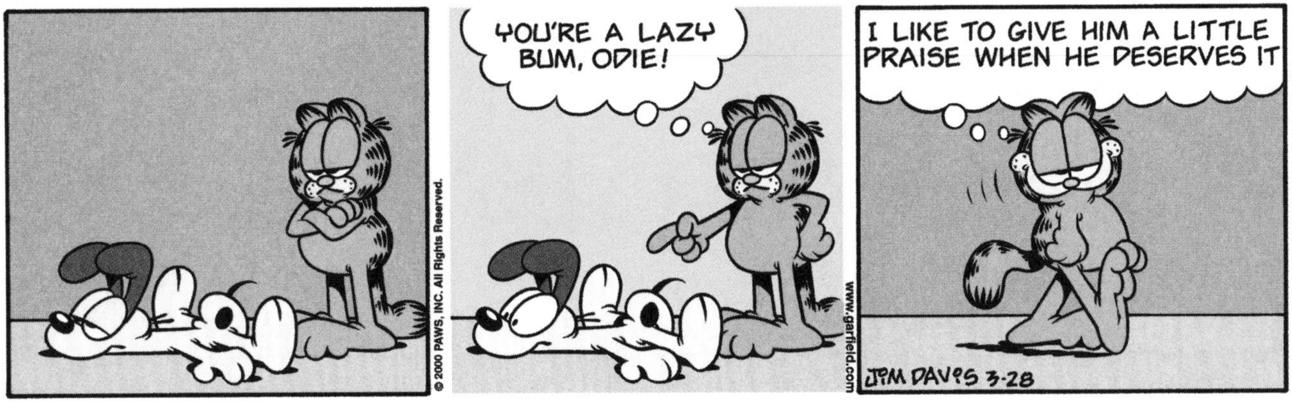
© 2000 PAWS, INC. All Rights Reserved.
YOU'RE A LAZY BUM, ODIE!
www.garfield.com
I LIKE TO GIVE HIM A LITTLE PRAISE WHEN HE DESERVES IT
JIM DAVIS 3-28

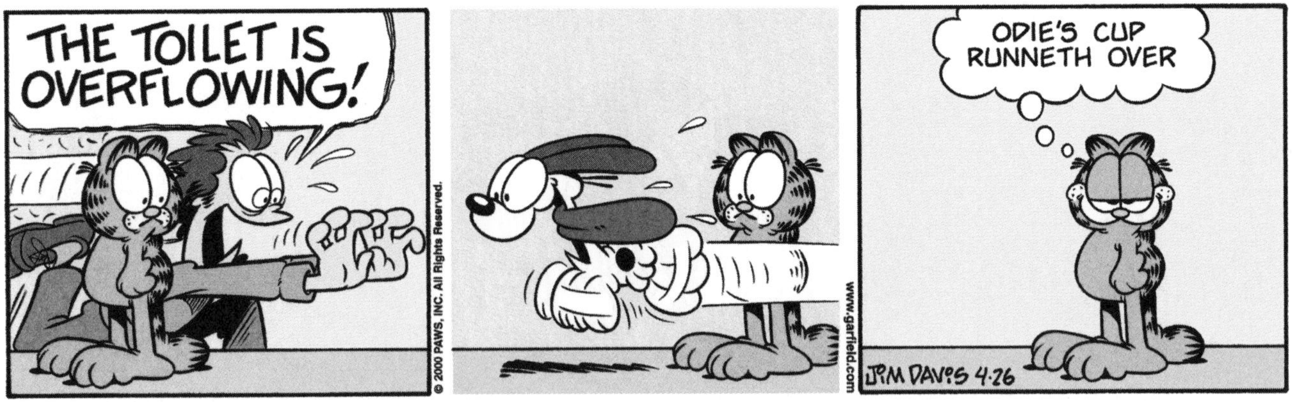
THE TOILET IS OVERFLOWING!
© 2000 PAWS, INC. All Rights Reserved.
www.garfield.com
ODIE'S CUP RUNNETH OVER
JIM DAVIS 4-26

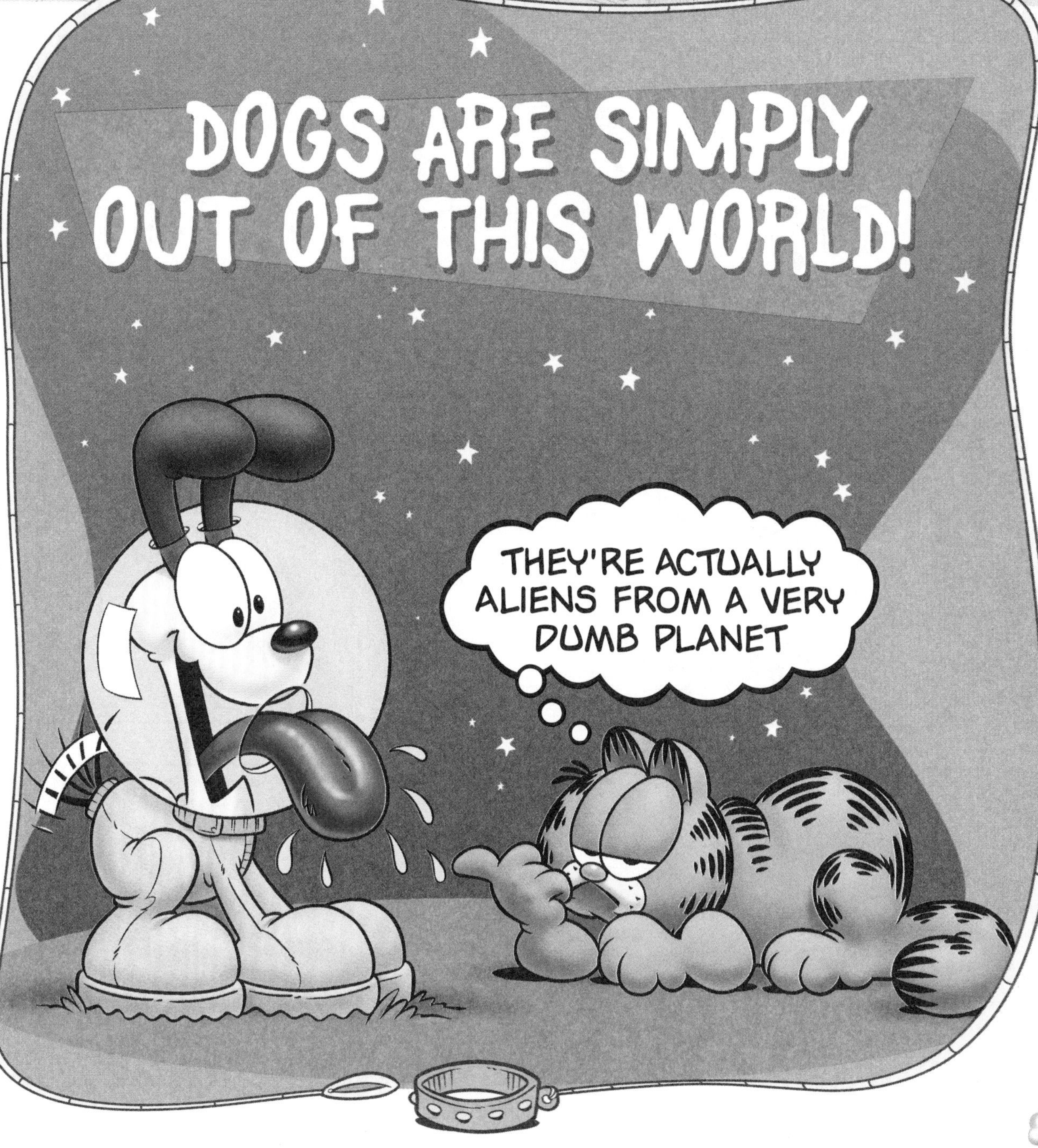
DOGS ARE SIMPLY OUT OF THIS WORLD!
THEY'RE ACTUALLY ALIENS FROM A VERY DUMB PLANET

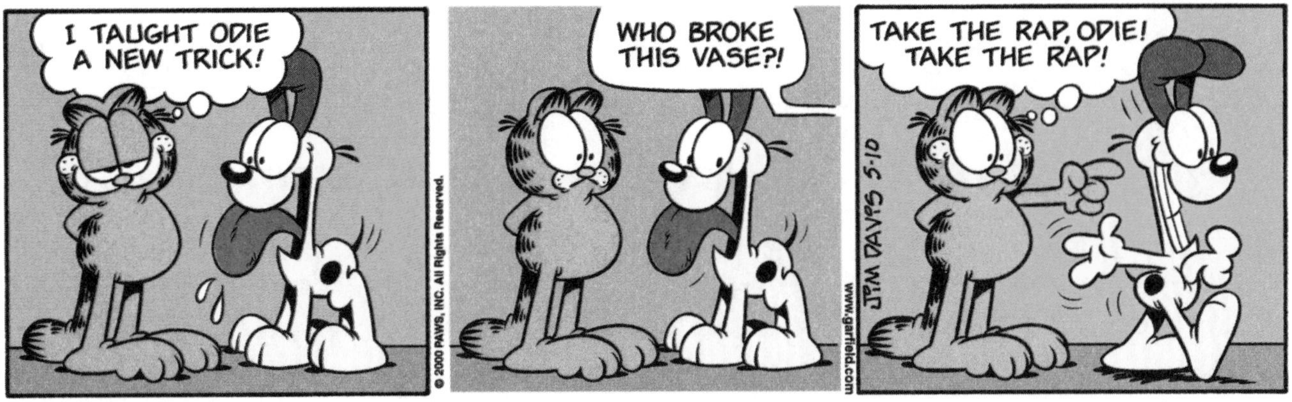
I TAUGHT ODIE A NEW TRICK!
WHO BROKE THIS VASE?!
TAKE THE RAP, ODIE! TAKE THE RAP!
© 2000 PAWS, INC. All Rights Reserved.
www.garfield.com
JIM DAVIS 5-10

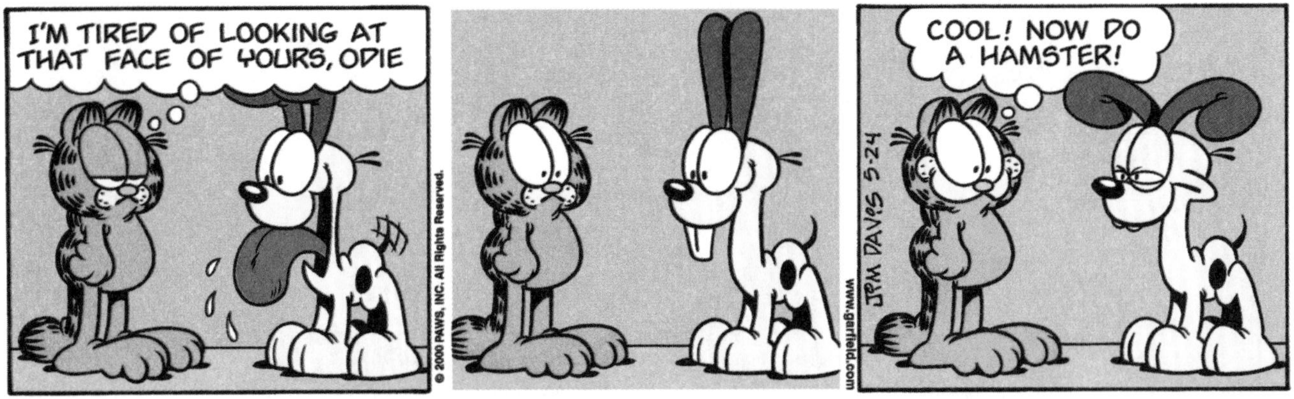
I'M TIRED OF LOOKING AT THAT FACE OF YOURS, ODIE
COOL! NOW DO A HAMSTER!
© 2000 PAWS, INC. All Rights Reserved.
www.garfield.com
JIM DAVIS 5-24

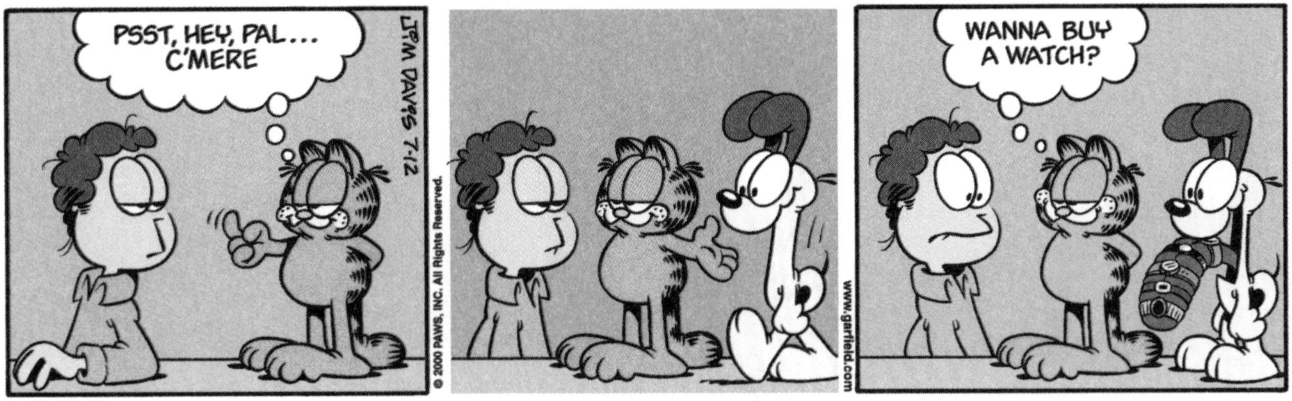
PSST, HEY, PAL... C'MERE
WANNA BUY A WATCH?
© 2000 PAWS, INC. All Rights Reserved.
www.garfield.com
JIM DAVIS 7-12

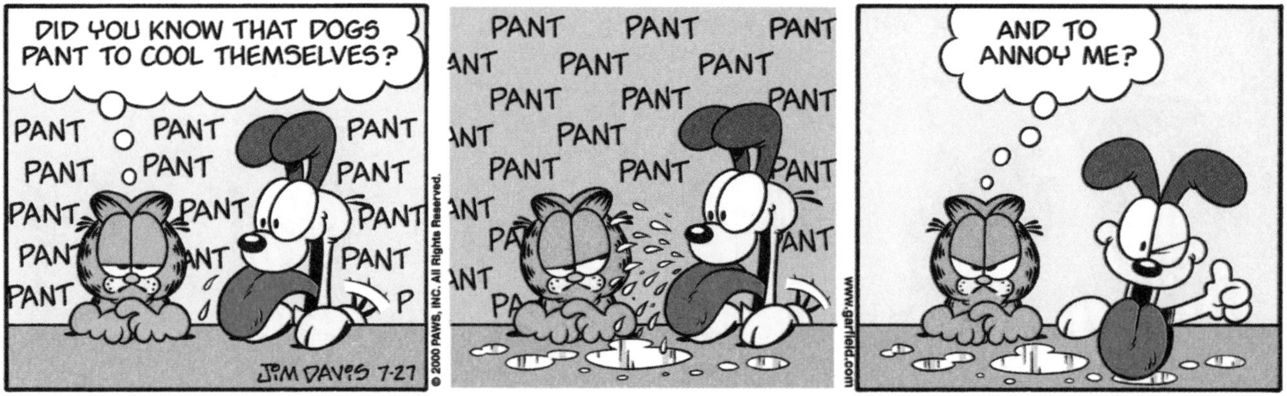
DID YOU KNOW THAT DOGS PANT TO COOL THEMSELVES?
PANT PANT PANT
PANT PANT PANT
PANT PANT PANT
PANT PANT
PANT
JIM DAVIS 7-27
© 2000 PAWS, INC. All Rights Reserved.
PANT PANT PANT
PANT PANT
PANT PANT PANT
PANT
PANT PANT PANT
www.garfield.com
AND TO ANNOY ME?

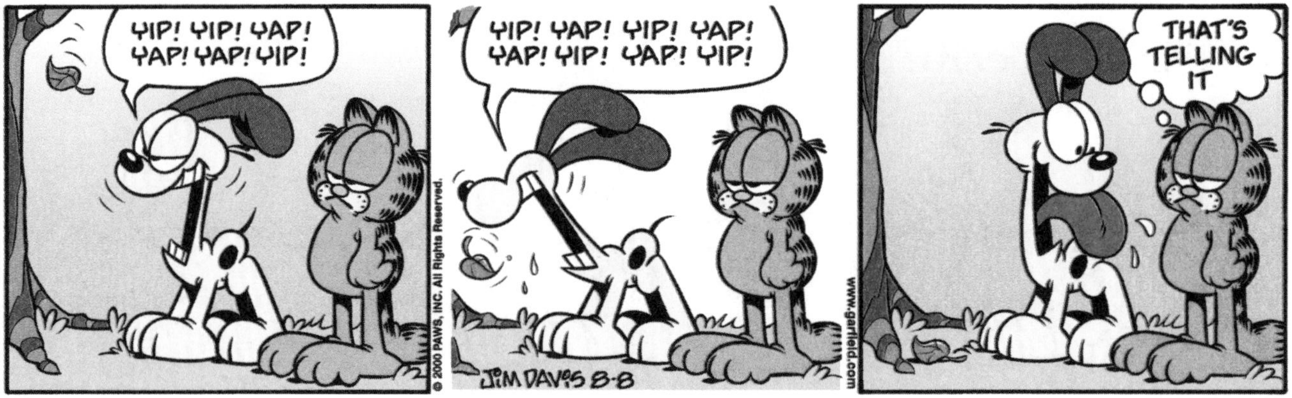
YIP! YIP! YAP! YAP! YAP! YIP!
© 2000 PAWS, INC. All Rights Reserved.
YIP! YAP! YIP! YAP! YAP! YIP! YAP! YIP!
JIM DAVIS 8-8
www.garfield.com
THAT'S TELLING IT

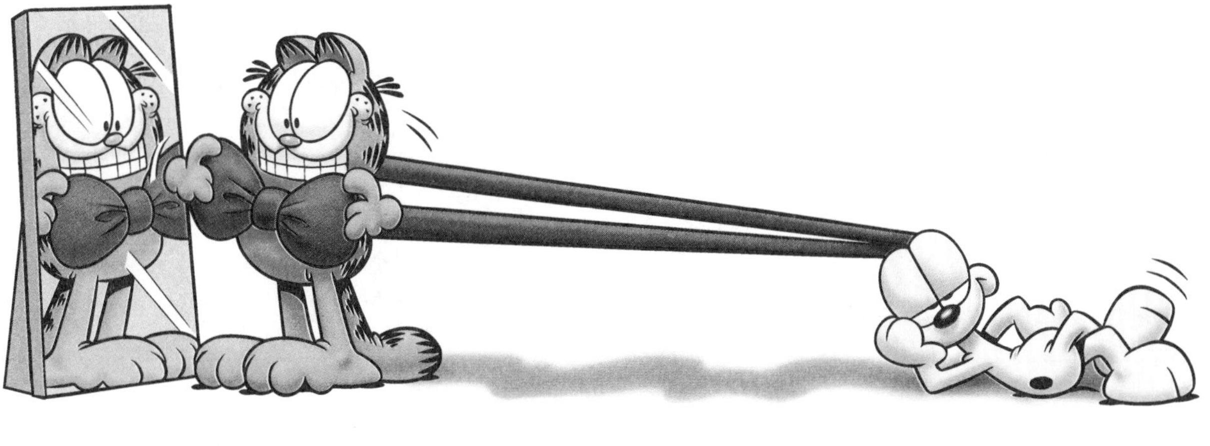

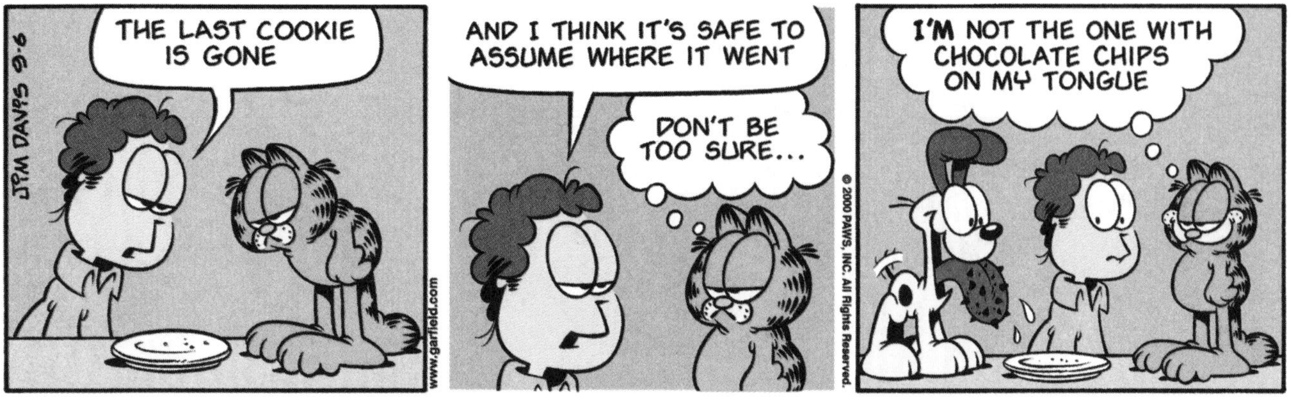
JIM DAVIS 9·6
THE LAST COOKIE IS GONE
www.garfield.com
AND I THINK IT'S SAFE TO ASSUME WHERE IT WENT
DON'T BE TOO SURE...
© 2000 PAWS, INC. All Rights Reserved.
I'M NOT THE ONE WITH CHOCOLATE CHIPS ON MY TONGUE

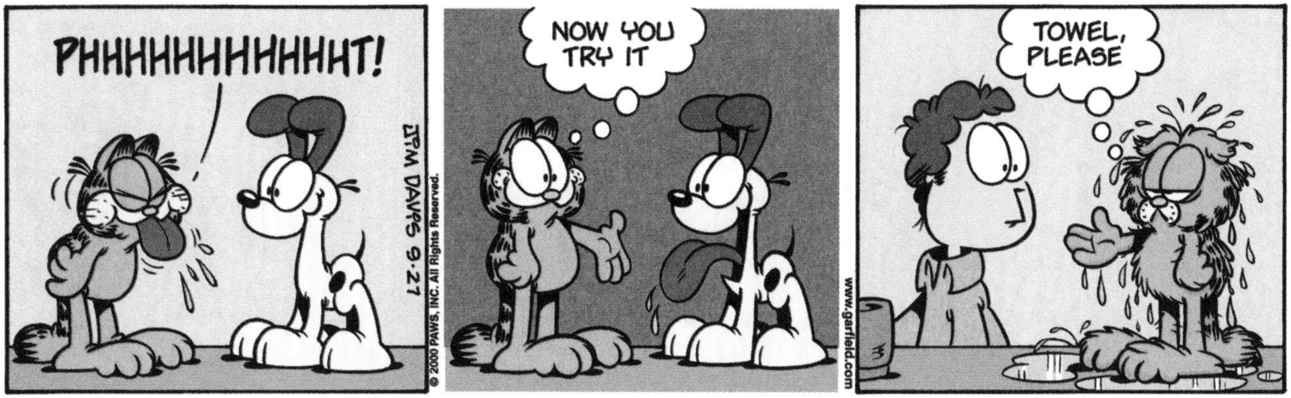
PHHHHHHHHHHHT!
JIM DAVIS 9·27
© 2000 PAWS, INC. All Rights Reserved.
NOW YOU TRY IT
www.garfield.com
TOWEL, PLEASE

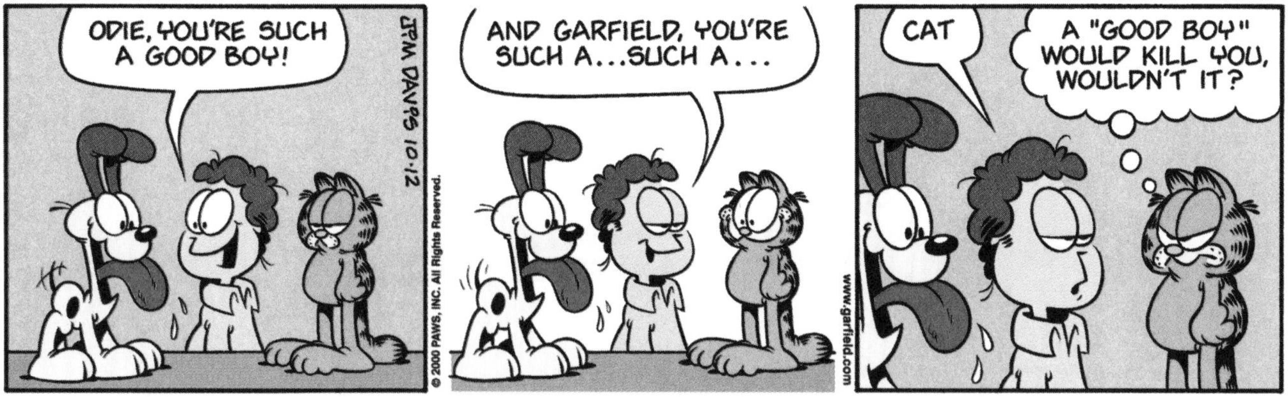
ODIE, YOU'RE SUCH A GOOD BOY!
JIM DAVIS 10·12
© 2000 PAWS, INC. All Rights Reserved.
AND GARFIELD, YOU'RE SUCH A...SUCH A...
www.garfield.com
CAT
A "GOOD BOY" WOULD KILL YOU, WOULDN'T IT?

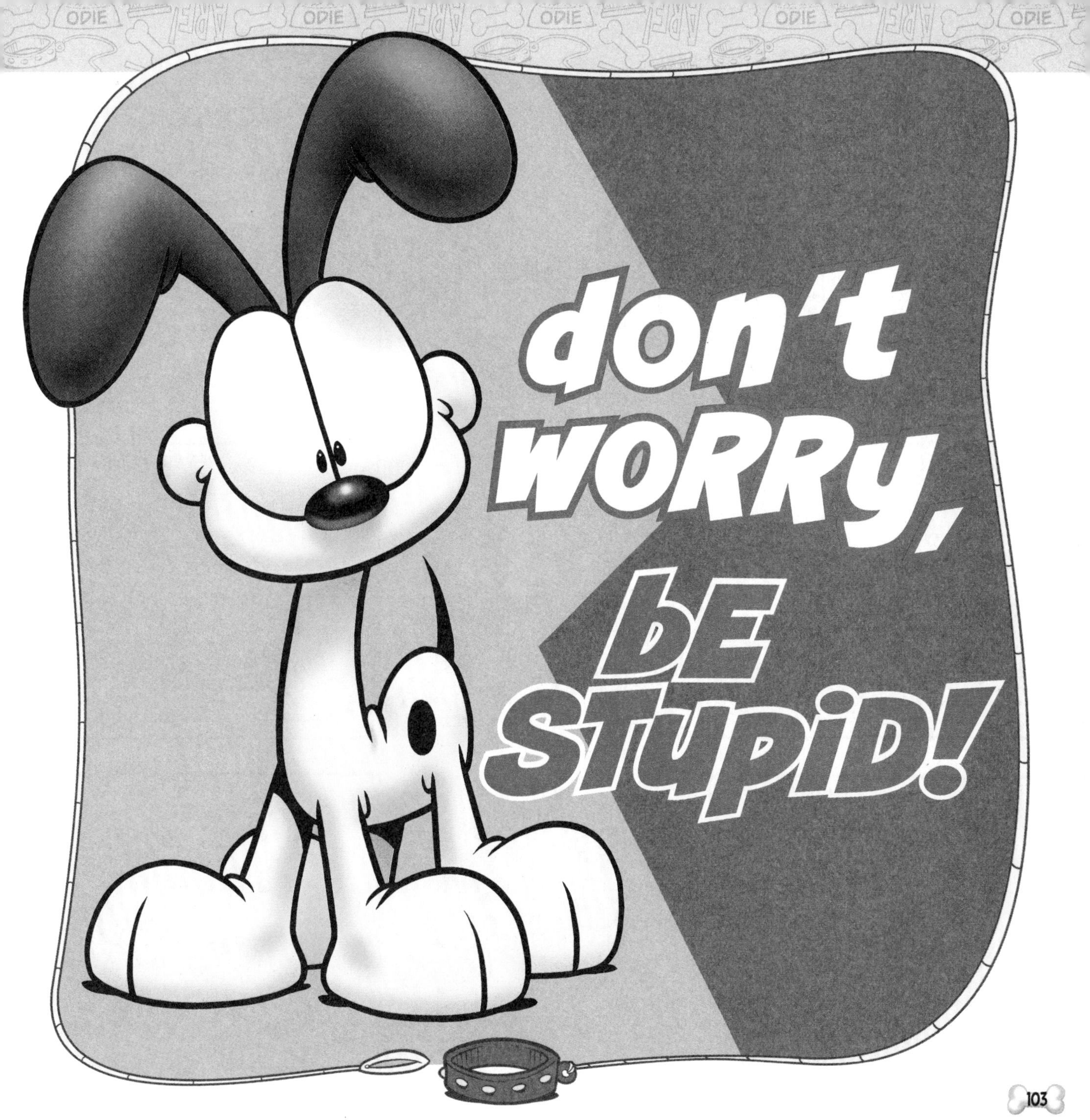
don't WORRy, bE STUPiD!

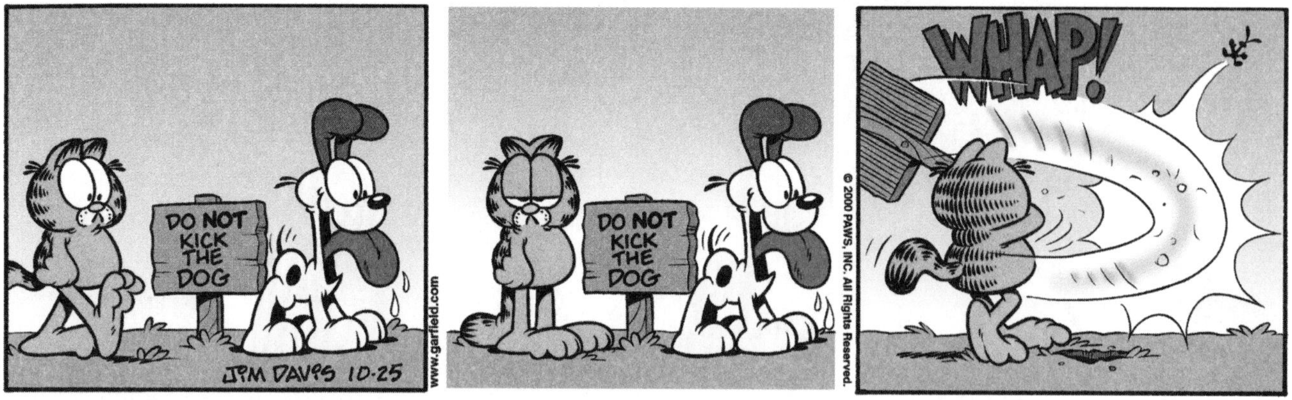
DO NOT KICK THE DOG
JIM DAVIS 10-25
www.garfield.com
DO NOT KICK THE DOG
© 2000 PAWS, INC. All Rights Reserved.
WHAP!

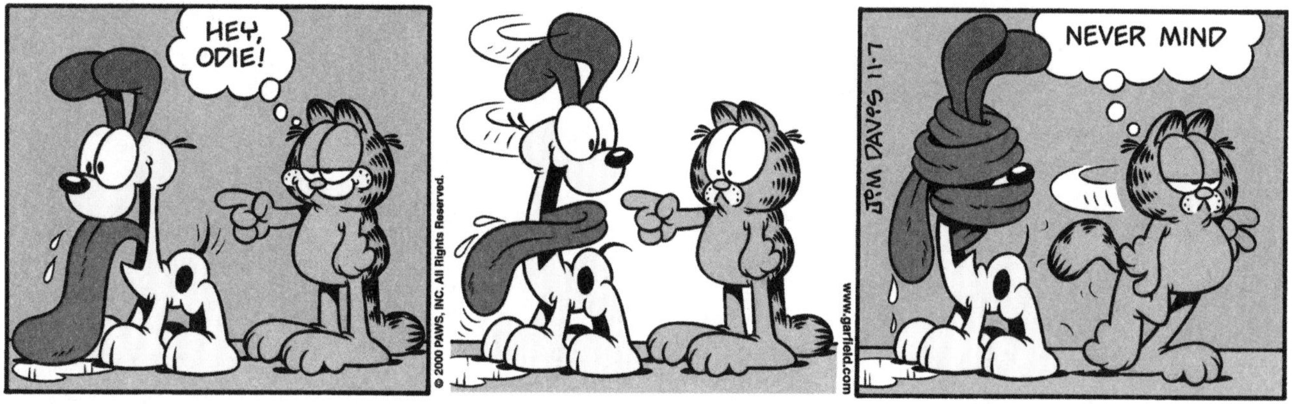
HEY, ODIE!
© 2000 PAWS, INC. All Rights Reserved.
www.garfield.com
JIM DAVIS 11-7
NEVER MIND

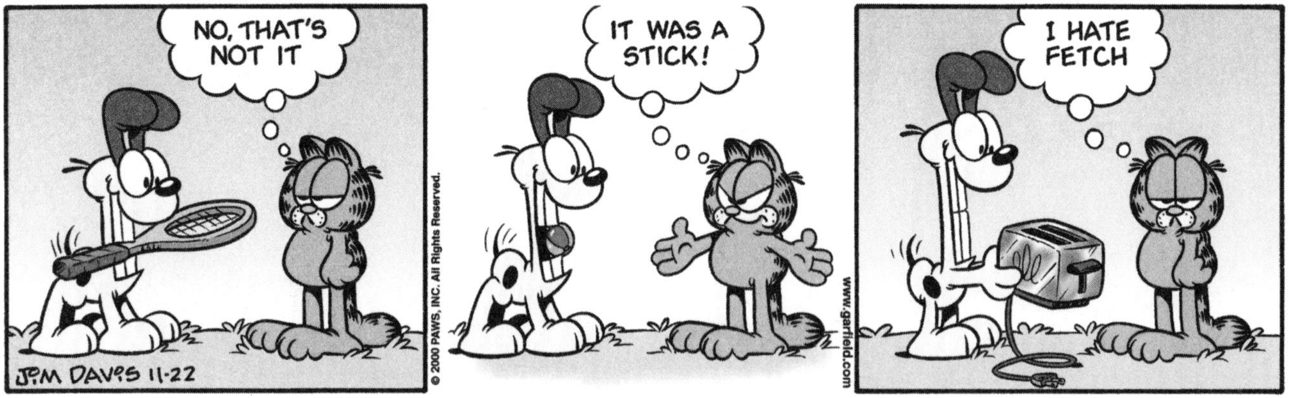
NO, THAT'S NOT IT
JIM DAVIS 11-22
© 2000 PAWS, INC. All Rights Reserved.
IT WAS A STICK!
www.garfield.com
I HATE FETCH

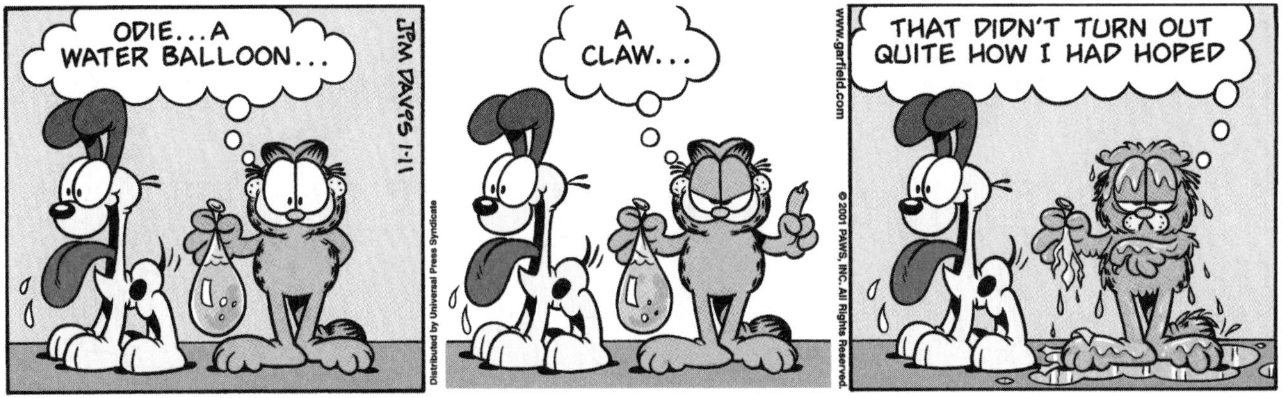
ODIE...A WATER BALLOON...
JIM DAVIS 1-11
A CLAW...
Distributed by Universal Press Syndicate
www.garfield.com
© 2001 PAWS, INC. All Rights Reserved.
THAT DIDN'T TURN OUT QUITE HOW I HAD HOPED

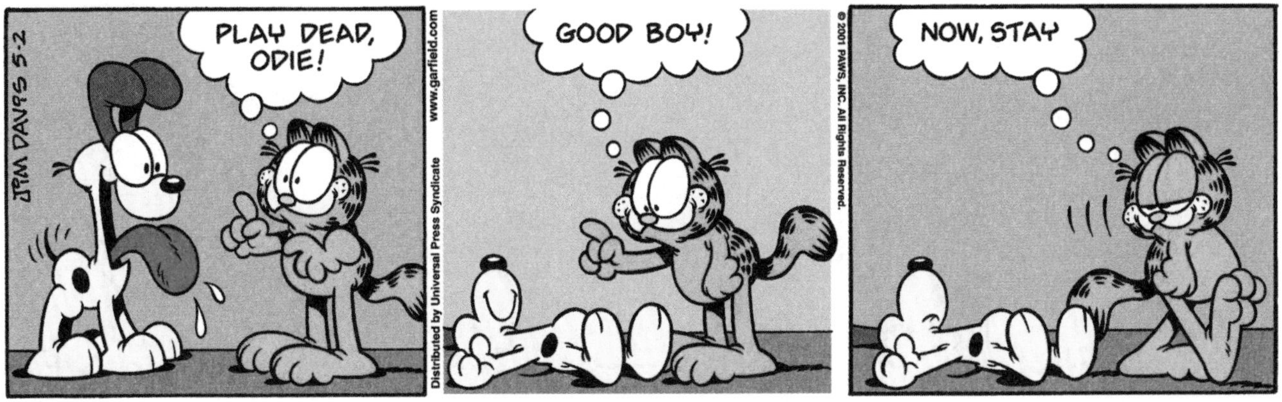
JIM DAVIS 5-2
PLAY DEAD, ODIE!
www.garfield.com
Distributed by Universal Press Syndicate
GOOD BOY!
© 2001 PAWS, INC. All Rights Reserved.
NOW, STAY

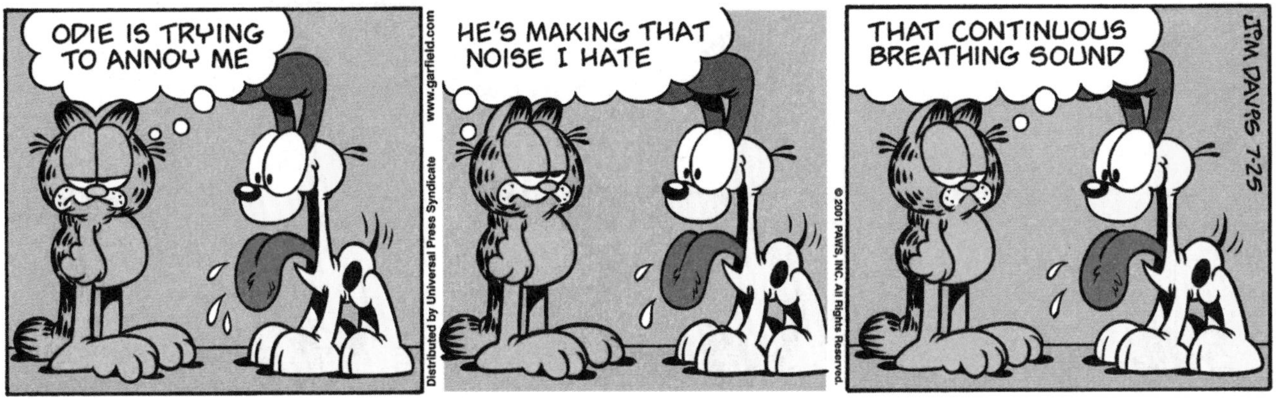
ODIE IS TRYING TO ANNOY ME
www.garfield.com
Distributed by Universal Press Syndicate
HE'S MAKING THAT NOISE I HATE
© 2001 PAWS, INC. All Rights Reserved.
THAT CONTINUOUS BREATHING SOUND
JIM DAVIS 7-25

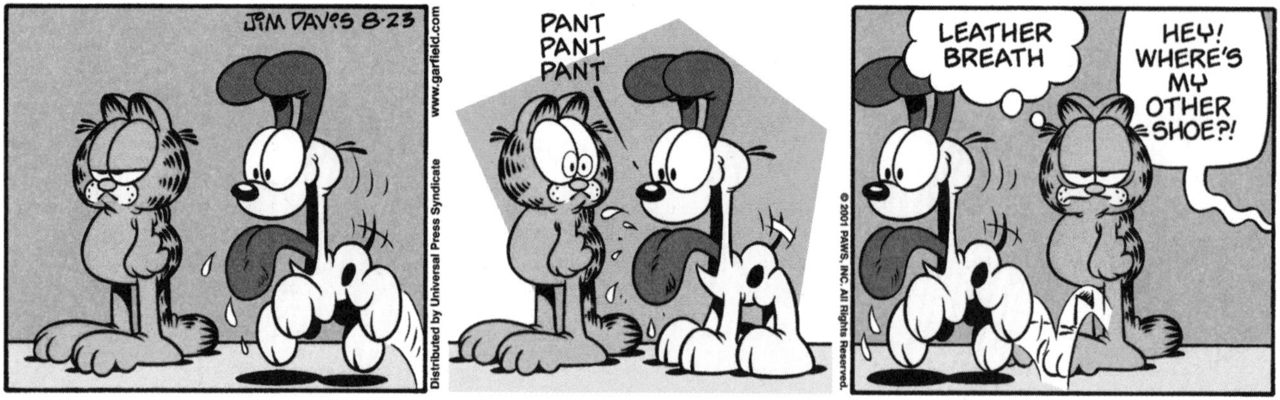
JIM DAVIS 8·23
www.garfield.com
Distributed by Universal Press Syndicate
PANT
PANT
PANT
© 2001 PAWS, INC. All Rights Reserved.
LEATHER BREATH
HEY! WHERE'S MY OTHER SHOE?!

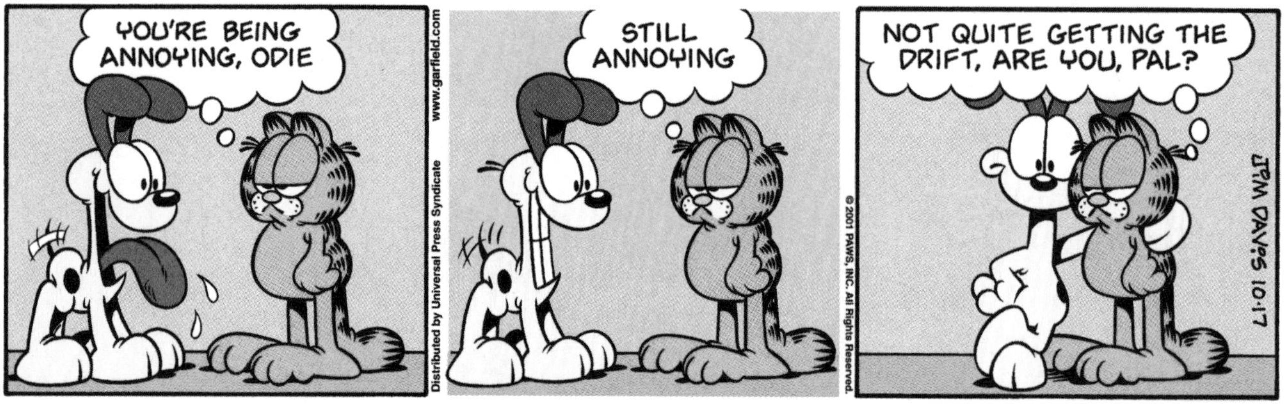
YOU'RE BEING ANNOYING, ODIE
www.garfield.com
Distributed by Universal Press Syndicate
STILL ANNOYING
© 2001 PAWS, INC. All Rights Reserved.
NOT QUITE GETTING THE DRIFT, ARE YOU, PAL?
JIM DAVIS 10·17

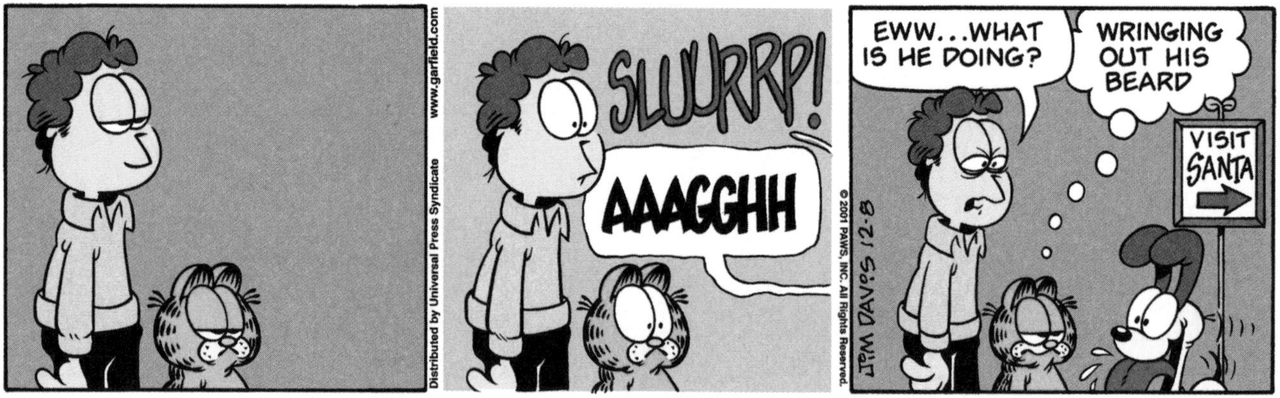
www.garfield.com
Distributed by Universal Press Syndicate
SLUURRP!
AAAGGHH
© 2001 PAWS, INC. All Rights Reserved.
JIM DAVIS 12·8
EWW...WHAT IS HE DOING?
WRINGING OUT HIS BEARD
VISIT SANTA

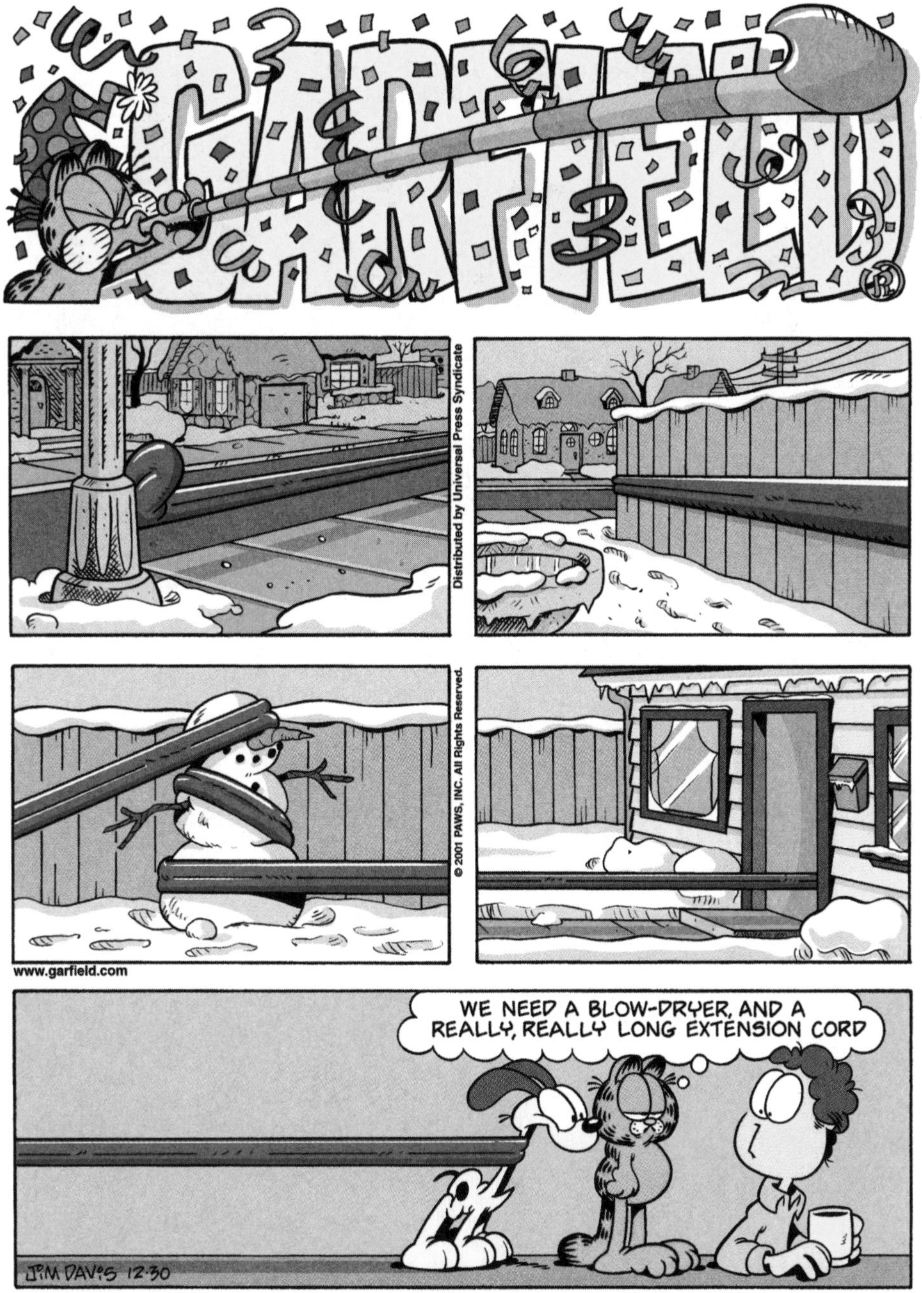
GARFIELD
Distributed by Universal Press Syndicate
© 2001 PAWS, INC. All Rights Reserved.
www.garfield.com
WE NEED A BLOW-DRYER, AND A REALLY, REALLY LONG EXTENSION CORD
JIM DAVIS 12-30

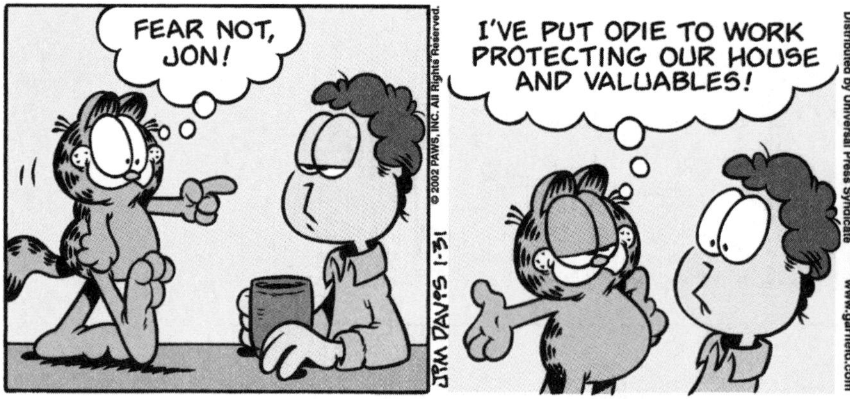
FEAR NOT, JON!
JPM DAVIS 1-31
© 2002 PAWS, INC. All Rights Reserved.
I'VE PUT ODIE TO WORK PROTECTING OUR HOUSE AND VALUABLES!
Distributed by Universal Press Syndicate
www.garfield.com
TAKE ANYTHING BUT THE FOOD

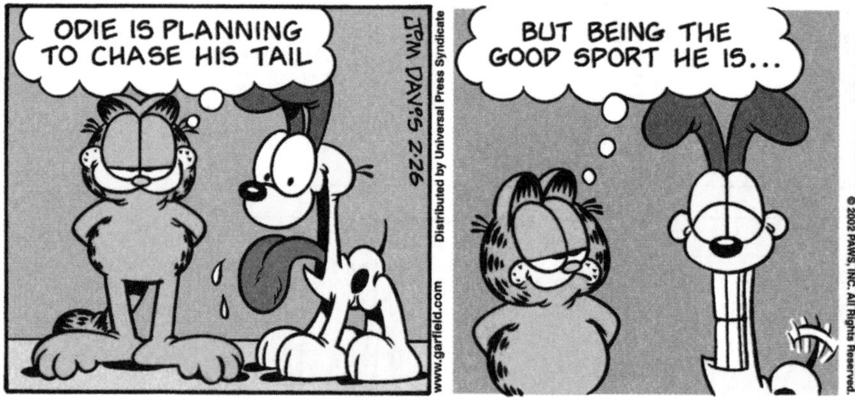
ODIE IS PLANNING TO CHASE HIS TAIL
JPM DAVIS 2-26
Distributed by Universal Press Syndicate
www.garfield.com
BUT BEING THE GOOD SPORT HE IS...
HE'S GOING TO GIVE IT A HEAD START
© 2002 PAWS, INC. All Rights Reserved.

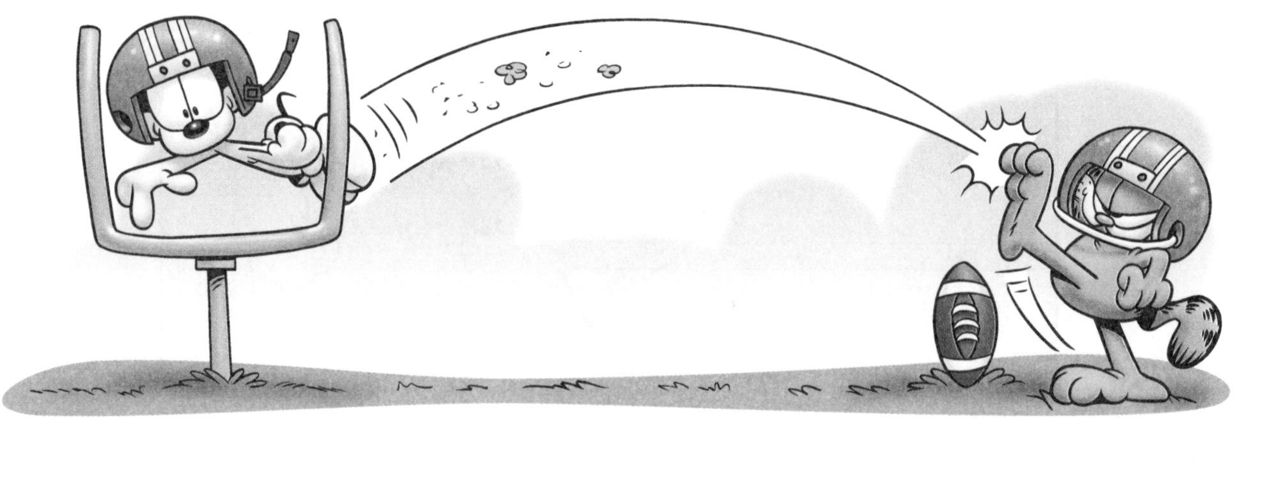

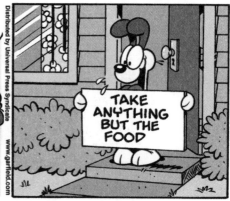

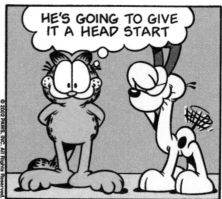

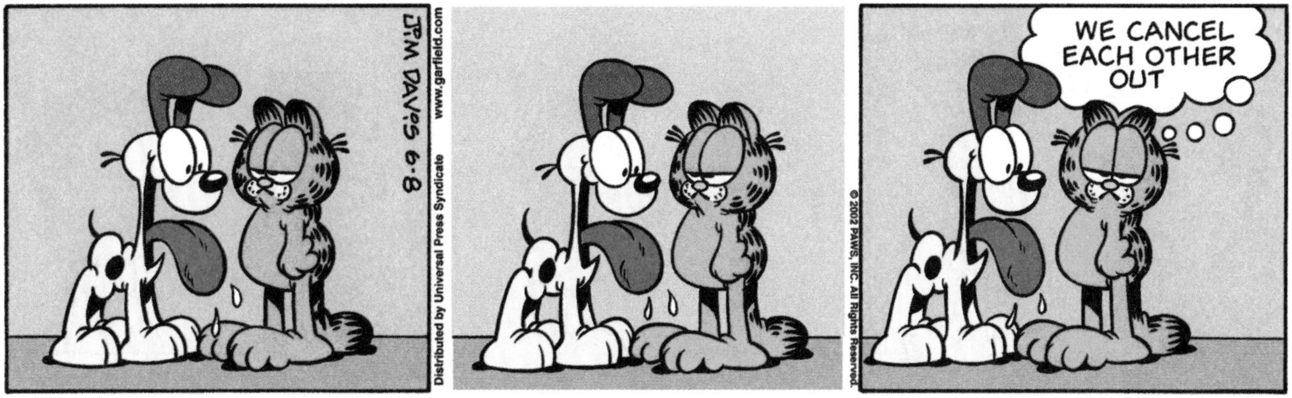
JIM DAVIS 6-8
www.garfield.com
Distributed by Universal Press Syndicate
© 2002 PAWS, INC. All Rights Reserved.
WE CANCEL EACH OTHER OUT

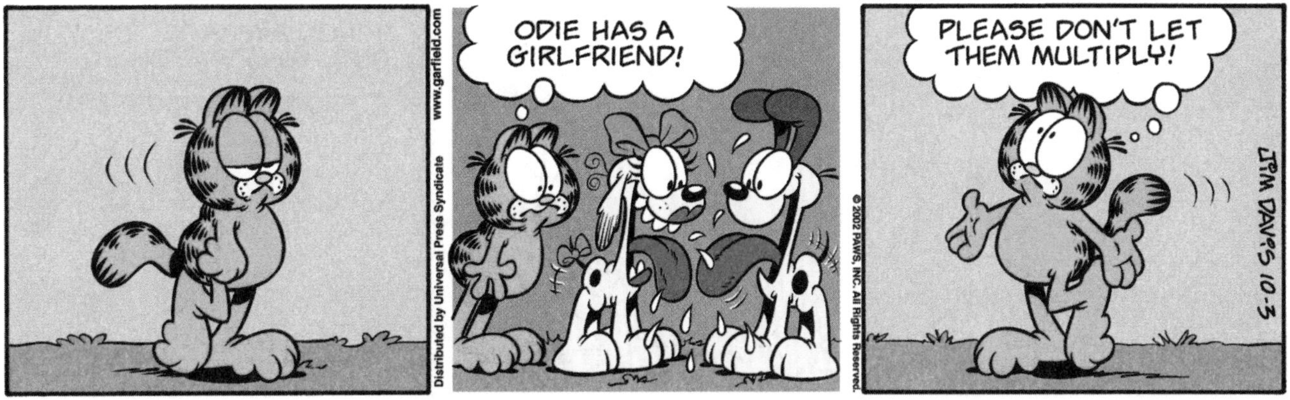
www.garfield.com
Distributed by Universal Press Syndicate
ODIE HAS A GIRLFRIEND!
© 2002 PAWS, INC. All Rights Reserved.
PLEASE DON'T LET THEM MULTIPLY!
JIM DAVIS 10-3

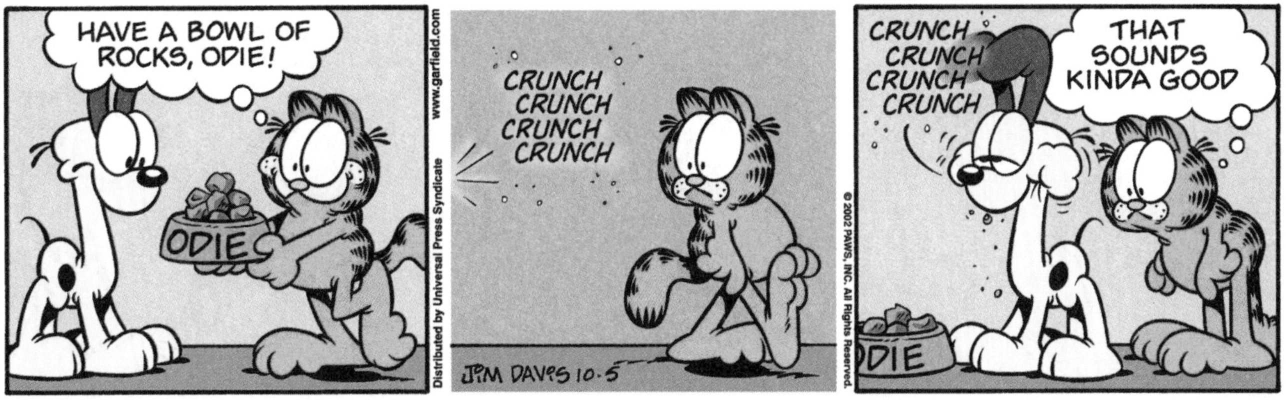
HAVE A BOWL OF ROCKS, ODIE!
ODIE
www.garfield.com
Distributed by Universal Press Syndicate
CRUNCH CRUNCH CRUNCH CRUNCH
JIM DAVIS 10-5
© 2002 PAWS, INC. All Rights Reserved.
CRUNCH CRUNCH CRUNCH CRUNCH
THAT SOUNDS KINDA GOOD
DIE

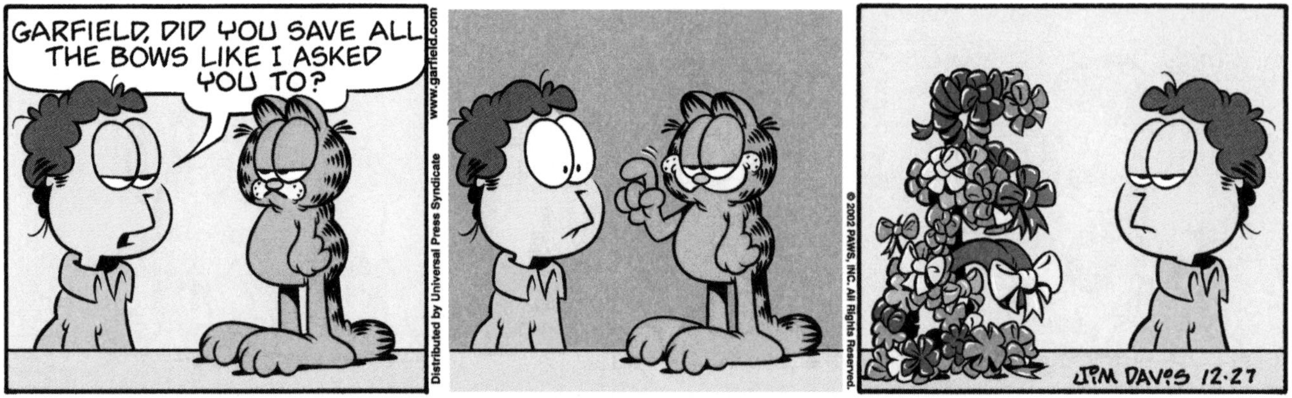
GARFIELD, DID YOU SAVE ALL THE BOWS LIKE I ASKED YOU TO?
www.garfield.com
Distributed by Universal Press Syndicate
© 2002 PAWS, INC. All Rights Reserved.
JIM DAVIS 12-27

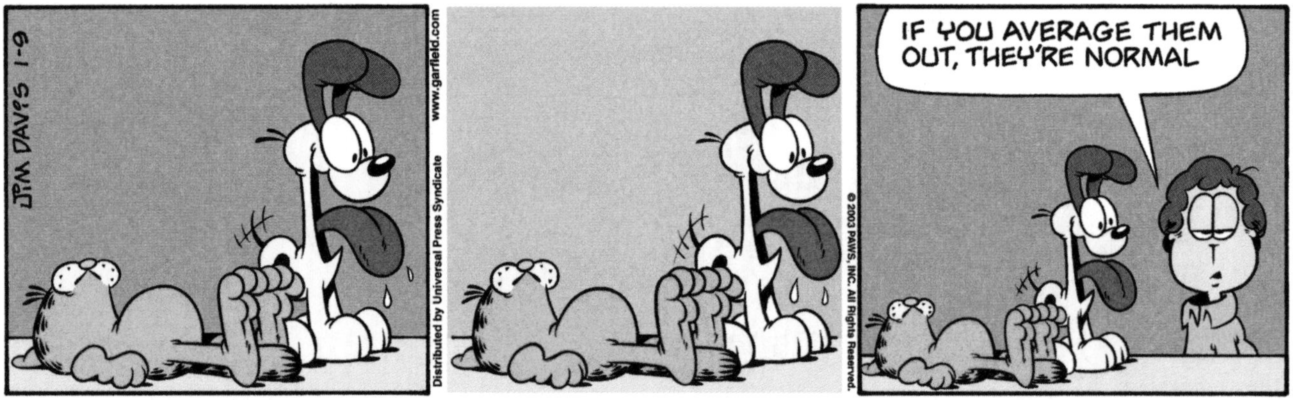
JIM DAVIS 1-9
www.garfield.com
Distributed by Universal Press Syndicate
© 2003 PAWS, INC. All Rights Reserved.
IF YOU AVERAGE THEM OUT, THEY'RE NORMAL

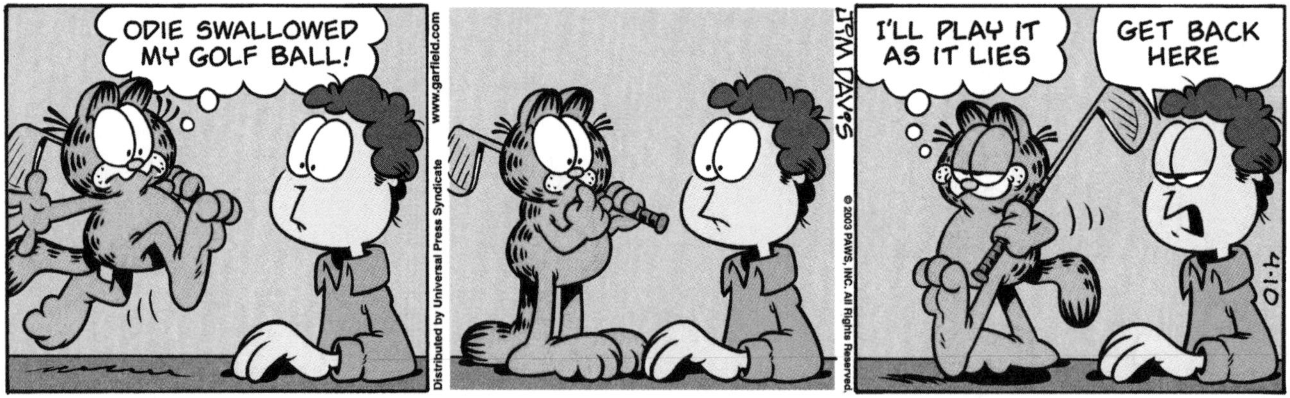
ODIE SWALLOWED MY GOLF BALL!
www.garfield.com
Distributed by Universal Press Syndicate
JIM DAVIS
© 2003 PAWS, INC. All Rights Reserved.
I'LL PLAY IT AS IT LIES
GET BACK HERE
4-10

PRACTICAL USES FOR ODIE'S DROOL

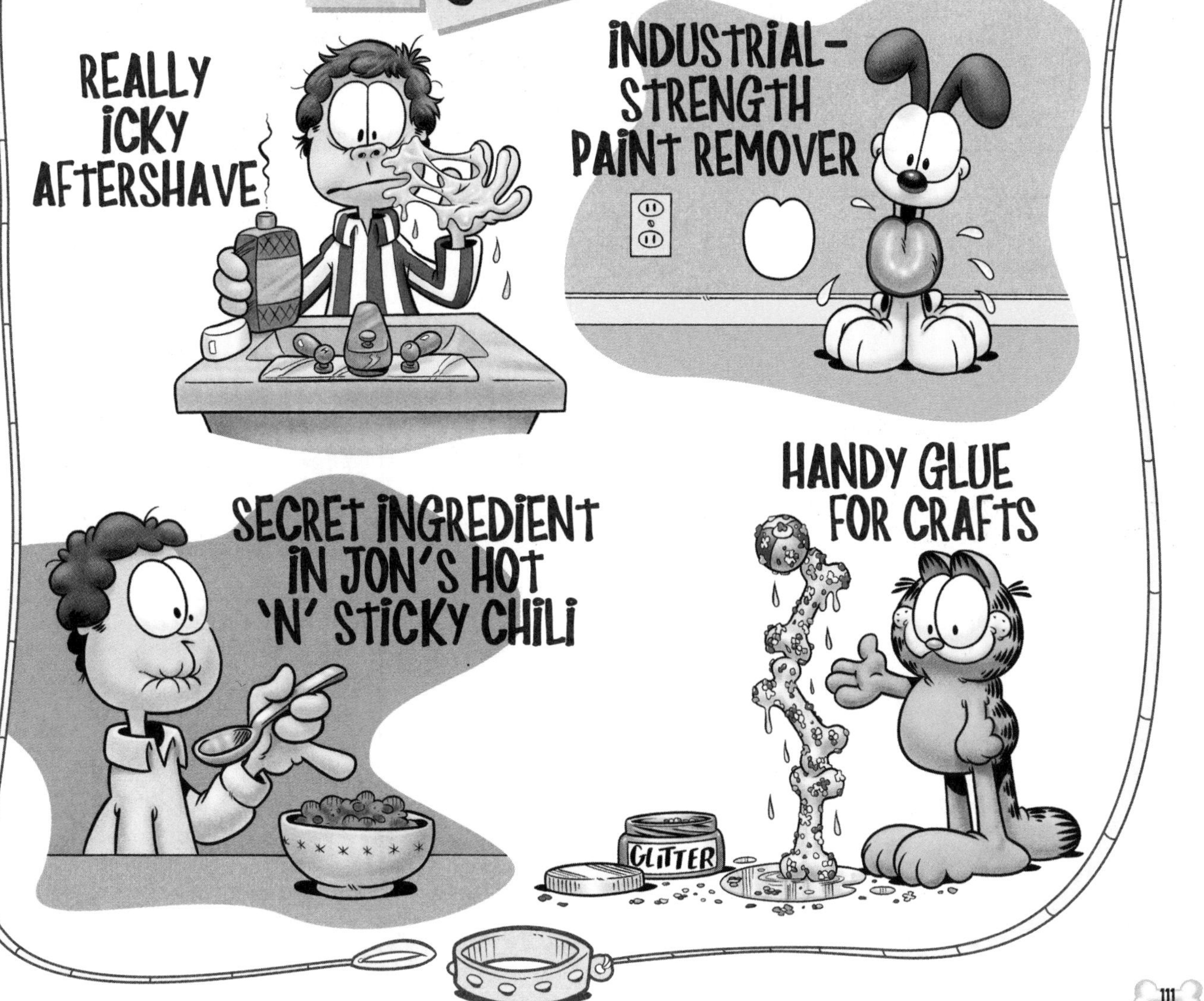
REALLY ICKY AFTERSHAVE
INDUSTRIAL-STRENGTH PAINT REMOVER
SECRET INGREDIENT IN JON'S HOT 'N' STICKY CHILI
HANDY GLUE FOR CRAFTS
GLITTER

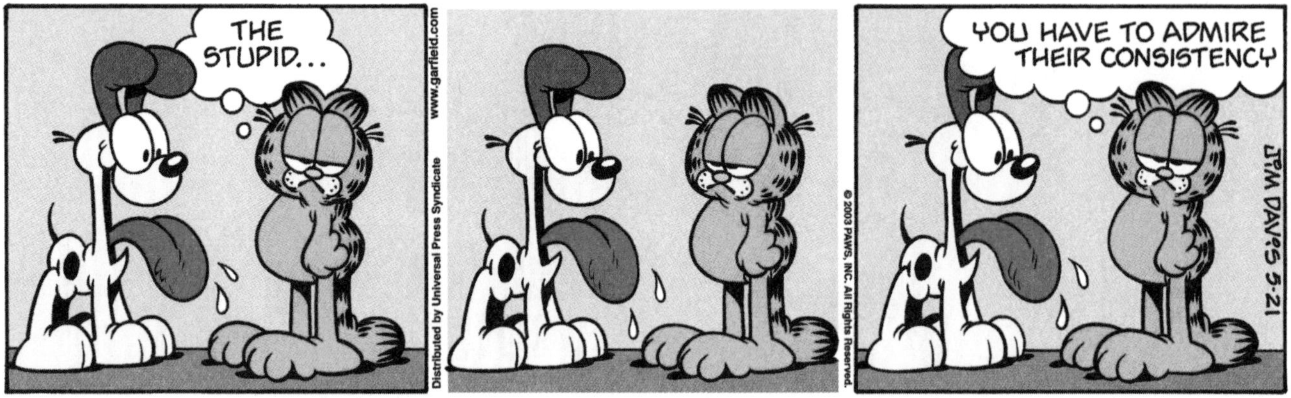
THE STUPID...
www.garfield.com
Distributed by Universal Press Syndicate
© 2003 PAWS, INC. All Rights Reserved.
YOU HAVE TO ADMIRE THEIR CONSISTENCY
JIM DAVIS 5-21

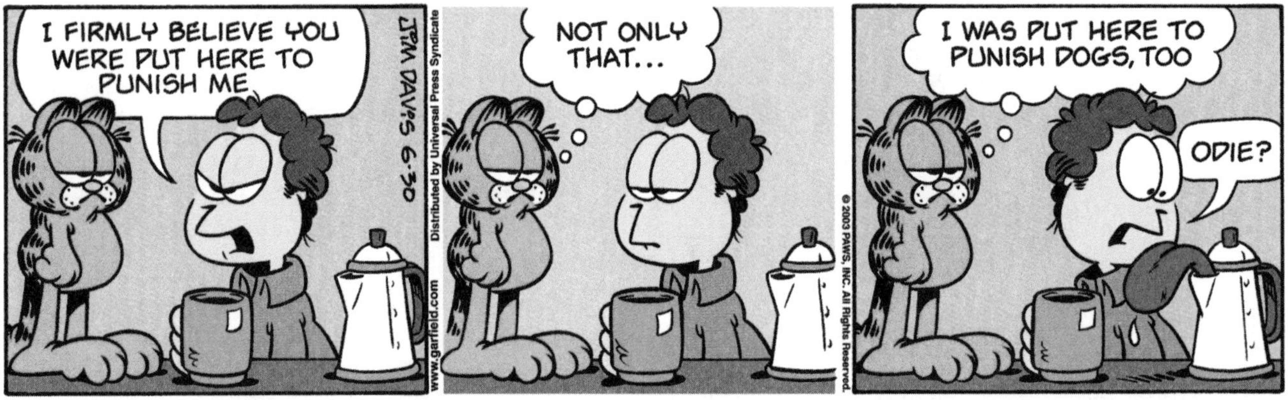
I FIRMLY BELIEVE YOU WERE PUT HERE TO PUNISH ME
JIM DAVIS 6-30
Distributed by Universal Press Syndicate
www.garfield.com
NOT ONLY THAT...
© 2003 PAWS, INC. All Rights Reserved.
I WAS PUT HERE TO PUNISH DOGS, TOO
ODIE?

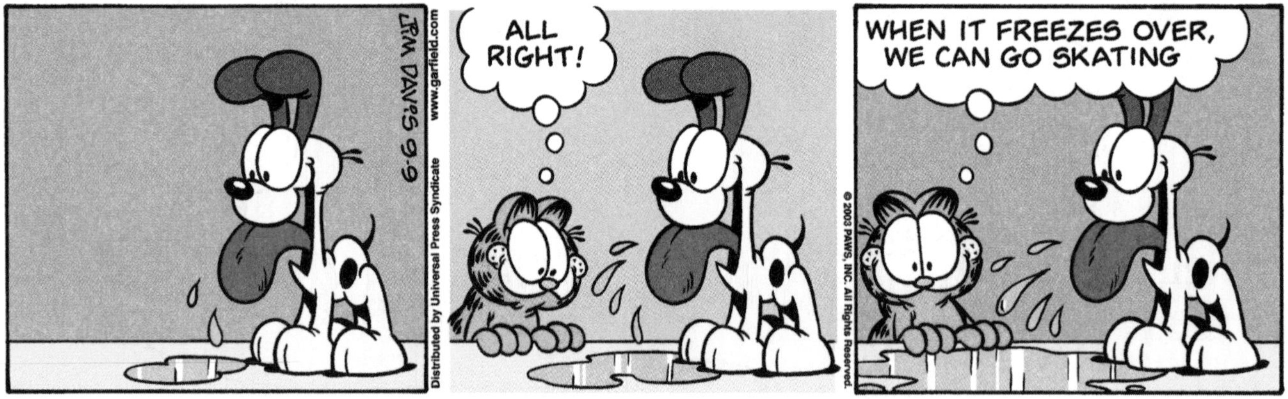
JIM DAVIS 9-9
www.garfield.com
Distributed by Universal Press Syndicate
ALL RIGHT!
© 2003 PAWS, INC. All Rights Reserved.
WHEN IT FREEZES OVER, WE CAN GO SKATING

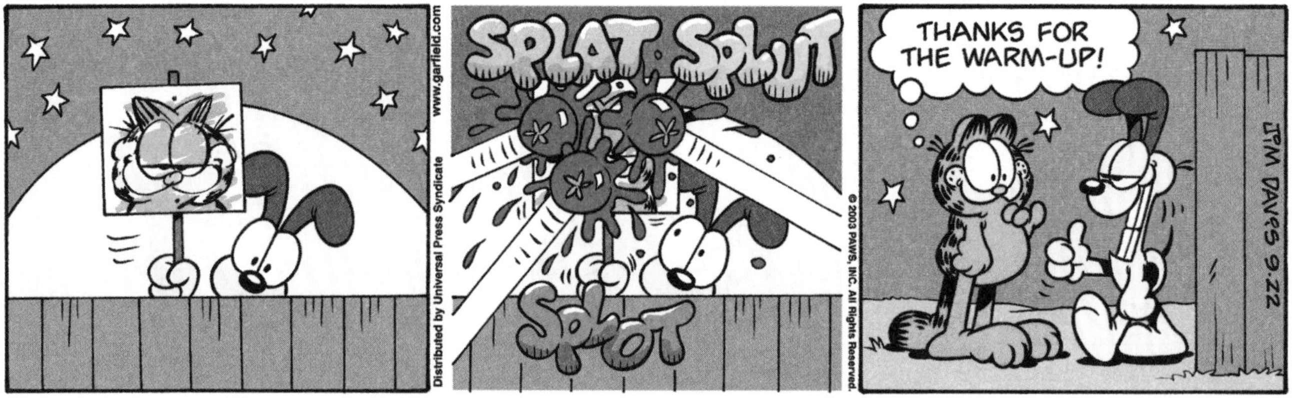
www.garfield.com
Distributed by Universal Press Syndicate
SPLAT SPLUT
SPLOT
© 2003 PAWS, INC. All Rights Reserved.
THANKS FOR THE WARM-UP!
JIM DAVIS 9-22

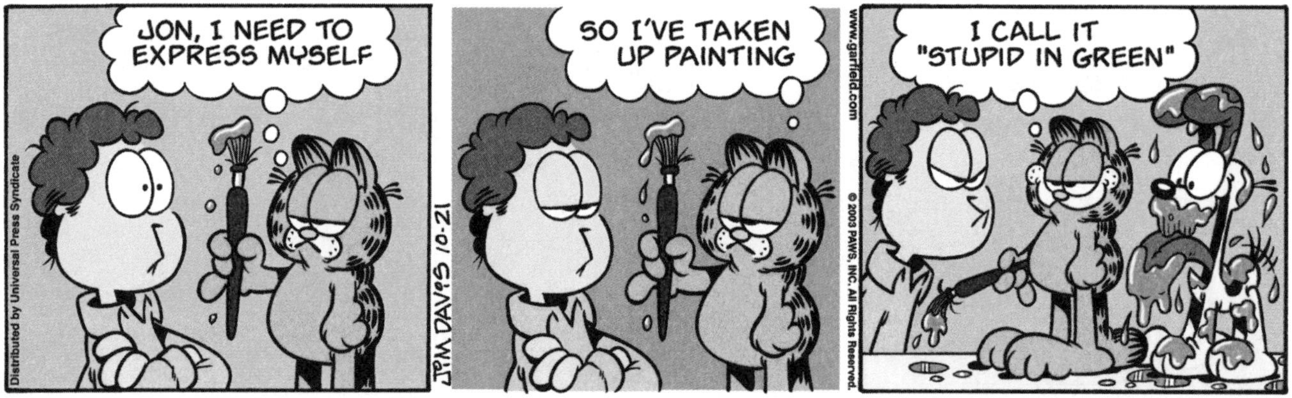
JON, I NEED TO EXPRESS MYSELF
Distributed by Universal Press Syndicate
JIM DAVIS 10-21
SO I'VE TAKEN UP PAINTING
www.garfield.com
© 2003 PAWS, INC. All Rights Reserved.
I CALL IT "STUPID IN GREEN"

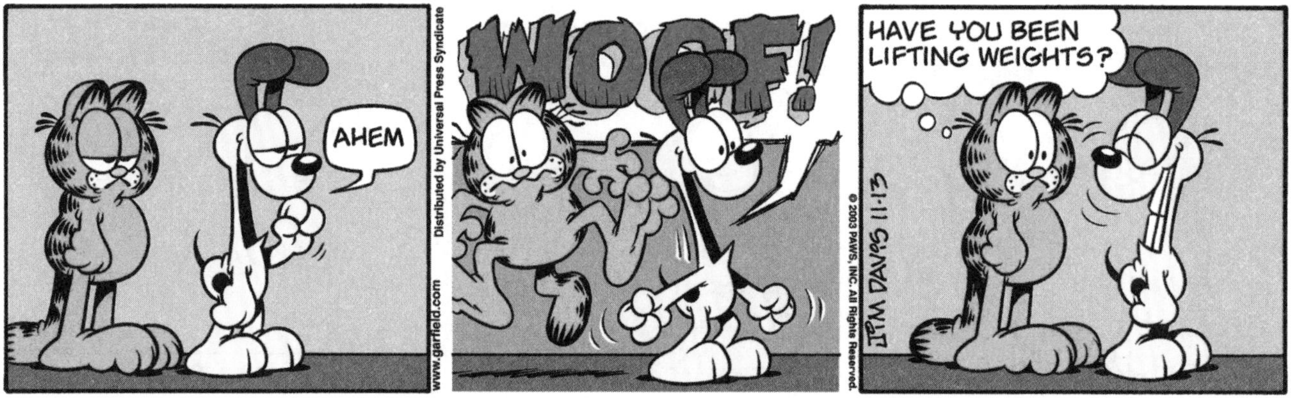
AHEM
Distributed by Universal Press Syndicate
www.garfield.com
WOOF!
© 2003 PAWS, INC. All Rights Reserved.
JIM DAVIS 11-13
HAVE YOU BEEN LIFTING WEIGHTS?

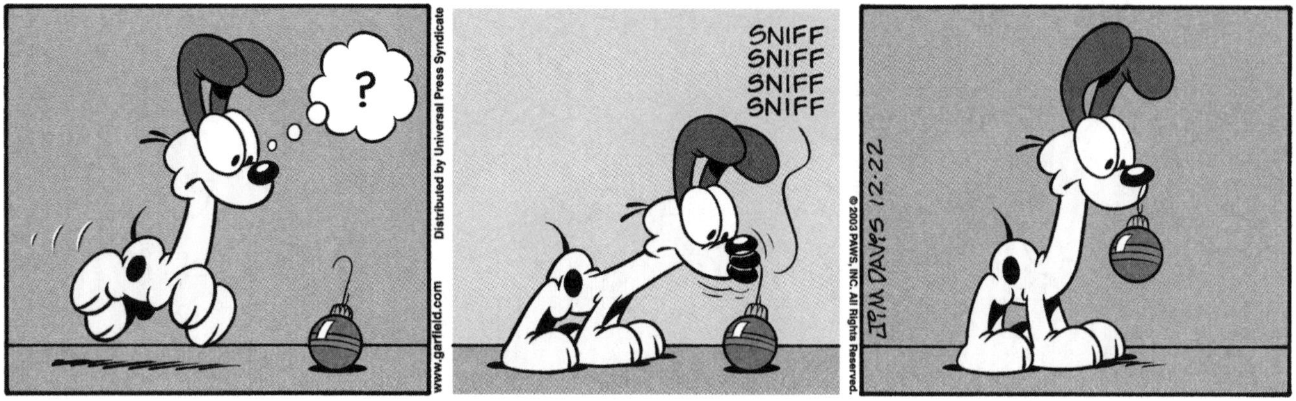
?
www.garfield.com Distributed by Universal Press Syndicate
SNIFF
SNIFF
SNIFF
SNIFF
© 2003 PAWS, INC. All Rights Reserved.
JIM DAVIS 12·22

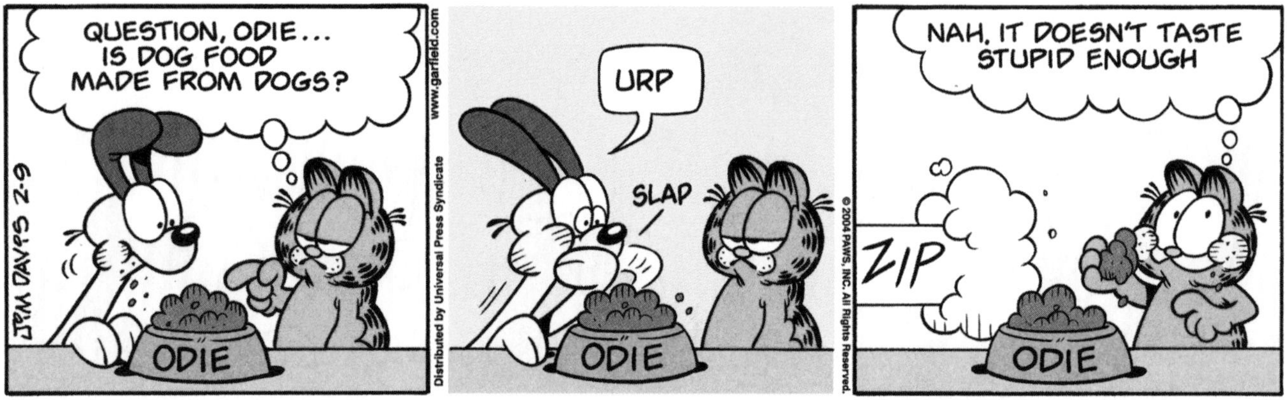
QUESTION, ODIE... IS DOG FOOD MADE FROM DOGS?
JIM DAVIS 2·9
ODIE
www.garfield.com Distributed by Universal Press Syndicate
URP
SLAP
ODIE
© 2004 PAWS, INC. All Rights Reserved.
NAH, IT DOESN'T TASTE STUPID ENOUGH
ZIP
ODIE

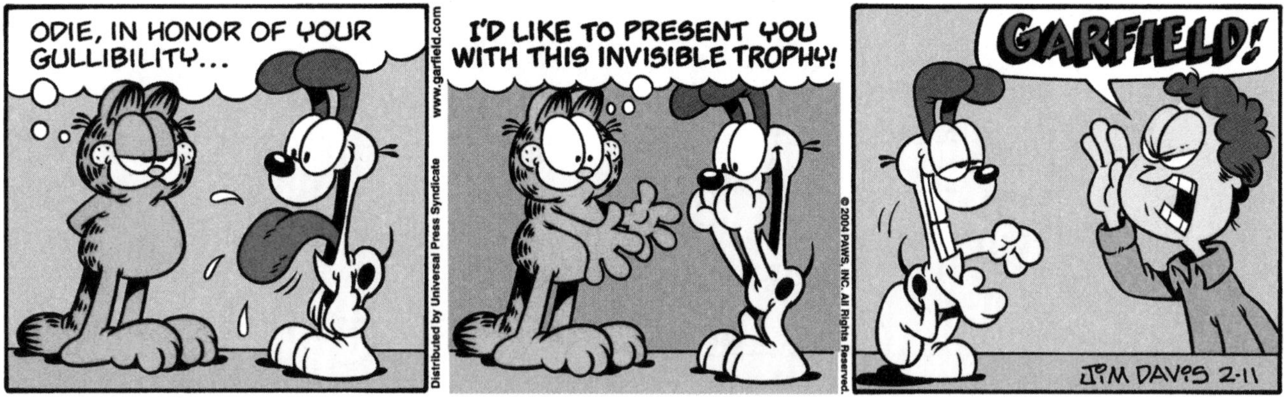
ODIE, IN HONOR OF YOUR GULLIBILITY...
www.garfield.com Distributed by Universal Press Syndicate
I'D LIKE TO PRESENT YOU WITH THIS INVISIBLE TROPHY!
© 2004 PAWS, INC. All Rights Reserved.
GARFIELD!
JIM DAVIS 2·11

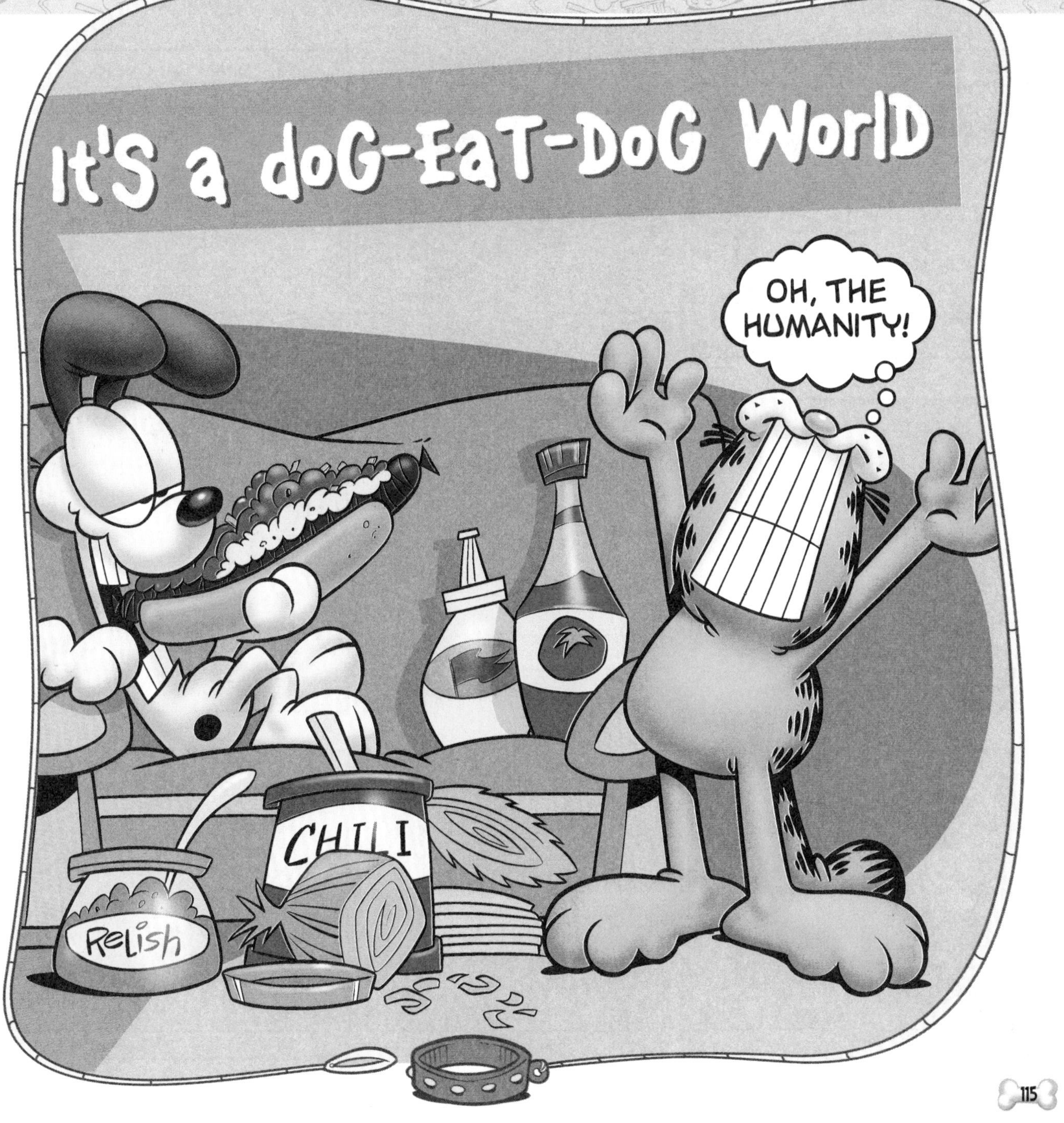
It's a doG-EaT-DoG WorlD
OH, THE HUMANITY!
CHILI
Relish

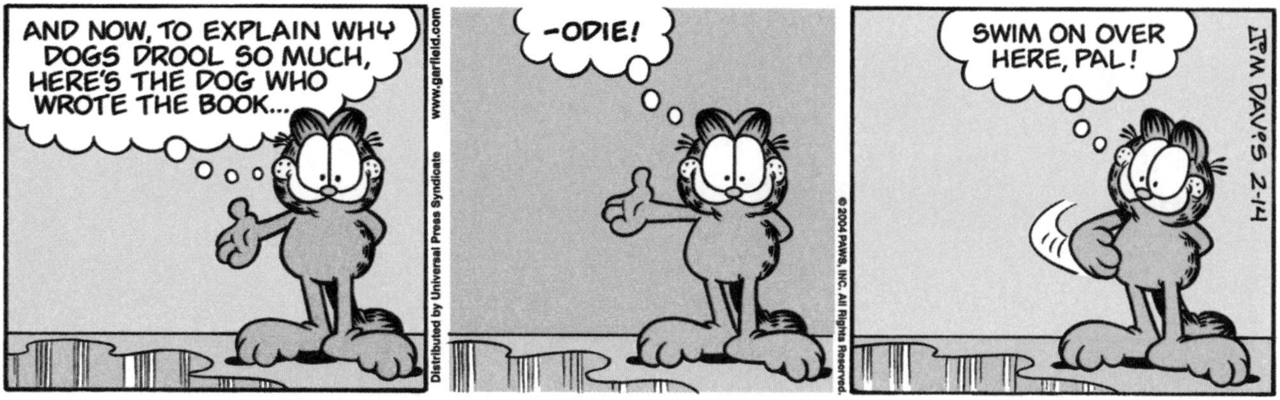
AND NOW, TO EXPLAIN WHY DOGS DROOL SO MUCH, HERE'S THE DOG WHO WROTE THE BOOK...
-ODIE!
SWIM ON OVER HERE, PAL!
JIM DAVIS 2-14
www.garfield.com
Distributed by Universal Press Syndicate
© 2004 PAWS, INC. All Rights Reserved.

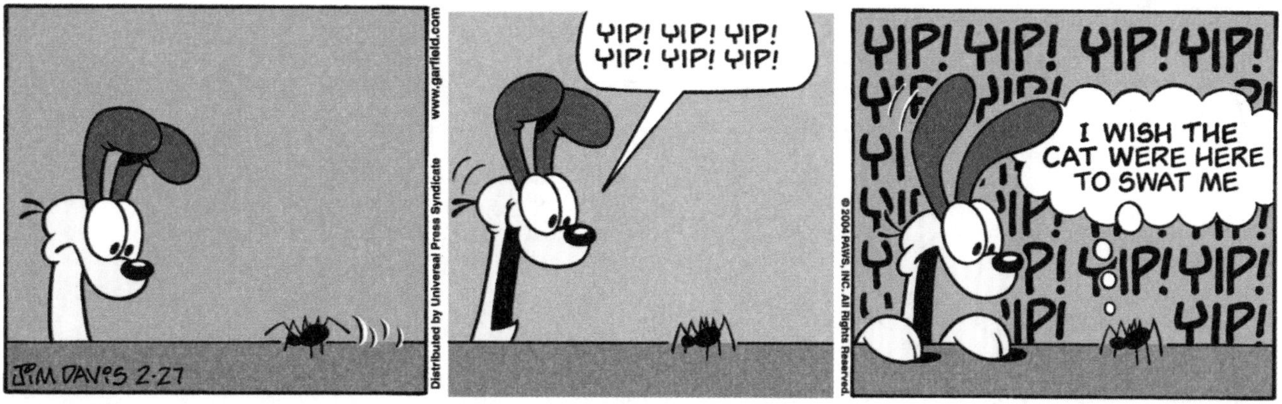
JIM DAVIS 2-27
YIP! YIP! YIP! YIP! YIP! YIP!
YIP! YIP! YIP! YIP!
I WISH THE CAT WERE HERE TO SWAT ME
www.garfield.com
Distributed by Universal Press Syndicate
© 2004 PAWS, INC. All Rights Reserved.

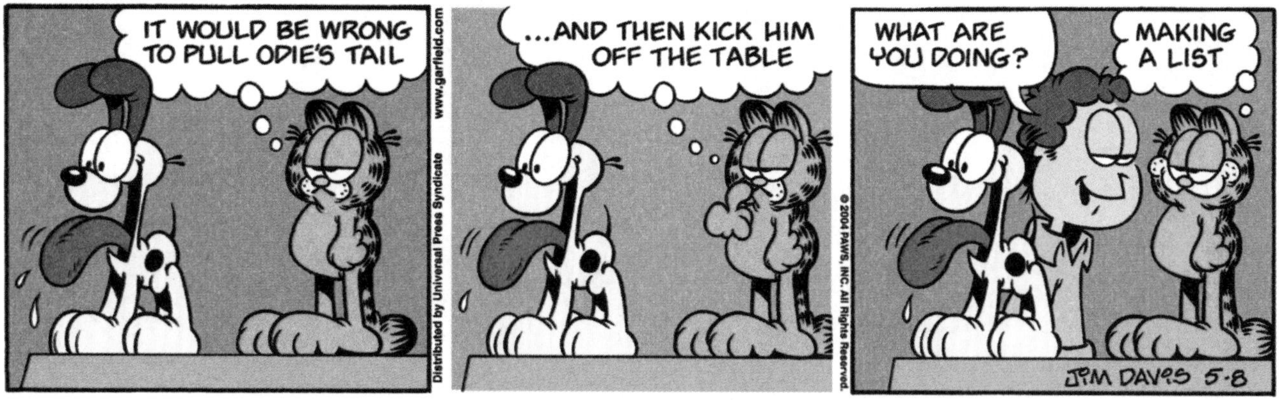
IT WOULD BE WRONG TO PULL ODIE'S TAIL
...AND THEN KICK HIM OFF THE TABLE
WHAT ARE YOU DOING?
MAKING A LIST
JIM DAVIS 5-8
www.garfield.com
Distributed by Universal Press Syndicate
© 2004 PAWS, INC. All Rights Reserved.

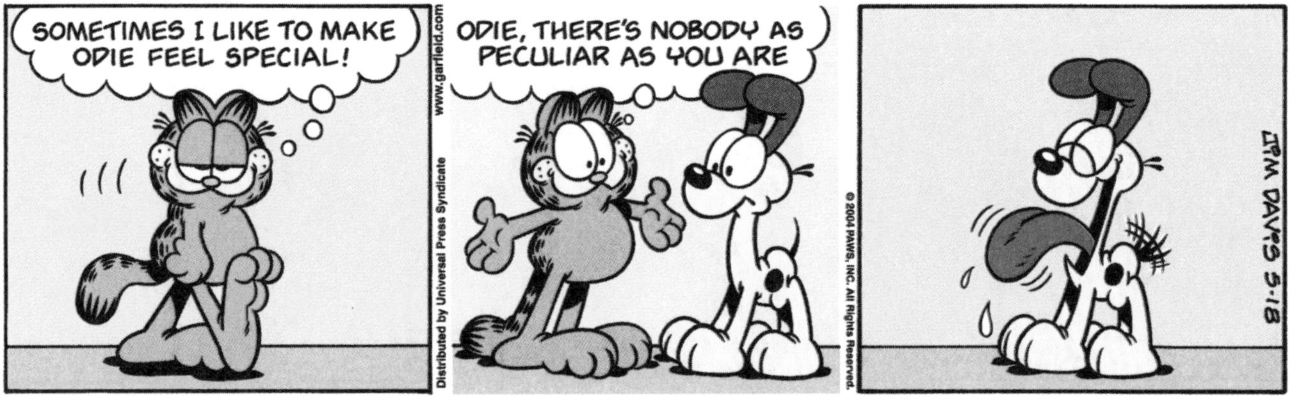
SOMETIMES I LIKE TO MAKE ODIE FEEL SPECIAL!
ODIE, THERE'S NOBODY AS PECULIAR AS YOU ARE
www.garfield.com
Distributed by Universal Press Syndicate
© 2004 PAWS, INC. All Rights Reserved.
JIM DAVIS 5-18

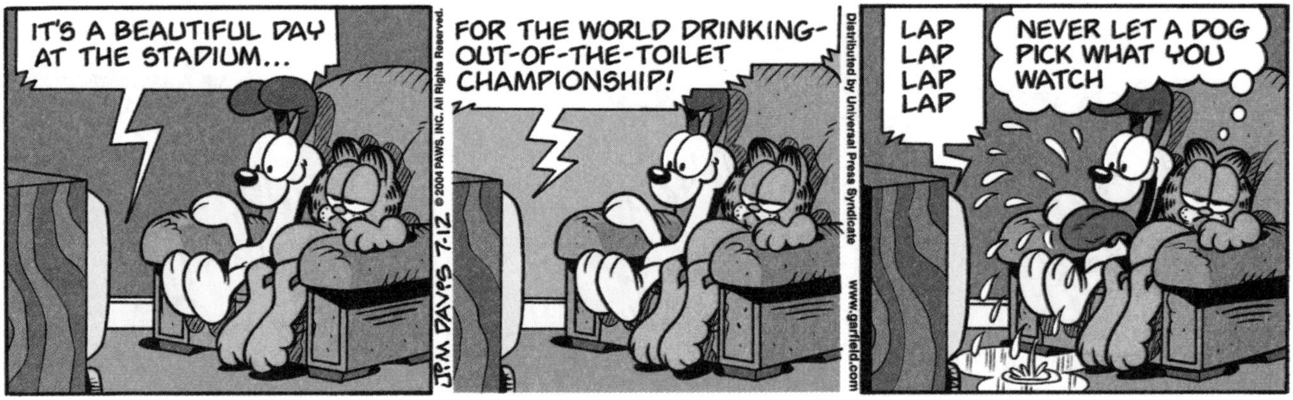
IT'S A BEAUTIFUL DAY AT THE STADIUM...
JIM DAVIS 7-12
© 2004 PAWS, INC. All Rights Reserved.
FOR THE WORLD DRINKING-OUT-OF-THE-TOILET CHAMPIONSHIP!
Distributed by Universal Press Syndicate
www.garfield.com
LAP LAP LAP LAP
NEVER LET A DOG PICK WHAT YOU WATCH

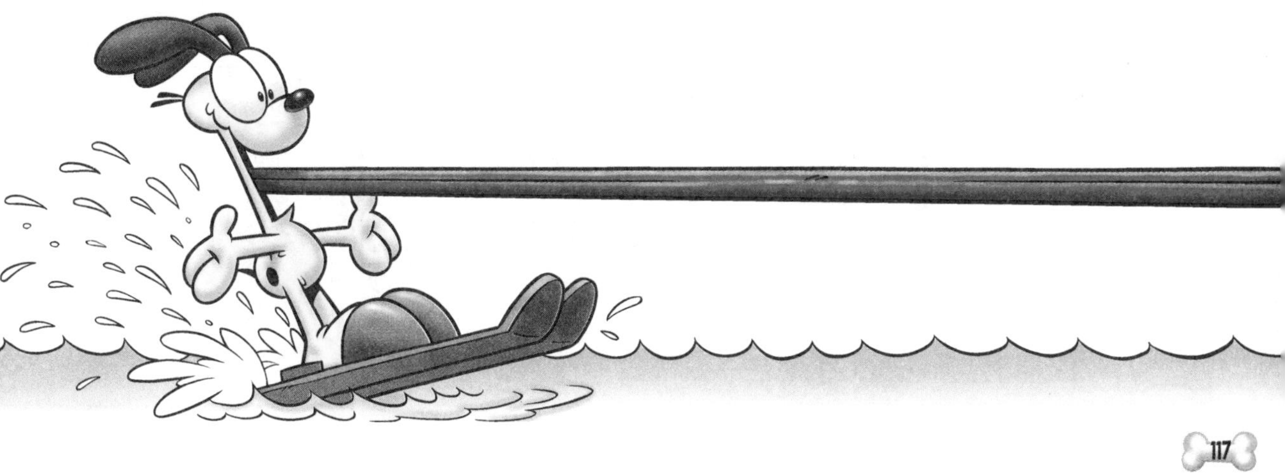

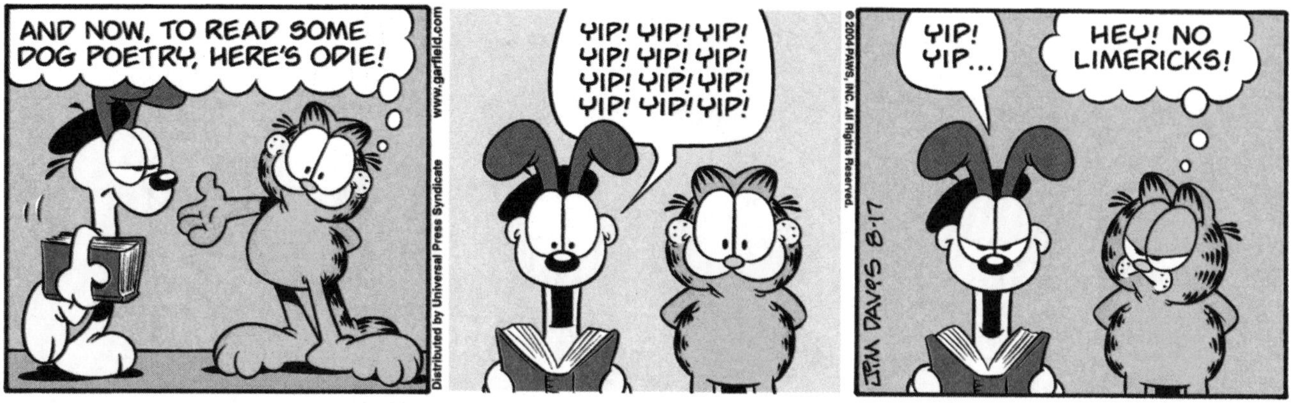
AND NOW, TO READ SOME DOG POETRY, HERE'S ODIE!
www.garfield.com
Distributed by Universal Press Syndicate
YIP! YIP! YIP! YIP! YIP! YIP! YIP! YIP! YIP! YIP! YIP! YIP!
© 2004 PAWS, INC. All Rights Reserved.
JIM DAVIS 8-17
YIP! YIP...
HEY! NO LIMERICKS!

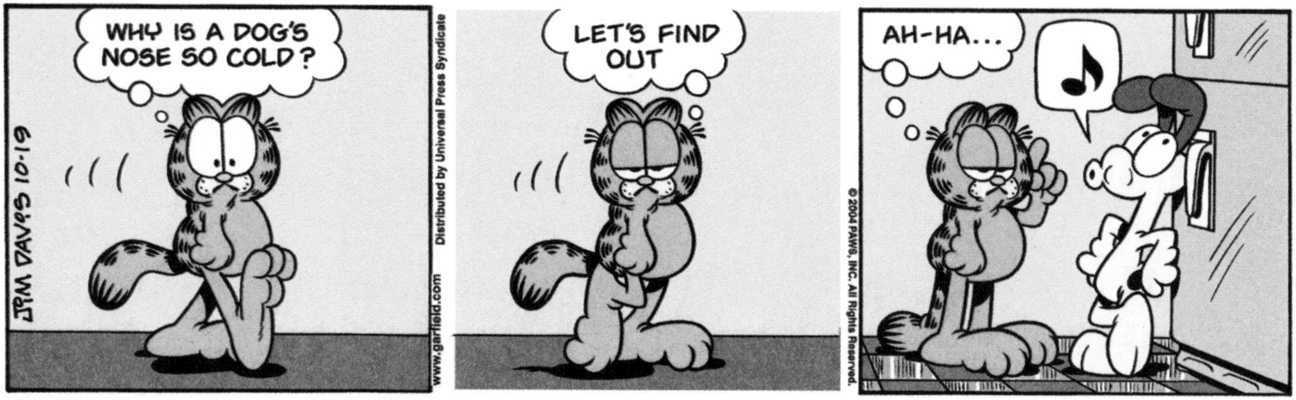
WHY IS A DOG'S NOSE SO COLD?
JIM DAVIS 10-19
Distributed by Universal Press Syndicate
www.garfield.com
LET'S FIND OUT
© 2004 PAWS, INC. All Rights Reserved.
AH-HA...

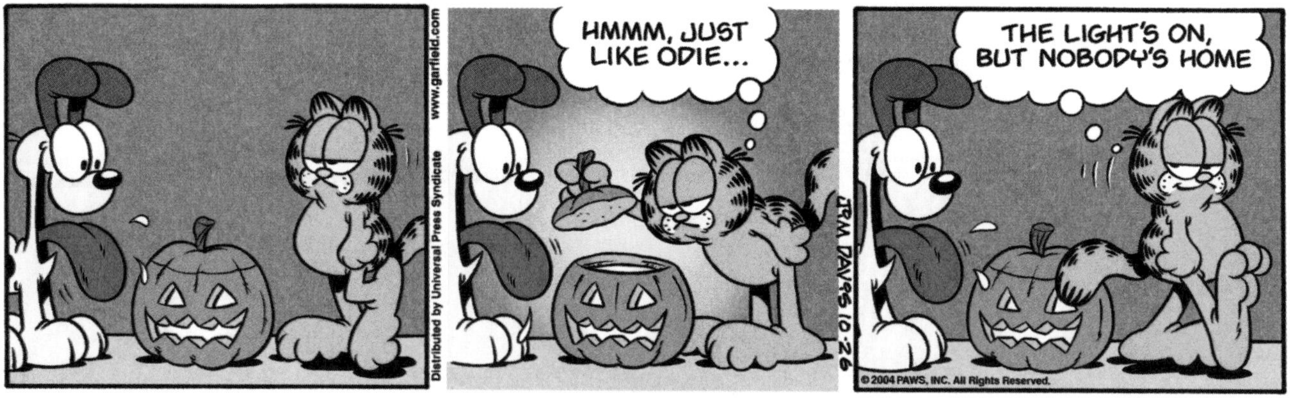
www.garfield.com
Distributed by Universal Press Syndicate
HMMM, JUST LIKE ODIE...
JIM DAVIS 10-26
THE LIGHT'S ON, BUT NOBODY'S HOME
© 2004 PAWS, INC. All Rights Reserved.

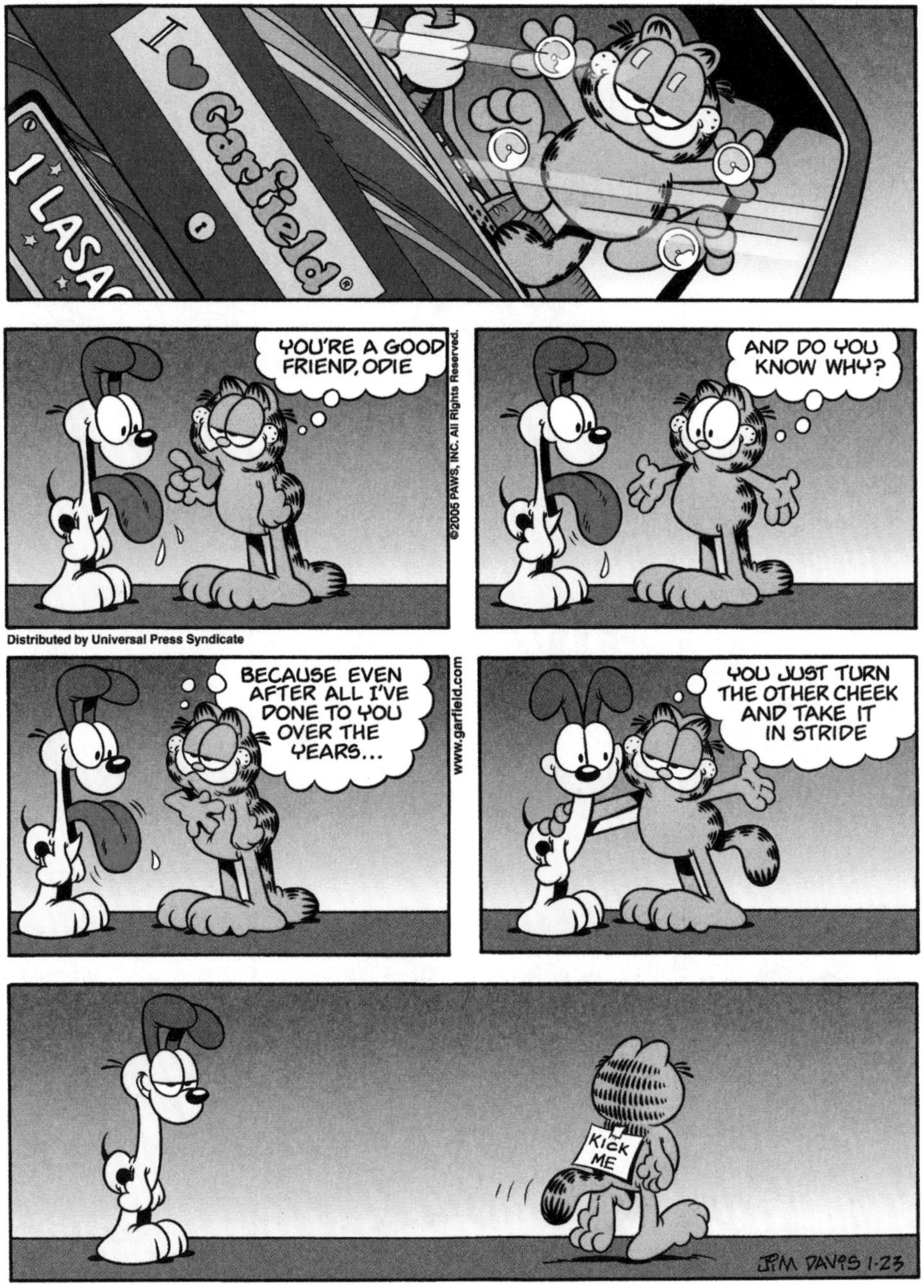
I ♥ Garfield®
YOU'RE A GOOD FRIEND, ODIE
©2005 PAWS, INC. All Rights Reserved.
AND DO YOU KNOW WHY?
Distributed by Universal Press Syndicate
BECAUSE EVEN AFTER ALL I'VE DONE TO YOU OVER THE YEARS...
www.garfield.com
YOU JUST TURN THE OTHER CHEEK AND TAKE IT IN STRIDE
KICK ME
JIM DAVIS 1-23

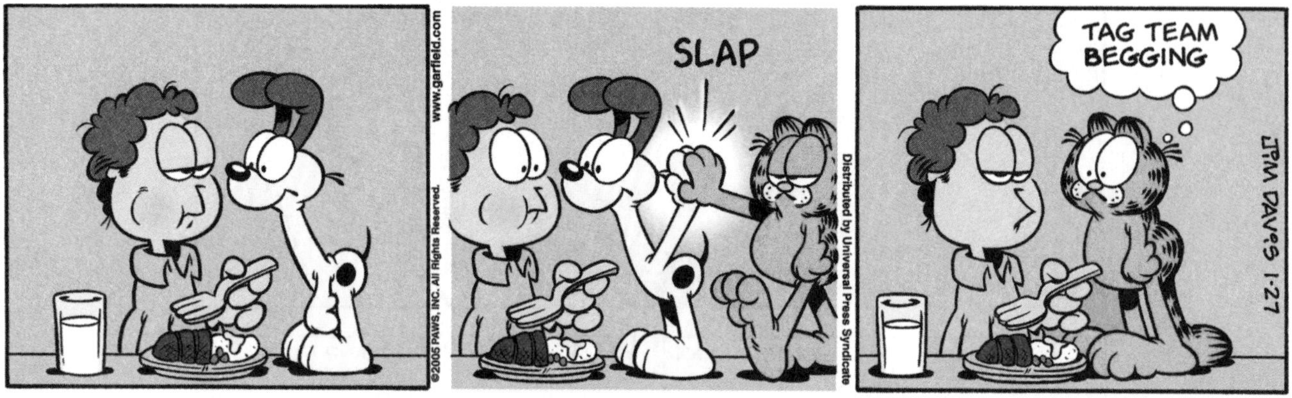
SLAP
TAG TEAM BEGGING
JIM DAVIS 1-27
©2005 PAWS, INC. All Rights Reserved. www.garfield.com
Distributed by Universal Press Syndicate

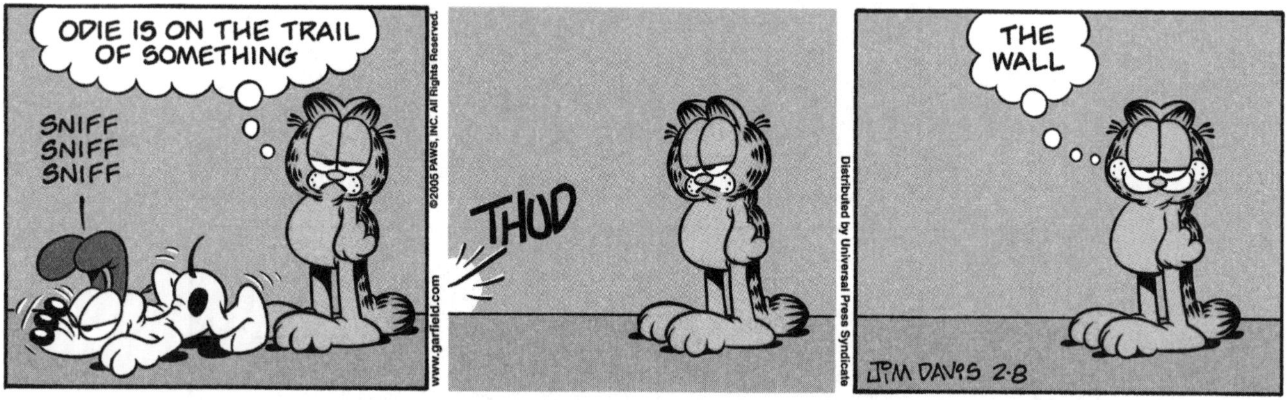
ODIE IS ON THE TRAIL OF SOMETHING
SNIFF SNIFF SNIFF
THUD
THE WALL
JIM DAVIS 2-8
©2005 PAWS, INC. All Rights Reserved. www.garfield.com
Distributed by Universal Press Syndicate

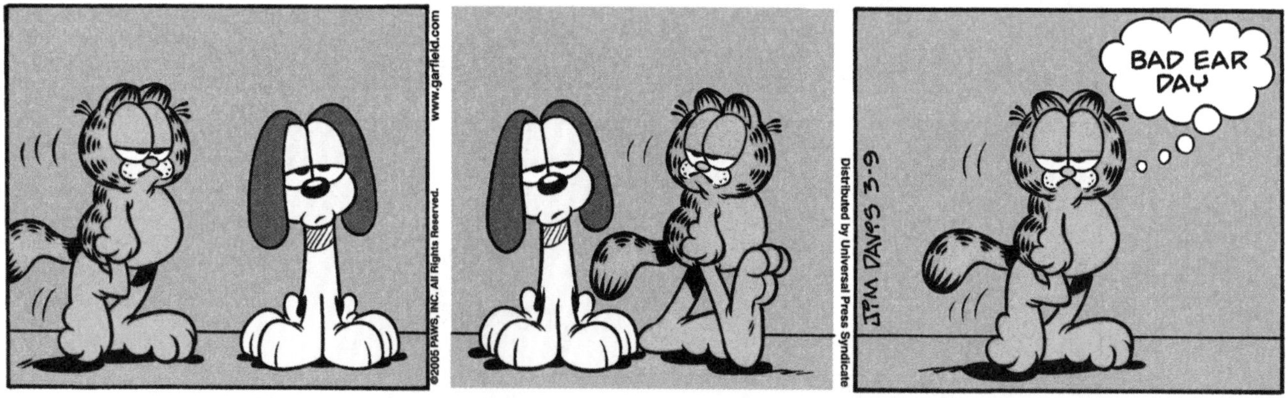
BAD EAR DAY
JIM DAVIS 3-9
©2005 PAWS, INC. All Rights Reserved. www.garfield.com
Distributed by Universal Press Syndicate

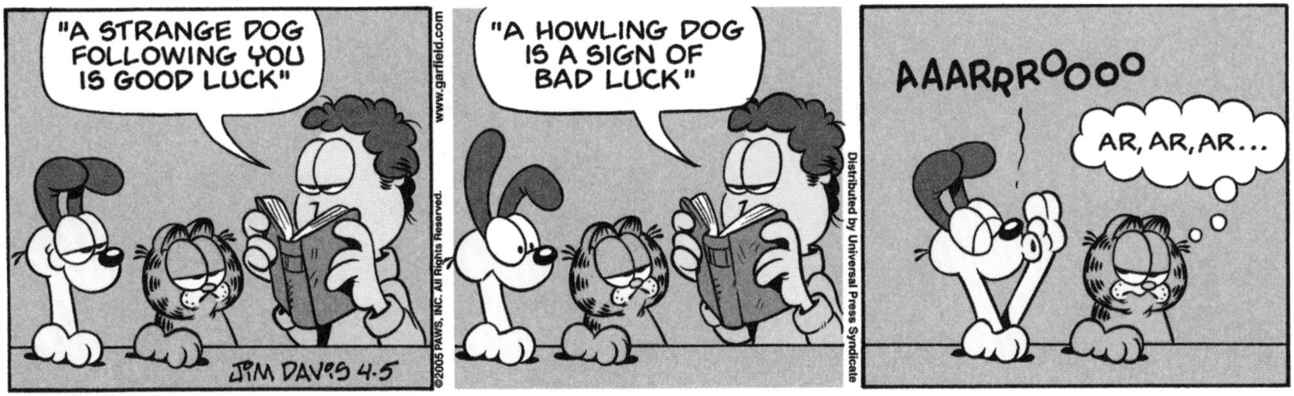
"A STRANGE DOG FOLLOWING YOU IS GOOD LUCK"
JIM DAVIS 4-5
©2005 PAWS, INC. All Rights Reserved. www.garfield.com
"A HOWLING DOG IS A SIGN OF BAD LUCK"
Distributed by Universal Press Syndicate
AAARRROOOO
AR, AR, AR...

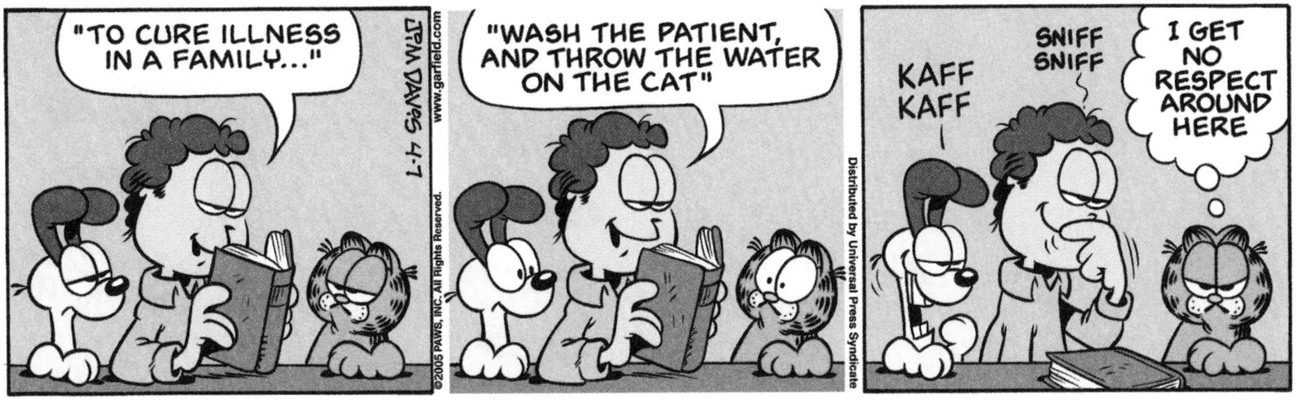
"TO CURE ILLNESS IN A FAMILY..."
JIM DAVIS 4-7
©2005 PAWS, INC. All Rights Reserved. www.garfield.com
"WASH THE PATIENT, AND THROW THE WATER ON THE CAT"
Distributed by Universal Press Syndicate
KAFF KAFF
SNIFF SNIFF
I GET NO RESPECT AROUND HERE

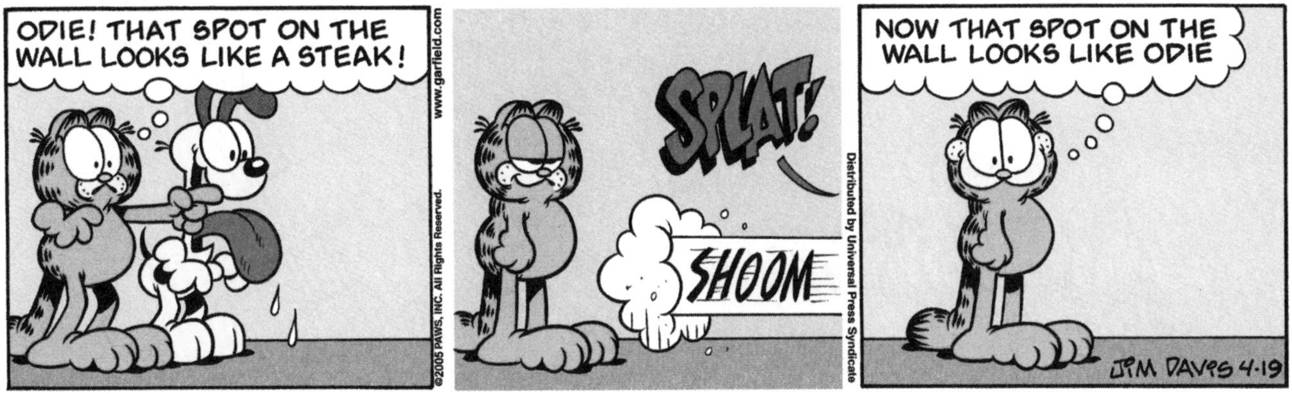
ODIE! THAT SPOT ON THE WALL LOOKS LIKE A STEAK!
©2005 PAWS, INC. All Rights Reserved. www.garfield.com
SPLAT!
SHOOM
Distributed by Universal Press Syndicate
NOW THAT SPOT ON THE WALL LOOKS LIKE ODIE
JIM DAVIS 4-19

OUTTAKES

WHEN WE WENT DIGGING FOR MATERIAL, WE WEREN'T SURE WHAT WE'D FIND. WE MANAGED TO UNEARTH A FEW GEMS, ALONG WITH SOME STUFF THAT SHOULD HAVE PROBABLY STAYED BURIED. ODIE SHOWS HIS DECIDEDLY ODD SIDE IN THESE UNEDITED, AND PREVIOUSLY UNPUBLISHED, STRIPS AND SKETCHES.

JIM DAVIS

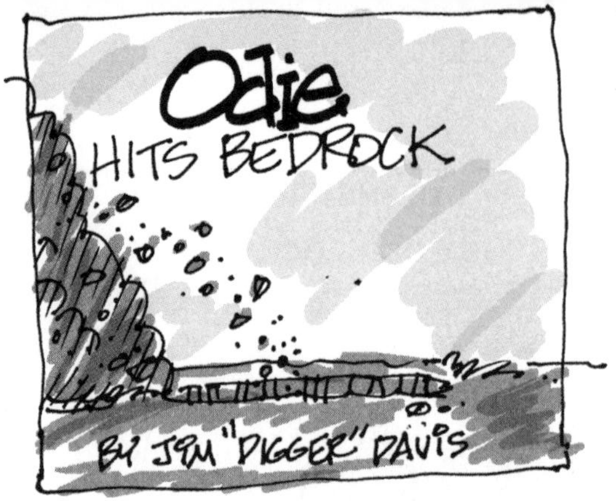
Odie
HITS BEDROCK
BY JIM "DIGGER" DAVIS

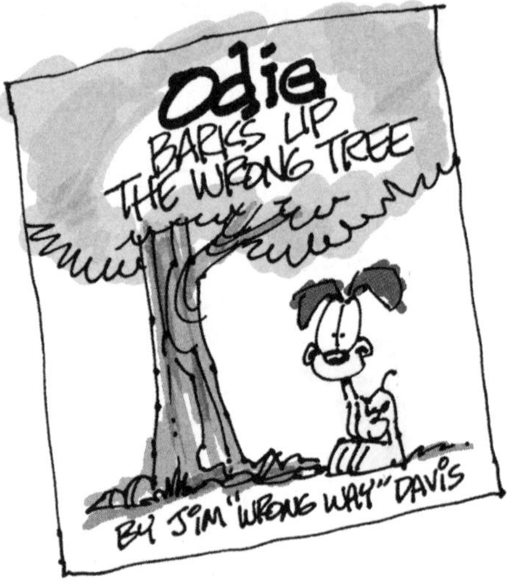
Odie
BARKS UP THE WRONG TREE
BY JIM "WRONG WAY" DAVIS

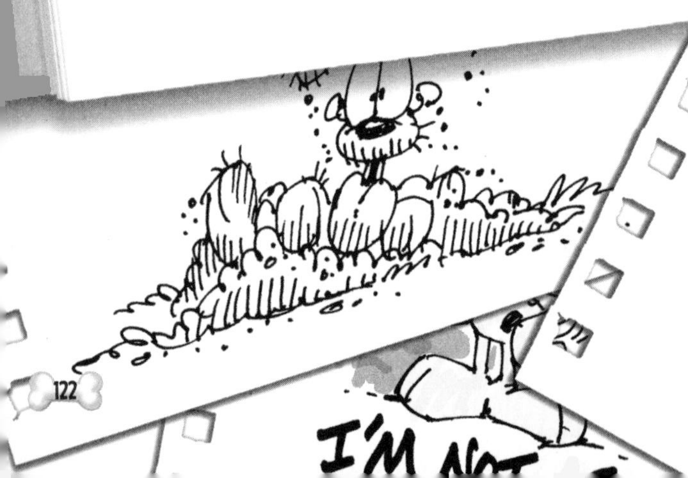
I'M

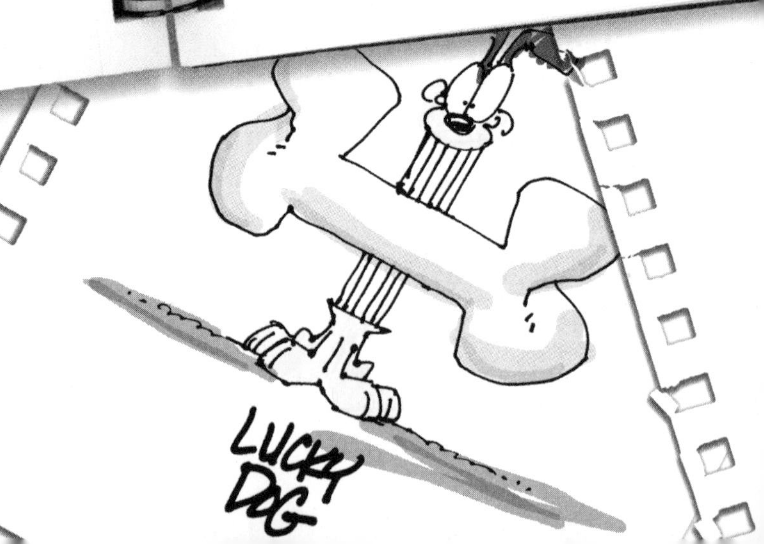
LUCKY DOG

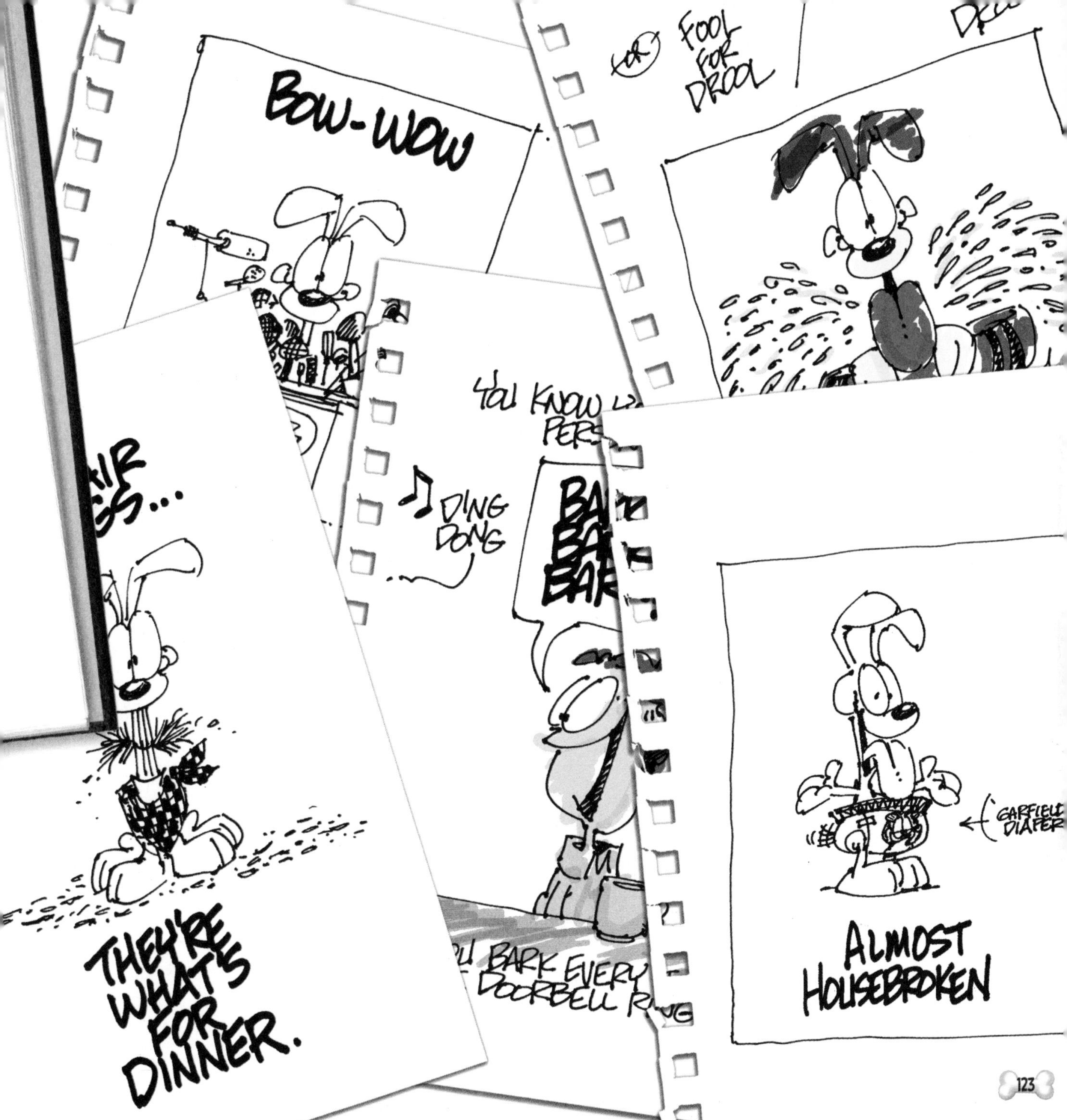
BOW-WOW
FOOL FOR DROOL
DING DONG
THEY'RE WHAT'S FOR DINNER.
ALMOST HOUSEBROKEN

ODDLY ODIE! REJECTED COMIC STRIPS

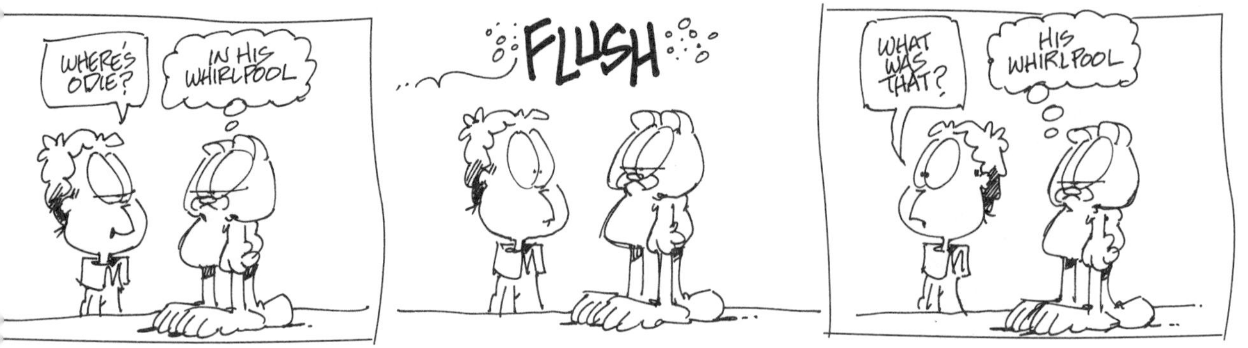
WHERE'S ODIE?
IN HIS WHIRLPOOL
FLUSH
WHAT WAS THAT?
HIS WHIRLPOOL

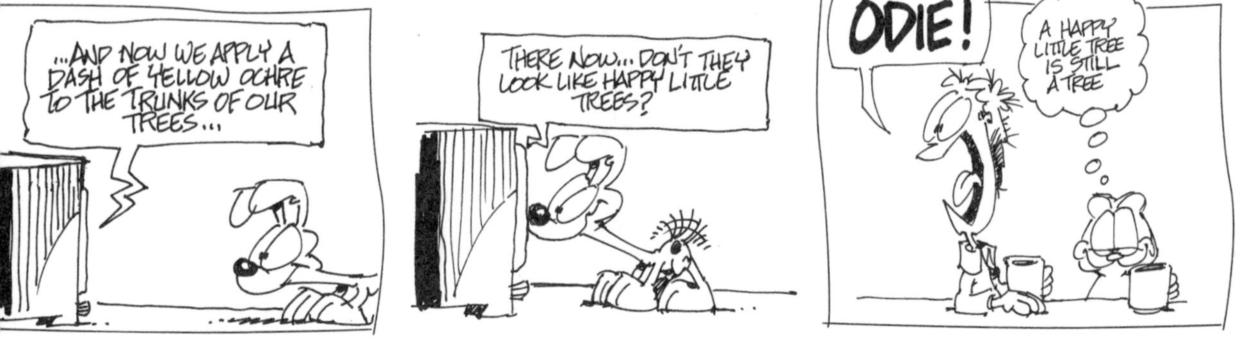
...AND NOW WE APPLY A DASH OF YELLOW OCHRE TO THE TRUNKS OF OUR TREES...
THERE NOW... DON'T THEY LOOK LIKE HAPPY LITTLE TREES?
ODIE!
A HAPPY LITTLE TREE IS STILL A TREE

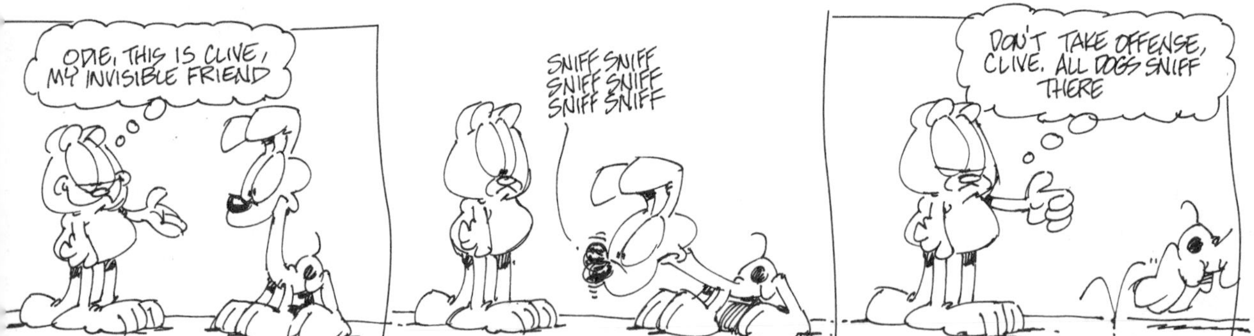
ODIE, THIS IS CLIVE, MY INVISIBLE FRIEND
SNIFF SNIFF SNIFF SNIFF SNIFF SNIFF
DON'T TAKE OFFENSE, CLIVE. ALL DOGS SNIFF THERE

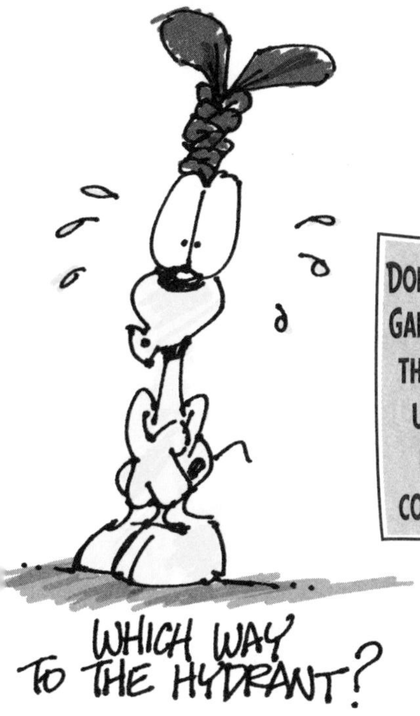
WHICH WAY
TO THE HYDRANT?

DON'T TELL PETA! GARFIELD CROSSES THE LINE IN THIS UNUSED—AND UNUSABLE—COVER CONCEPT.

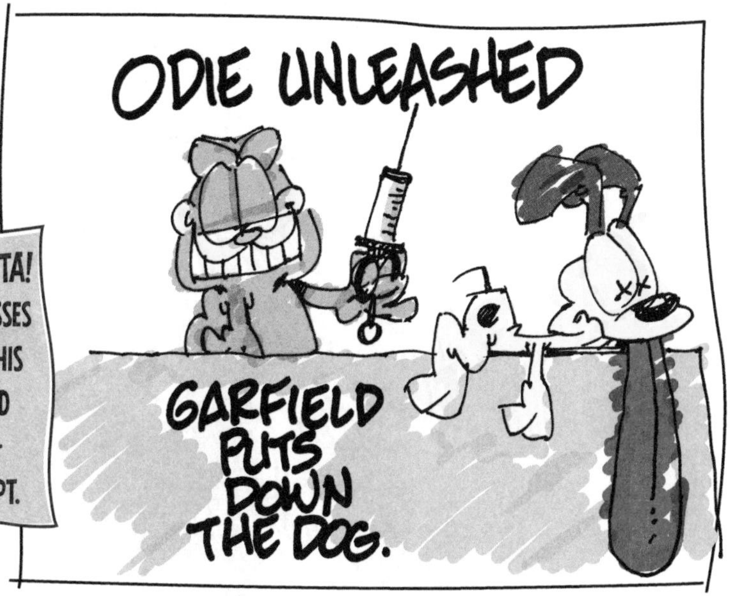
ODIE UNLEASHED
GARFIELD PUTS DOWN THE DOG.

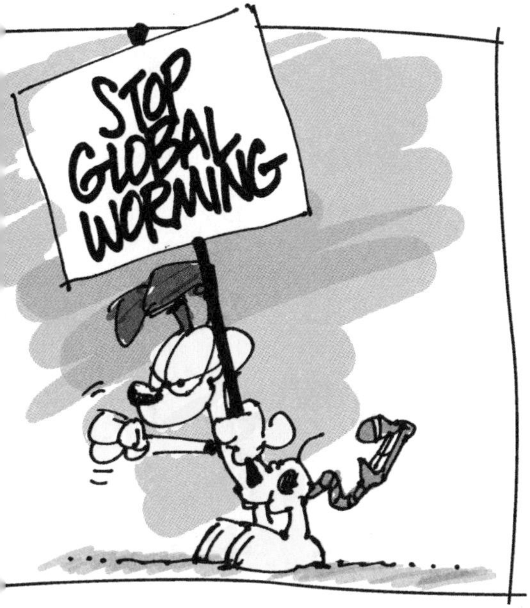
STOP GLOBAL WORMING

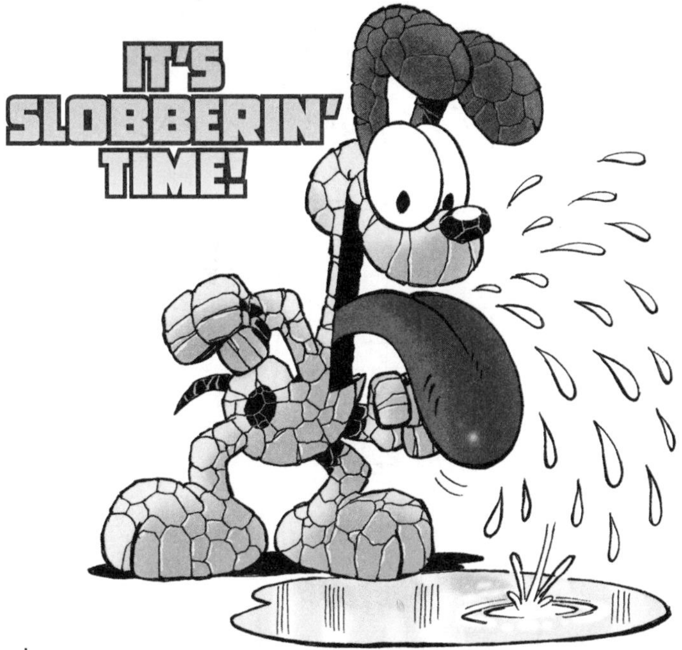
IT'S SLOBBERIN' TIME!

WITH APOLOGIES TO BEN GRIMM: ODIE AS THE THING FROM THE *FANTASTIC FOUR* COMIC BOOK.

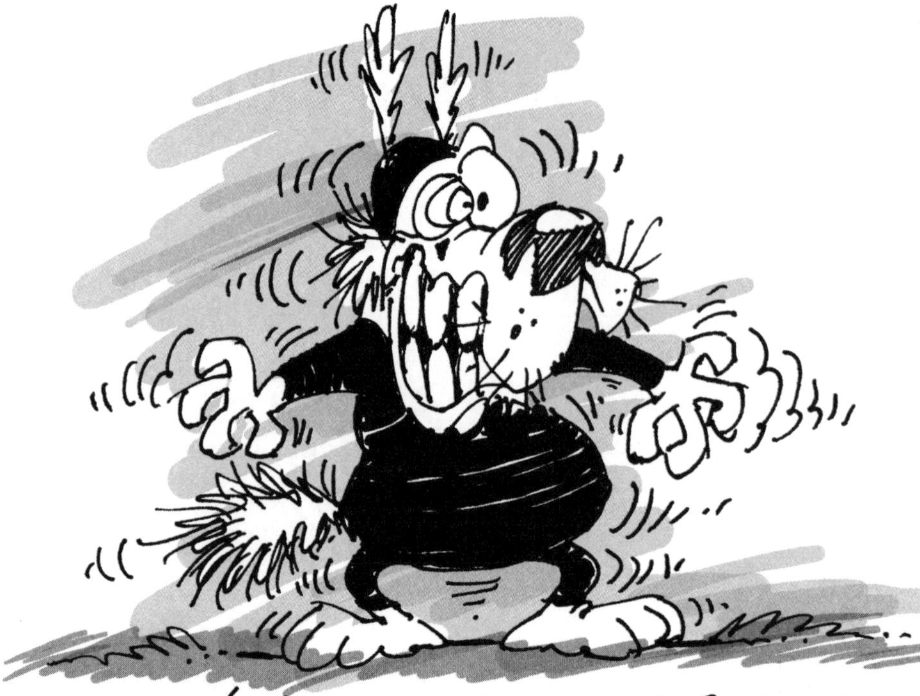

DOG MIMING AN INVISIBLE FENCE.

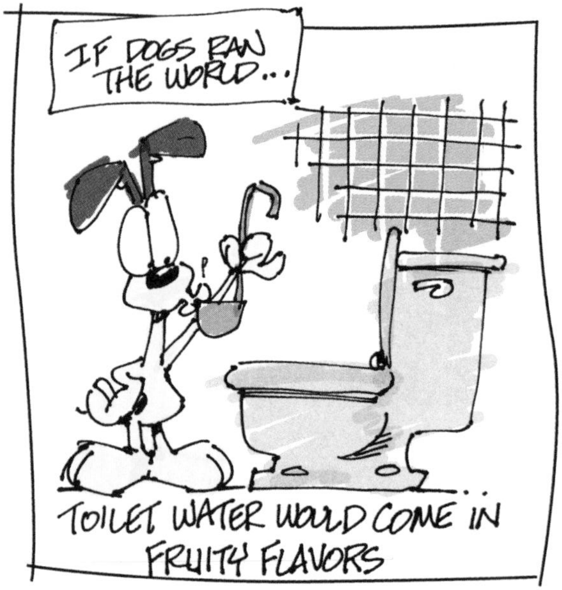
IF DOGS RAN THE WORLD...
TOILET WATER WOULD COME IN FRUITY FLAVORS

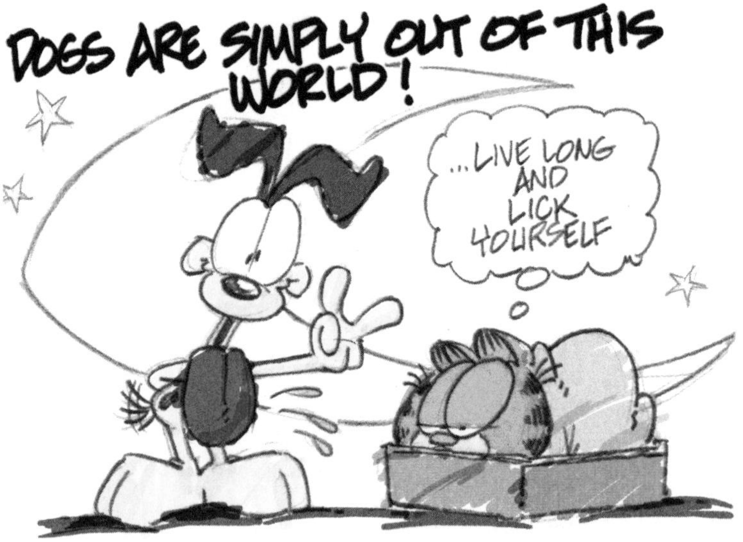
DOGS ARE SIMPLY OUT OF THIS WORLD!
...LIVE LONG AND LICK YOURSELF

BAD DOG! REJECTED BOOK-COVER DESIGNS

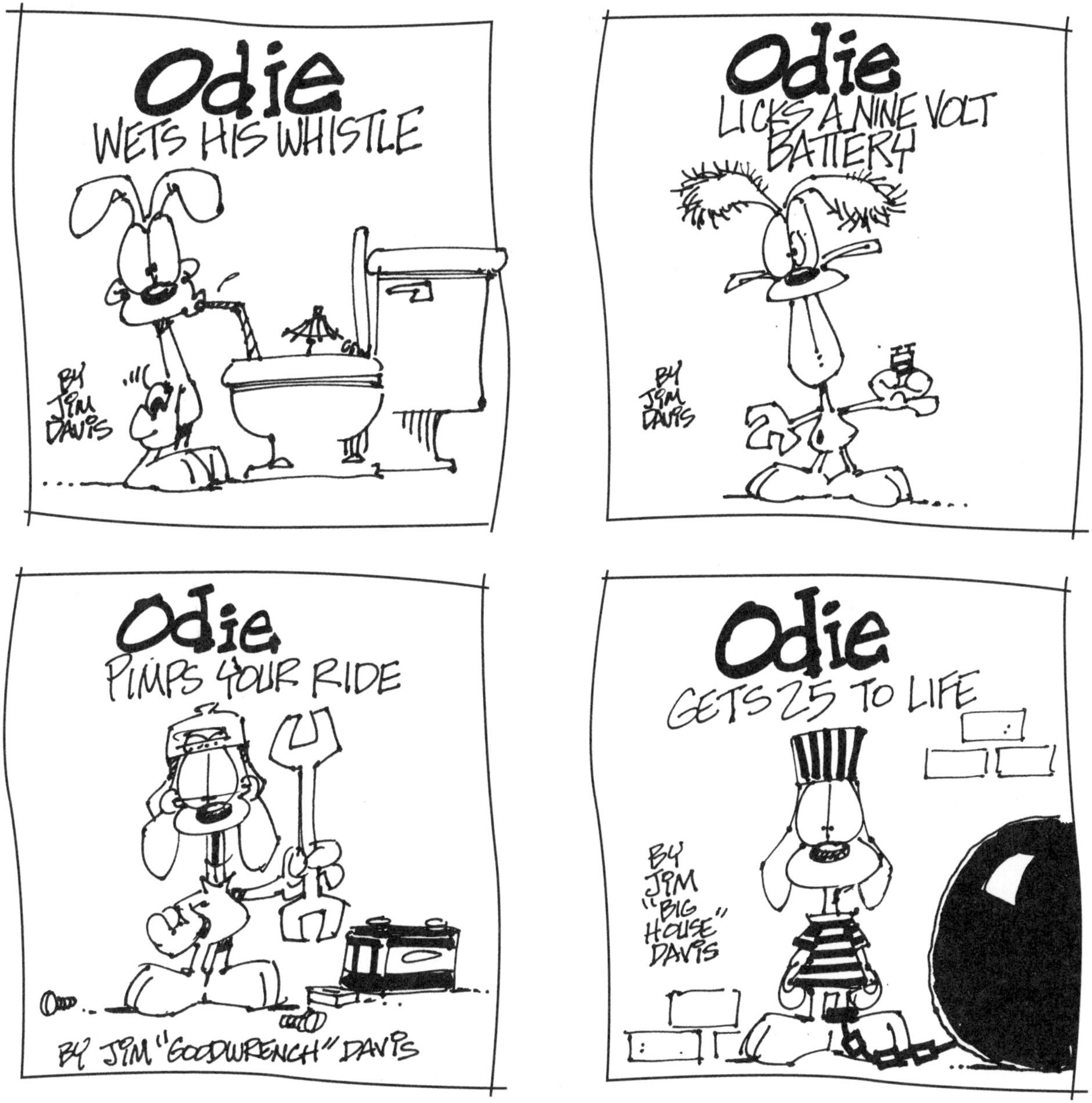
Odie
WETS HIS WHISTLE
BY JIM DAVIS
Odie
LICKS A NINE VOLT BATTERY
BY JIM DAVIS
Odie
PIMPS YOUR RIDE
BY JIM "GOODWRENCH" DAVIS
Odie
GETS 25 TO LIFE
BY JIM "BIG HOUSE" DAVIS

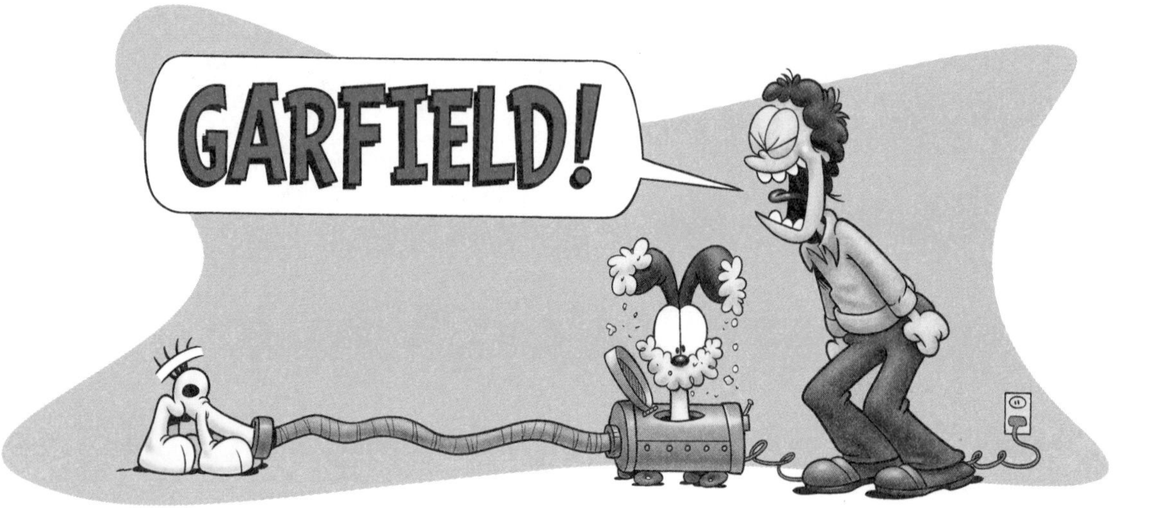
GARFIELD!